CHANGE MANAGEMENT
training

ATD Workshop Series

CHANGE MANAGEMENT
training

ELAINE BIECH

PRESS

Alexandria, Virginia

ATD Press is an internationally renowned source of insightful and practical information on talent development, workplace learning, and professional development.

ATD Press
1640 King Street
Alexandria, VA 22314

Ordering information for print edition: Books published by ATD Press can be purchased by visiting ATD's website at td.org/books or by calling 800.628.2783 or 703.683.8100.

Library of Congress Control Number: 2016936134 (print edition only)

ISBN-10: 1-60728-087-6
ISBN-13: 978-1-60728-087-3
e-ISBN: 978-1-60728-119-1

ATD Press Editorial Staff:
Director: Kristine Luecker
Manager: Christian Green
Community of Practice Manager, Learning & Development: Amanda Smith

Trainers Publishing House (TPH) Staff:
Publisher: Cat Russo
Project, Editorial, and Production Management: Jacqueline Edlund-Braun
TPH Copyeditor: Tora Estep
Rights Associate and Data Manager: Nancy Silva
Cover and Text Design: Ana Ilieva Foreman/Design
Composition: Kristin Goble, PerfecType, Nashville, TN, and Debra Deysher, Double D Media, Reading, PA

Cover art: Shutterstock
Presentation Slide and Handout Art: Fotolia
Printed by Data Reproductions Corporation, Auburn Hills, MI, www.datarepro.com

For Shane, Thad, and Dan

The men who changed my life for the better

The ATD Workshop Series

Whether you are a professional trainer who needs to pull together a new training program next week, or someone who does a bit of training as a part of your job, you'll find the ATD Workshop Series is a timesaver.

Topics deliver key learning on today's most pressing business needs, including training for change management, coaching, communication skills, customer service, emotional intelligence, facilitation, leadership, new employee orientation, new supervisors, presentation skills, project management, and time management. The series is designed for busy training and HR professionals, consultants, and managers who need to deliver training quickly to optimize performance now.

Each ATD Workshop book provides all the content and trainer's tools you need to create and deliver compelling training guaranteed to

- **enhance** learner engagement
- **deepen** learner understanding
- **increase** learning application.

Each book in the series offers innovative and engaging programs designed by leading experts and grounded in design and delivery best practices and theory. It is like having an expert trainer helping you with each step in the workshop process. The straightforward, practical instructions help you prepare and deliver the workshops quickly and effectively. Flexible timing options allow you to choose from half-day, one-day, and two-day workshop formats, or to create your own, using the tips and strategies presented for customizing the workshops to fit your unique business environment. Each ATD Workshop book also comes with guidance on leveraging learning technologies to maximize workshop design and delivery efficiency and access to all the training materials you will need, including activities, handouts, tools, assessments, and presentation slides.

Contents

Foreword

In 2002, we launched the ASTD Trainer's WorkShop Series—a collection of books authored by practitioners that focused on the design and delivery of training on popular soft-skills topics. The creation of this series was a departure for us. These workshops-in-a-book were created to help internal trainers expedite their program delivery by using appropriate and exceptionally designed content that could be adapted and repurposed.

These topics, dealing with issues ranging from customer service to leadership to manager skills, continue to be important training programs offered in companies and organizations of all sizes and across the globe. The ASTD Trainer's WorkShop Series has helped more than 60,000 trainers and occasional trainers deliver top-notch programs that meet business needs and help drive performance.

And while many things about the delivery of soft-skills training have not changed in the last decade, there have been advances in technology and its use in training. So, when we began talking about how to refresh this popular series, we knew we needed to incorporate technology and new topics. We also wanted to make sure that the new series was cohesively designed and had input from author-practitioners who are, after all, the heart and soul of this series.

In this series, we are pleased to feature the work of outstanding trainers and innovators in the field of talent management—none more so than that of Elaine Biech. *Change Management Training* is her second book in the ATD Workshop Series. In 2015 she lent her expertise to *New Supervisor Training*. Inside each of the titles in the series, you'll find innovative content and fresh program agendas to simplify your delivery of key training topics. You'll also find consistency among titles, with each presented in a contemporary manner, designed by peers, and reflecting the preferences of training professionals who conduct workshops.

We hope that you find tremendous value in the ATD Workshop Series.

Tony Bingham
President & CEO
Association for Talent Development (ATD)
May 2016

Introduction
How to Use This Book

What's in This Chapter

- Why change management development is important
- What you need to know about training
- Estimates of time required
- A broad view of what the book includes

Why Is Change Management Training Important?

Change happens—whether we want it or not. Sometimes we can plan for it, but often we can't. Sometimes the best we can do is to make sense of change, make the best choices change offers, and make things happen. People and organizations who are the most successful predict and prepare for change—even *creating* change that benefits them.

What's Changing? Everything. Even managing change has changed! Today's organizations operate in a volatile, uncertain, complex, ambiguous (VUCA) world (Johansen 2012). Our organizations face more complex continuous change than ever before. Being adaptable to quickly adjust to continuous change as well as being expert at leading through complex change are more important than ever. Change is a way of life, and proficient navigation in its turbulent waters is a strategic imperative. Simply put, managing change is a *required* skill for all leaders, managers, and employees.

You've heard the statistics. Even though change management has been a recognized discipline for more than half a century, studies continue to report the high failure rates for organizational change projects. *Harvard Business Review* reports that "most studies still show a 60-70 percent failure rate" (Ashkenas 2013). Gallup confirms that this statistic has been constant since the 1970s (Leonard and Coltea 2013). What's going on?

Change Is Changing. Until recently an organization addressed changes one at a time, using fundamental tools and processes. Change teams had time to follow an eight-step process, gather data, and create a vision for each change project. We continue to implement a change management approach that was designed for single-issue changes. But the VUCA environment allows us neither the time nor the ease to rely on a set of basic tools any longer.

Organizations are challenged by the constant bombardment, faster pace, and convoluted complexity of change. Organizations require change-ready employees and change-savvy managers at the ready. And organizations must build a capacity for continuous change. These challenges require a different skill set. Choices and consequences are no longer as clear as they once were.

Change-Savvy Managers Are Critical to Success. Managers have a key role to play to ensure an organization's future success. Recent research by Accenture shows that business unit managers *play the most significant role in effectively implementing change* in organizations (Parry 2015). Today's managers need to understand their expanded role, practice new management techniques, and demystify the people side of change.

Organizations Must Foster Change-Ready Employees. The Conference Board reported in its 2015 annual survey that "organizations must focus on behavioral change to make change more sustainable and become agile. It is about helping people embrace and adopt change by building personal competencies . . . It is about instilling personal responsibility and accountability for change at every level. . . .The focus should be on developing change leaders at all levels, not just reactive change managers" (Mitchell et al. 2015).

Change How We Change. The bottom line is that we need to change *how* we change: how we make choices, how we make things happen, even how we perceive change. Change is neither good nor bad. The most successful organizations are proactive about change. They look for ways to turn obstacles into opportunities.

The workshops in *Change Management Training* provide an essential component in preparing organizations and their leaders to thrive in a VUCA world. The innovative, engaging two-day, full-day, and half-day programs give you all the tools and resources you need to develop change-savvy managers who can ensure success for their organizations, satisfaction for their direct reports, and job fulfillment for themselves.

What Do I Need to Know About Training?

The ATD Workshop Series is designed to be adaptable for many levels of both training facilitation and topic expertise. Circle the answers in this quick assessment that most closely align with your state of expertise.

QUICK ASSESSMENT: HOW EXPERT DO I NEED TO BE?			
Question	**Authority**	**Developing Expertise**	**Novice**
What is your level of expertise as a facilitator?	• More than 5 years of experience • Consistently receive awesome evaluations • Lead highly interactive sessions with strong participant engagement	• From 1 to 5 years of experience • Catch myself talking too much • May feel drained after training • Participants sometimes sit back and listen instead of engage	• Less than 1 year of experience • No idea what to do to be successful • Eager to develop a facilitative style
How proficient are you with the topic?	• Well versed • Have taken courses • Read books/ authored articles • Created training materials • Am sought out by peers on this topic • It is my passion	• On my way • Have taken courses • Read books • Created workshop materials • Would benefit from the book's support tools	• I can spell it! • Had a course in school • Received feedback from respected colleagues indicating I have a natural inclination for this topic (but feel a bit like an imposter)

Two-fold novice: Your best bet is to stick closely to the materials as they are designed. Spend extra time with the content to learn as much as possible about it. Read the examples and sample stories, and plan examples of your own to share. Also, closely read Chapter 8 on training delivery, and consider practicing with a colleague before delivering the program. Take comfort in the tested materials you are holding and have confidence in your ability to apply them!

Developing your expertise in one or both areas: Logical choices for you may include using the outline and materials, and then including material you have developed that is relevant to the topic *and* your participants' workplace needs. Or, take the core content of the materials and revise the learning techniques into interactive approaches you have used with success in the past. Play to your strengths and develop your growth areas using the resources in this volume that complement your existing skills.

Authority twice over: Feel free to adapt the agendas and materials as you see fit and use any materials that you have already developed, or simply incorporate training activities, handouts, and so forth from this volume into your own agenda. Enjoy the benefits of ready-to-use processes and support tools and have fun tailoring them to your preferences and organizational needs.

How Much Time Will Preparation Take?

Putting together and facilitating a training workshop, even when the agendas, activities, tools, and assessments are created for you, can be time consuming. For planning purposes, estimate about four days of preparation time for a two-day course.

What Are the Important Features of the Book?

Section I includes the various workshop designs (from two days to a half day) with agendas and thumbnails from presentation slides as well as a chapter on customizing the workshop for your circumstances. The chapters included are

- Chapter 1. Two-Day Workshop (16 hours program time) + Agenda + PPT (thumbnails)
- Chapter 2. One-Day Workshop (8 hours program time) + Agenda + PPT (thumbnails)
- Chapter 3. Half-Day Workshop (4 hours program time) + Agenda + PPT (thumbnails)
- Chapter 4. Customizing the Change Management Workshops.

The workshop chapters include advice, instructions, workshop at-a-glance tables, as well as full program agendas.

Section II is standard from book to book in the ATD Workshop Series as a way to provide a consistent foundation of training principles. This section's chapters follow the ADDIE model—the classic instructional design model named after its steps (analysis, design, development, implementation, and evaluation). The chapters are based on best practices and crafted with input from experienced training practitioners. They are meant to help you get up to speed as quickly as possible. Each chapter includes several additional recurring features to help you understand the concepts and ideas presented. The Bare Minimum gives you the bare bones of what you need to know about the topic. Key Points summarize the most important points of each chapter. What to Do Next guides you to your next action steps. And, finally, the Additional Resources and References sections at the end of each chapter give you options for further reading to broaden your understanding of training design and delivery. Section II chapters include

- Chapter 5. Identifying Needs for Change Management Training
- Chapter 6. Understanding the Foundations of Training Design
- Chapter 7. Leveraging Technology to Maximize and Support Design and Delivery
- Chapter 8. Delivering Your Change Management Workshop: Be a Great Facilitator
- Chapter 9. Evaluating Workshop Results.

Section III covers information about post-workshop learning:

- Chapter 10. Follow-Up for Change Management Training.

Section IV includes all the supporting documents and online guidance:

- Chapter 11. Learning Activities
- Chapter 12. Assessments
- Chapter 13. Handouts
- Chapter 14. Online Supporting Documents and Downloads.

The book includes everything you need to prepare for and deliver your workshop:

- **Agendas,** the heart of the series, are laid out in three columns for ease of delivery. The first column shows the timing, the second gives the presentation slide number and image for quick reference, and the third gives instructions and facilitation notes. These are designed to be straightforward, simple agendas that you can take into the training room and use to stay on track. They include cues on the learning activities, notes about tools or handouts to include, and other important delivery tips. You can download the agendas from the website (see Chapter 14) and print them out for easy use.

- **Learning activities,** which are more detailed than the agendas, cover the objectives of the activity, the time and materials required, the steps involved, variations on the activity in some cases, and wrap-up or debriefing questions or comments.

- **Assessments, handouts, and tools** are the training materials you will provide to learners to support the training program. These can include scorecards for games, instructions, reference materials, samples, self-assessments, and so forth.

- **Presentation media** (PowerPoint slides) are deliberately designed to be simple so that you can customize them for your company and context. They are provided for your convenience. Chapter 7 discusses different forms of technology that you can incorporate into your program, including different types of presentation media.

All the program materials are available for download, customization, and duplication. See Chapter 14 for instructions on how to access the materials.

How Are the Agendas Laid Out?

The following agenda is a sample from the two-day workshop.

Day One: (8:00 a.m. to 4:00 p.m.)

TIMING	SLIDES	ACTIVITIES/NOTES/CONSIDERATIONS
8:00 a.m. (10 min)	Slide 1A ATD Workshop Change Management Training Day One	**Welcome and Introduction** Arrive 1 hour before the session starts to ensure that the room is set up, equipment works, and materials are arranged for participants. This gives you time to make participants feel truly welcomed. Chatting with them builds a trusting relationship and opens them up for learning.
8:10 a.m. (20 min)	Slide 2 My Change Manager Role Is Like a ... · Sail · Rudder · Tiller · Hull · Compass	**Learning Activity 1: Managers Navigate Constant, Complex Change** • **Handout 1: Managers Navigate Constant, Complex Change** This activity is the icebreaker. It will introduce participants to the content, to each other, and to the action orientation of this workshop. It is meant to be lively and noisy. Follow the instructions in the learning activity. NOTE: The workshop uses a nautical theme. The pictures, terminology, activities, and titles all add to the fun and intrigue. Please feel free to add your own touches, such as toy sailboats, sailors' "knot puzzles," or other things that your participants will enjoy.
8:30 a.m. (10 min)	Slide 3 Quote Me · Select a quote · What guides you? · Your thoughts about change	**Learning Activity 2: Quote Me** • **Quote Me Cards** In this activity, participants will select a change quote printed on a card that resonates with them and continue to get to know the people at their tables. Follow instructions in the learning activity.

How Do I Use This Book?

If you've ever read a "Choose Your Own Adventure" book, you will recognize that this book follows a similar principle. Think back to the self-assessment at the beginning of this introduction:

- If you chose *authority*, you can get right to work preparing one of the workshops in Section I. Use Section II as a reference. Each of the chapters in Section II features a sidebar or other information written by the author who has much experience in the topic under consideration. This advice can help guide your preparation, delivery, and evaluation of training.

- If you chose *developing expertise*, read Section II in depth and skim the topic content.

- If you chose *novice at training and the topic*, then spend some serious time familiarizing yourself with both Sections I and II of this volume as well as the topic content.

Once you have a general sense of the material, assemble your workshop. Select the appropriate agenda and then modify the times and training activities as needed and desired. Assemble the materials and familiarize yourself with the topic, the activities, and the presentation media.

Key Points

- The workshops in this book are designed to be effective at all levels of trainer expertise.

- Good training requires an investment of time.

- The book contains everything you need to create a workshop, including agendas, learning activities, presentation media, assessments, handouts, and tools.

What to Do Next

- Review the agendas presented in Section I and select the best fit for your requirements, time constraints, and budget.

- Based on your level of expertise, skim or read in-depth the chapters in Section II.

- Consider what kind of follow-up learning activities you will want to include with the workshop by reviewing Section III.

References

Ashkenas, R. (2013). "Change Management Needs to Change." *Harvard Business Review*, April 16. https://hbr.org/2013/04/change-management-needs-to-cha.

Biech, E. (2008). *10 Steps to Successful Training*. Alexandria, VA: ASTD Press.

Biech, E., ed. (2014). *ASTD Handbook: The Definitive Reference for Training & Development*, 2nd edition. Alexandria, VA: ASTD Press.

Emerson, T., and M. Stewart. (2011). *The Learning and Development Book.* Alexandria, VA: ASTD Press.

Johansen, B. (2012). *Leaders Make the Future.* San Francisco: Berrett-Koehler.

Leonard, D., and C. Coltea. (2013). "Most Change Initiatives Fail—But They Don't Have To." *Gallup Business Journal*, May 24. http://www.gallup.com/businessjournal/162707/change-initiatives-fail-don.aspx.

McCain, D.V. (2015). *Facilitation Basics*, 2nd edition. Alexandria, VA: ATD Press.

Mitchell, M., et al. (2015). *The Conference Board CEO Challenge: 2015.* New York: The Conference Board.

Parry, W. (2015). *Big Change, Best Path: Successfully Managing Organizational Change.* London: Kogan Page.

SECTION I

The Workshops

Chapter 1
Two-Day Change Management Training Workshop

What's in This Chapter

- Objectives of the two-day Change Management Training Workshop
- Summary chart for the flow of content and activities
- Two-day program agenda

Whether you choose a two-day, one-day, half-day, or custom-designed workshop format, time spent helping managers develop the skills required to manage change will be a solid investment for your organization. Managing change has—well—changed! Today's organizations operate in a volatile, uncertain, complex, ambiguous (VUCA) world, and continuous, multifarious, and sometimes complicated change is at the helm. Managing change for their organizations is more important than ever for managers. Understanding their expanded role, practicing new management techniques, and demystifying the people side of change are critical skills for contemporary managers.

And there are other advantages for bringing managers together to address change management. Participants get to know each other, build rapport, and reflect on and practice skills they are learning. They also have a greater opportunity to network with other participants so that they have ready lifelines to call when they return to the job. Moreover, managers who attend from the same company will recognize the importance of working across departments to coordinate the complex, continuous changes their organizations face daily.

A well-designed workshop accounts for and anticipates the natural and predictable "low energy" times during the day. It is essential to incorporate activities that engage participants and get them out of their seats and actively participating in relevant and meaningful experiential activities, small group discussion, and practice. Facilitating a two-day (or longer) workshop requires the facilitator to have a high level of energy, focus, and a keen ability to read the energy level of the participants. Keep the participants engaged and the energy high by managing the flow of activities, presentations, personal reflection, and small- or large-group discussions. Variety is the key. To add to the interest and variety, the workshop is based on a nautical theme, using pictures and words to hold participants' attention.

This chapter provides a comprehensive two-day workshop agenda focused on helping managers manage their organizations' change today and in the future. The workshop presents a four-phase model and allows time for practice plus tips, templates, and checklists to support managers back on the job. Day One focuses on assessing the organization and clarifying the process for employees. Day Two focuses on implementing the current change and building capacity for future change.

Two-Day Workshop Objectives

By the end of the two-day workshop, participants will be able to

- Assess their change management areas of strength and areas requiring improvement
- Create a plan to determine organizational/departmental readiness
- Clarify the fundamentals of change management
- Lead a change management initiative in their department
- Manage change from an operational and an employee perspective
- Build change capacity for their organization
- Evaluate a change initiative from three result perspectives: effort, organization, and personal.

                                               CHANGE MANAGEMENT training

Two-Day Workshop Overview

Day One Overview

TOPICS	TIMING
Workshop Opening: The Changing World of Change	
Welcome and Introduction	10 minutes
Learning Activity 1: Managers Navigate Constant, Complex Change	20 minutes
Learning Activity 2: Quote Me	10 minutes
Learning Objectives	10 minutes
Workshop Guidelines	5 minutes
Assessment 1: Rate Your Managing Change Skills	30 minutes
Learning Activity 3: Is Change a Sinking Ship?	20 minutes
BREAK	**15 minutes**
Phase I: Assess the Situation	
Learning Activity 4: Ensure the Fundamentals Are in Place	75 minutes
Learning Activity 5: Make Up Your Mind!	15 minutes
Learning Activity 6: Determine Organizational Readiness	30 minutes
LUNCH	**60 minutes**
Learning Activity 7: Establish a Sense of Urgency	30 minutes
Learning Activity 8: Snap, Snap, Change	15 minutes
Phase II: Accept Leadership Accountability	
Learning Activity 9: What's Leadership Accountability?	15 minutes
Open Your Fist	5 minutes
Learning Activity 10: Optimize Communication	25 minutes
BREAK	**15 minutes**
Learning Activity 11: Navigate Resistance to Change	30 minutes
Learning Activity 12: Work Is a Juggling Act	15 minutes
Learning Activity 13: Tools to Manage Relationships	20 minutes
Day One Debrief: My MVT (Most Valuable Tip) of the Day	10 minutes
TOTAL	**480 minutes (8 hours)**

Day Two Overview

TOPICS	TIMING
Learning Activity 14: A Different Perspective	10 minutes
Learning Activity 15: Angles, Tangles, and Dangles	20 minutes
Learning Activity 16: Oceans of Respect for Good Role Models	50 minutes
Phase III: Attain Implementation Progress	
Cross Your Arms, Fold Your Hands	5 minutes

TOPICS	TIMING
Involve and Engage Others	20 minutes
BREAK	**15 minutes**
Learning Activity 17: Full Speed Ahead to Generate Gains	40 minutes
Learning Activity 18: Naval Slang Energizer	20 minutes
Learning Activity 19: Test the Waters With Ideas for Change-Ready Employees	60 minutes
LUNCH	**60 minutes**
Phase IV: Advance to Future Initiatives	
Institutionalize Changes	10 minutes
Evaluate the Change Results	15 minutes
Learning Activity 20: Smooth Sailing	60 minutes
BREAK	**15 minutes**
Learning Activity 21: Build Capacity for Continuous Change and My Next Steps	45 minutes
Learning Activity 22: Change That Tune	10 minutes
Learning Activity 23: Nothing Will Change If You Don't	20 minutes
Close: Sending You Off	5 minutes
TOTAL	**480 minutes (8 hours)**

Two-Day Workshop Agenda: Day One

The focus of Day One is communication and guiding the work.

Day One: (8:00 a.m. to 4:00 p.m.)

TIMING	SLIDES	ACTIVITIES/NOTES/CONSIDERATIONS
8:00 a.m. (10 min)	Slide 1A ATD Workshop Change Management Training Day One	**Welcome and Introduction** Arrive 1 hour before the session starts to ensure that the room is set up, equipment works, and materials are arranged for participants. This gives you time to make participants feel truly welcomed. Chatting with them builds a trusting relationship and opens them up for learning.

8:10 a.m. (20 min)	Slide 2 My Change Manager Role Is Like a ... · Sail · Rudder · Tiller · Hull · Compass	**Learning Activity 1: Managers Navigate Constant, Complex Change** • **Handout 1: Managers Navigate Constant, Complex Change** This activity is the icebreaker. It will introduce participants to the content, to each other, and to the action orientation of this workshop. It is meant to be lively and noisy. Follow the instructions in the learning activity. NOTE: The workshop uses a nautical theme. The pictures, terminology, activities, and titles all add to the fun and intrigue. Please feel free to add your own touches, such as toy sailboats, sailors' "knot puzzles," or other things that your participants will enjoy.
8:30 a.m. (10 min)	Slide 3 Quote Me · Select a quote · What guides you? · Your thoughts about change	**Learning Activity 2: Quote Me** • **Quote Me Cards** In this activity, participants will select a change quote printed on a card that resonates with them and continue to get to know the people at their tables. Follow instructions in the learning activity.
8:40 a.m. (10 min)	Slide 4 Learning Objectives · Assess your change management skills · Determine organizational readiness · Clarify change fundamentals · Lead a change management initiative · Manage operational and employee focus · Build organizational change capacity · Evaluate a change initiative three ways	**Learning Objectives** • **Handout 2: Change Management Training Objectives** • **Handout 3: A Manager's Model for Change** Review the global objectives on the slide and Handout 2. Explain that the session has 29 handouts and 23 experiential activities to help participants delve more deeply into the content. Ask if they are looking for specific information or solutions in the workshop.
	Slide 5 Manager's Change Model	Use this slide to introduce the Manager's Change Model and give the participants the big picture of the content covered in the workshop (Handout 3).

8:50 a.m. (5 min)	Slide 6	**Workshop Guidelines**
	Workshop Guidelines · Start & end on time · Ask questions · Offer ideas · Breaks · Get involved	This slide lays out basic ground rules for the workshop. Ask participants what else they would like to include and add anything you think is pertinent.
8:55 a.m. (30 min)	Slide 7	**Assessment 1: Rate Your Managing Change Skills**
	Rate Your Skills · Complete the assessment · Respond to the questions · Pair with someone for feedback ABILITY	• **Handout 4: Rate Your Managing Change Skills** This assessment gives participants another picture of what is expected of them. Tell them to complete the assessment in Handout 4, respond to the open-ended questions, and then pair with someone to share feedback. Lead a group discussion around their assessment results. Optional: You could ask participants to complete the assessment before the workshop to introduce them to the topic.
9:25 a.m. (20 min)	Slide 8	**Learning Activity 3: Is Change a Sinking Ship?**
	Is Change a Sinking Ship? It's a VUCA world Volatile Uncertain Complex Ambiguous . . . or a sunken treasure?	• **Handout 5: Is Change a Sinking Ship?** • **Handout 6: It's Time to Change How We Change!** This activity explores the past record of managing change and how it has changed today. Both handouts are information dense, and you will want to read and digest them thoroughly prior to the workshop so that you can lead a quick but informative discussion. If you are not familiar with VUCA, get yourself up to speed quickly. You'll find interesting information with just a quick search on the Internet.
	Slide 9	Use Slides 9 and 10 to guide you through Handouts 5 and 6. They will help you punctuate and reinforce the learning discussion generated by this activity.
	Change Can Be a Sunken Treasure · Fundamentals are important— but not everything · Inform employees— but listen more · Build organizational change capacity— but create change-ready employees too	

	Slide 10	

9:45 a.m. (15 min)	Slide 11 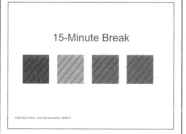	**BREAK** During the break, take time to meet and greet participants who may have arrived late.
10:00 a.m. (75 min)	Slide 12 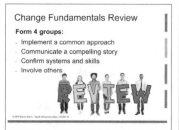	**Learning Activity 4: Ensure the Fundamentals Are in Place** • **Handout 7a: Ensure the Fundamentals Are in Place** • **Handout 7b: Fundamental 1** • **Handout 7c: Fundamental 2** • **Handout 7d: Fundamental 3** • **Handout 7e: Fundamental 4** This activity will help participants quickly review the foundational elements of change management. In Learning Activity 3, they learned that managing change is very different today than in the past. It is no longer a single, spaced initiative; it is ongoing, constant, and complex. Given that this workshop is for managers, many of your participants will most likely have had the basics of using a model, developing a communication plan, ensuring systems are in place, and getting others involved. However, some may not be familiar with these basics, and this activity will give everyone a quick-and-dirty overview. And of course it serves as a good review for those who may have forgotten the fundamentals. Be sure to substitute your organization's content, tools, and information as appropriate. Follow the instructions in the learning activity.

	Slide 13 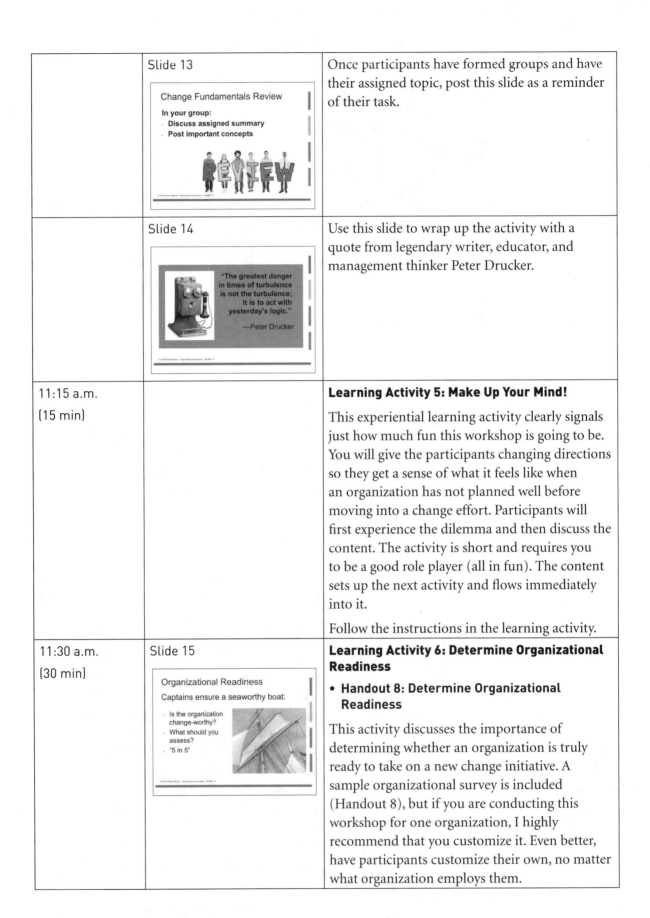	Once participants have formed groups and have their assigned topic, post this slide as a reminder of their task.
	Slide 14	Use this slide to wrap up the activity with a quote from legendary writer, educator, and management thinker Peter Drucker.
11:15 a.m. (15 min)		**Learning Activity 5: Make Up Your Mind!**
		This experiential learning activity clearly signals just how much fun this workshop is going to be. You will give the participants changing directions so they get a sense of what it feels like when an organization has not planned well before moving into a change effort. Participants will first experience the dilemma and then discuss the content. The activity is short and requires you to be a good role player (all in fun). The content sets up the next activity and flows immediately into it.
		Follow the instructions in the learning activity.
11:30 a.m. (30 min)	Slide 15	**Learning Activity 6: Determine Organizational Readiness**
		• **Handout 8: Determine Organizational Readiness**
		This activity discusses the importance of determining whether an organization is truly ready to take on a new change initiative. A sample organizational survey is included (Handout 8), but if you are conducting this workshop for one organization, I highly recommend that you customize it. Even better, have participants customize their own, no matter what organization employs them.

12:00 p.m. (60 min)	Slide 16 60-Minute Lunch	**LUNCH**
1:00 p.m. (30 min)	Slide 17 Sense of Urgency **Two Methods Are Necessary:** ½ increase energy, excitement ½ reduce fear, anger, complacency Index cards 4 minutes	**Learning Activity 7: Establish a Sense of Urgency** • **Handout 9a: Establish a Sense of Urgency** • **Handout 9b: Deep Dives** • **Supplemental Handout: What Floats Your Boat?** • **Supplemental Resource: Ways to Establish a Sense of Urgency** This activity is just what you need right after lunch because it incorporates something I created called a *lingo line*, where the participants facilitate the information flow for you. Follow the instructions in the learning activity.
	Slide 18 What Floats Your Boat? Ideas and actions you want to remember	Use this slide to wrap up this activity. Pass out the What Floats Your Boat? sheet, which is designed for them to capture ideas they want to remember when they return to work. Suggest they choose one idea they will do as a result of this exercise. Explain that throughout the workshop you will periodically remind them to capture their great ideas on this sheet.
1:30 p.m. (15 min)		**Learning Activity 8: Snap, Snap, Change** This activity is a combination energizer and experiential activity to show how it feels when change creates stress in an organization. Practice this before the session with some colleagues. It can be tricky. Follow the instructions in the learning activity.

1:45 p.m. (15 min)	Slide 19 What's Leadership Accountability? **On your index card, list:** · **One specific action that defines _leadership accountability_**	**Learning Activity 9: What's Leadership Accountability?** Use this lively activity to help you transition into phase two of the manager's change model: accept leadership accountability. When it comes to change, there are always questions about leadership and accountability, and so a few minutes spent here will help your participants focus on practical things they can do to demonstrate leadership accountability. Assure participants that there are no right or wrong answers. Follow the instructions in the learning activity.
2:00 p.m. (5 min)	Slide 20 Our Words of Change **Positive or Negative?** · Cancel · Terminate · Plan · Alter · Uncertain · Modify · Start over · Indefinite · Different · Reschedule · Reorganize · Substitute · Urgency · Replace	**Open Your Fist** Ask participants to pair up and select one person to be A and the other B. Ask As to make a fist and to place it in front of the other person. Tell Bs they have 13 seconds, without drawing blood and limiting violence, to open As' fists. Say: "Ready, set, go." Call time at 13 seconds. How many used force? What other ways did Bs use to try to open As' fists? How many just asked the As to open their fists? State: "My language may have led you there. Using words such as _fist, blood_, and _violence_ may have suggested that _force_ was necessary. As we move into a communication discussion, think about the words we use." Show the slide and ask how many of these words connected with change feel positive? Thank you Elliott Masie for this idea!

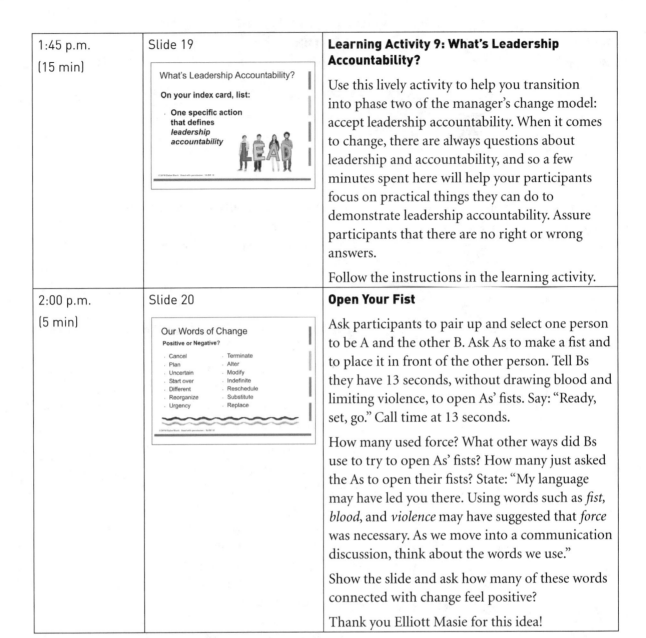

2:05 p.m. (25 min)	Slide 21 Optimize Communication Or . . . What's a metaphor? "Like sitting in a dingy during a tsunami!" Got the picture?	**Learning Activity 10: Optimize Communication** • **Handout 10: Your Communication Plan** • **Handout 11: Optimize Your Communication Plan With Social Media** In Learning Activity 10 we find a lively activity that perfectly accompanies a topic that is talked (no pun intended) to death: communication. Refer to Handout 10 and ask participants about the purpose of a communication plan. Ask them to share what communication advice they would have for change leaders. Discuss their answers briefly. This activity will give them experience with using metaphor as a powerful communication tool. Follow the instructions in the learning activity.
	Slide 22 Your team has been hired for the important "Brussel Sprout Relaunch." · Create campaign slogan giving the sprout: · Its rightful splendor and pride · Its valuable place in the world · Draw a picture representing the slogan · 10 minutes	Have participants work as teams to use metaphors to create a communication or marketing statement for a very unlikely candidate: the lowly brussels sprout. Expect fun.
	Slide 23 Common Metaphor Themes · Geography · Disasters · Community · Hurricane, storm · Family · Solar system · Growing · Animals · Sports · Body parts · Ocean, sea, water · Transportation · Racing · Heroics · Mountain climbing · Building · Trips or journeys · Working, jobs	Use this slide to list common metaphor themes to help the groups get started on their relaunch campaign.
	Slide 24 How Do You Use Social Media? SOCIAL MEDIA	Social media is one of the newer tools in the communication toolkit. Use Handout 11 to help participants explore using social media to manage change more effectively. Ask them to share how they are already using social media to optimize their communication plans. Remind them to write the ideas they want to remember on their What Floats Your Boat? sheets.

	Slide 25 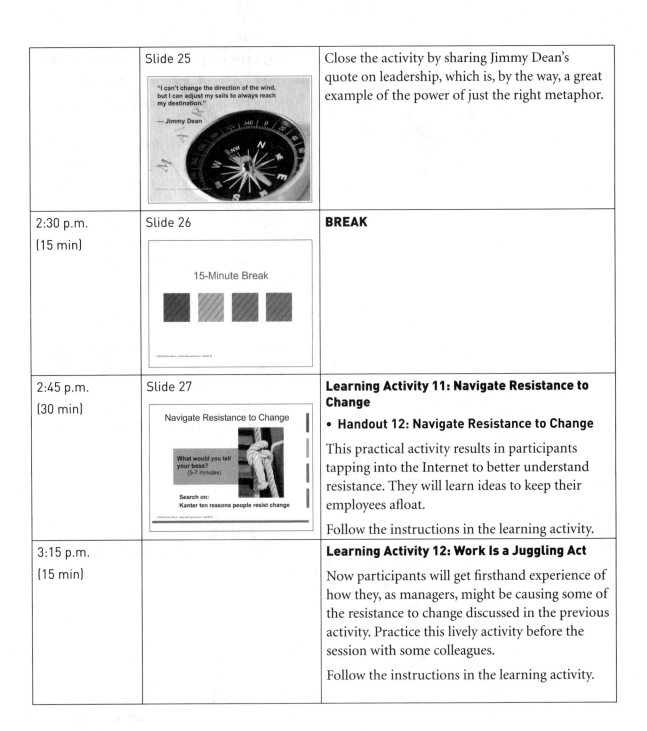	Close the activity by sharing Jimmy Dean's quote on leadership, which is, by the way, a great example of the power of just the right metaphor.
2:30 p.m. (15 min)	Slide 26 15-Minute Break	**BREAK**
2:45 p.m. (30 min)	Slide 27 Navigate Resistance to Change What would you tell your boss? (5-7 minutes) Search on: Kanter ten reasons people resist change	**Learning Activity 11: Navigate Resistance to Change** • **Handout 12: Navigate Resistance to Change** This practical activity results in participants tapping into the Internet to better understand resistance. They will learn ideas to keep their employees afloat. Follow the instructions in the learning activity.
3:15 p.m. (15 min)		**Learning Activity 12: Work Is a Juggling Act** Now participants will get firsthand experience of how they, as managers, might be causing some of the resistance to change discussed in the previous activity. Practice this lively activity before the session with some colleagues. Follow the instructions in the learning activity.

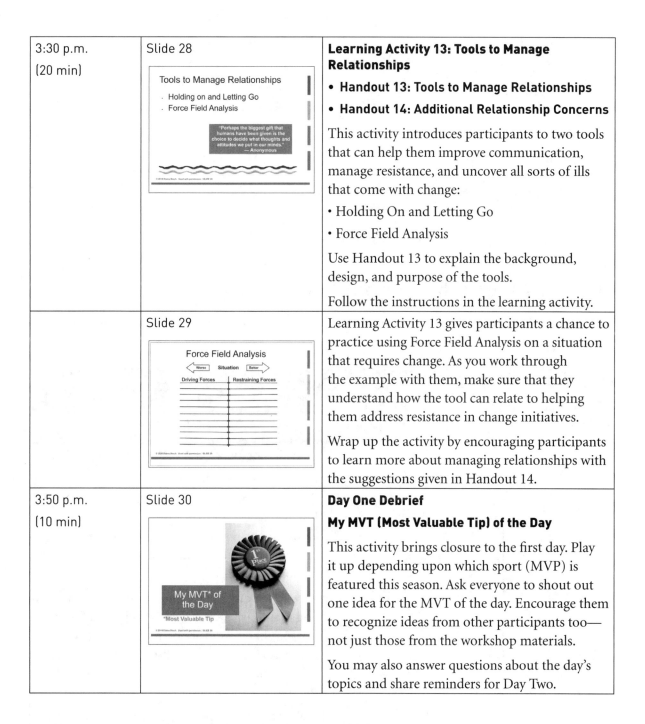

3:30 p.m. (20 min)	Slide 28	**Learning Activity 13: Tools to Manage Relationships** • **Handout 13: Tools to Manage Relationships** • **Handout 14: Additional Relationship Concerns** This activity introduces participants to two tools that can help them improve communication, manage resistance, and uncover all sorts of ills that come with change: • Holding On and Letting Go • Force Field Analysis Use Handout 13 to explain the background, design, and purpose of the tools. Follow the instructions in the learning activity.
	Slide 29	Learning Activity 13 gives participants a chance to practice using Force Field Analysis on a situation that requires change. As you work through the example with them, make sure that they understand how the tool can relate to helping them address resistance in change initiatives. Wrap up the activity by encouraging participants to learn more about managing relationships with the suggestions given in Handout 14.
3:50 p.m. (10 min)	Slide 30	**Day One Debrief** **My MVT (Most Valuable Tip) of the Day** This activity brings closure to the first day. Play it up depending upon which sport (MVP) is featured this season. Ask everyone to shout out one idea for the MVT of the day. Encourage them to recognize ideas from other participants too—not just those from the workshop materials. You may also answer questions about the day's topics and share reminders for Day Two.

What to Do Between Workshop Days

- Make notes about follow-up you need to do before the second day.

- Capture facilitator lessons learned from the first day of the workshop and adjust materials or your facilitation plan for the second day, if necessary.

- Address equipment, room setup, catering, or other learning environment issues you may not have been able to address during the workshop.

- Ensure that you have printed the Supplemental Handouts required for Learning Activities 18, 20, and 22. These handouts are included with the corresponding learning activities in Chapter 11 and require a close hold by you until the appropriate time within the activity.

- Debrief with your cofacilitator, if appropriate.

- Gather together the materials required for Day Two's activities.

- Move participants for Day Two's opening activity. (Follow the instructions in Learning Activity 14 for an easy way to do this.)

- Get a good night's sleep to ensure that you are refreshed and ready for Day Two.

Two-Day Workshop Agenda: Day Two

The focus of Day Two is leading the workforce, coaching employee performance, and developing yourself.

Day Two: (8:00 a.m. to 4:00 p.m.)

TIMING	SLIDES	ACTIVITIES/NOTES/CONSIDERATIONS
8:00 a.m. (10 min)	Slide 31	**Learning Activity 14: A Different Perspective** Launch right into this opening activity. It is designed to help participants experience what it is like to have the environment changed without warning. For this to work, you will need to have moved their materials at the end of Day One's session. Play up the drama of the situation. Say: "What? You moved where you were sitting? What is this—a change workshop or something?" It makes the point, and the discussion it generates will be beneficial. You can decide if you will allow them to return to their original seats. Follow the instructions in the learning activity.
8:10 a.m. (20 min)	Slide 32	**Learning Activity 15: Angles, Tangles, and Dangles** This activity gives participants an opportunity to review what they learned from a positive and questioning perspective. It also helps them identify the content that needs to be reinforced or explored for better understanding. Follow the instructions in the learning activity.

8:30 a.m. (50 min)	Slide 33	**Learning Activity 16: Oceans of Respect for Good Role Models**
	Respect for Good Role Models **Behaviors That Drive** Commitment · Rate your behaviors +/- · Find a partner · Review 15 minutes **Behaviors That Drive** Change · Review with your partner · What effect on success of change? · How can you exhibit each? © 2010 Elaine Biech. Used with permission / SLIDE 33	• **Handout 15: Oceans of Respect for Good Role Models** This activity helps participants understand how imperative role modeling is to the success of change efforts. Use this activity to expose them to research that supports the behaviors that are expected of them. Because they probably have some "personal changing" to do, ample time is allotted for self-reflection and partner activities to reinforce these behaviors in their manager toolkit. Be supportive during this activity by mingling during their small group discussions. Encourage them to continue their discussions with their partners after the workshop. Follow the instructions in the learning activity.
9:20 a.m. (5 min)		**Cross Your Arms, Fold Your Hands** These two quick activities bring participants back to why change can be difficult. First, tell participants to cross their arms, look at how they are crossed, and then cross them with the *opposite* arm on top. Keep talking with them about how it feels, why, how they ended up with these feelings—any topic that keeps their arms folded the wrong way as long as possible. Soon you will see people separating their arms. For some, crossing their arms in a different way will be so uncomfortable that they can barely listen to you. Make the point that if they are that uncomfortable with such a little thing as crossing their arms, imagine how their employees must feel with the larger changes foisted upon them. Second, make the same point by asking participants to fold their hands and then refold them with the *opposite* thumb on top. How long are they able to do this? Let them know that these are both good activities they can take back to their people to help them understand their teams' discomfort and difficulty with change.

9:25 a.m. (20 min)	Slide 34 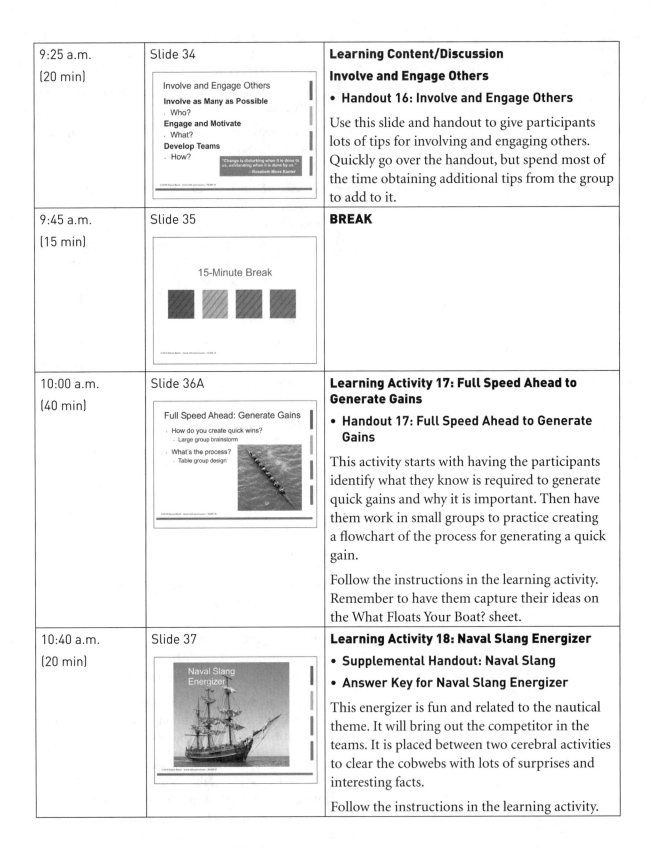	**Learning Content/Discussion** **Involve and Engage Others** • **Handout 16: Involve and Engage Others** Use this slide and handout to give participants lots of tips for involving and engaging others. Quickly go over the handout, but spend most of the time obtaining additional tips from the group to add to it.
9:45 a.m. (15 min)	Slide 35	**BREAK**
10:00 a.m. (40 min)	Slide 36A	**Learning Activity 17: Full Speed Ahead to Generate Gains** • **Handout 17: Full Speed Ahead to Generate Gains** This activity starts with having the participants identify what they know is required to generate quick gains and why it is important. Then have them work in small groups to practice creating a flowchart of the process for generating a quick gain. Follow the instructions in the learning activity. Remember to have them capture their ideas on the What Floats Your Boat? sheet.
10:40 a.m. (20 min)	Slide 37	**Learning Activity 18: Naval Slang Energizer** • **Supplemental Handout: Naval Slang** • **Answer Key for Naval Slang Energizer** This energizer is fun and related to the nautical theme. It will bring out the competitor in the teams. It is placed between two cerebral activities to clear the cobwebs with lots of surprises and interesting facts. Follow the instructions in the learning activity.

11:00 a.m. (60 min)	Slide 38 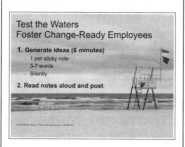	**Learning Activity 19: Test the Waters With Ideas for Change-Ready Employees** • **Handout 18: Foster Change-Ready Employees** Start the activity by overviewing the highlights of Handout 18. Then introduce the affinity diagram tool to participants, which is a great way to get a large group of people to generate, organize, prioritize, and agree on a large number of ideas for a large topic. It is highly interactive and involves all the participants at the same time. Lead the group in a self-brainstorming exercise, generating ideas to answer this question: What are the issues involved in creating a change-ready workforce? Have them write their ideas on sticky notes, share them aloud, and post on the wall. If you have a room full of managers, they will have great ideas, and you will want to capture all of them. Follow the instructions in the learning activity.
	Slide 39A 	For the next step in this activity, have the participants group all the ideas that were generated into like categories. They remain silent during this step. In the final step, you will lead them in prioritizing the groups of ideas. Wrap up the activity by discussing what will happen with their good work. For example, if they have a list of informal learning opportunities or a list of topics employees require, what can they do to ensure that the content moves to the next step? Someone may volunteer to write down the content for a permanent record. If so, be sure that the person receives all the notes.
12:00 p.m. (60 min)	Slide 40 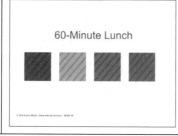	**LUNCH**

1:00 p.m. (10 min)	Slide 41 	**Learning Content/Discussion** **Institutionalize Changes** • **Handout 19: Institutionalize Changes** Use this slide and handout to explain what *institutionalizing change* means and provide lots of ideas to help change put down roots in their organizations. Lead a quick discussion and ask for a couple of additional ideas. The handout is meant to be a resource that participants can use back on their jobs.
1:10 p.m. (15 min)	Slide 42 	**Learning Content/Discussion** **Evaluate the Change Results** • **Handout 20: Evaluate the Change Results** This handout provides examples and discusses the three types of evaluations organizations should complete after change efforts. Some organizations have an ongoing evaluation process because change never stops. The handout includes two assessments for participants to use to evaluate the change process and themselves as leaders of change. Invite them to revisit these assessments at the end of every change initiative to gather lessons learned.
1:25 p.m. (60 min)	Slide 43 	**Learning Activity 20: Smooth Sailing** **Supplemental Handouts:** • **Smooth Sailing Observer Sheet** • **Smooth Sailing Engineering Team Role** • **Smooth Sailing Marketing Team Role** • **Smooth Sailing Financial Team Role** • **Smooth Sailing Post-Leadership Meeting Debrief** This activity helps participants use everything they have learned in the workshop to analyze and solve problems that are exaggerated but realistic. It is a busy, fun, and chaotic activity. Its placement just before break is intentional because it may be difficult to get them to stop learning! Follow the instructions in the learning activity.

	Slide 44	Display this slide as you wrap up the activity. It provides an example of a paper boat design that actually floats. Debrief the activity using the discussion questions provided in the learning activity.
2:25 p.m. (15 min)	Slide 45	**BREAK**
2:40 p.m. (45 min)	Slide 46	**Learning Activity 21: Build Capacity for Continuous Change and My Next Steps** • **Handout 21: Build Capacity for Continuous Change** • **Handout 22: Action Planning: My Next Steps** • **Handout 24: Additional Reading for Your Continued Development** This activity enables participants to explore ideas that build capacity for an organization's continuous change. Its "speed-dating" format helps them gather ideas from colleagues for specific ideas they want to pursue back at their workplace. Follow the instructions in the learning activity.
	Slide 47	The content in the first part of this learning activity is a natural transition to creating an action plan to ensure that the managers actually implement the ideas they have learned. Ask them to capture their next step on the action planning handout (Handout 22). If you haven't already, this is also a good time to point out the reading list in Handout 24. You should be familiar with these or other books so that you can recommend appropriate materials to the participants to keep learning about change.

3:25 p.m. (10 min)	Slide 48 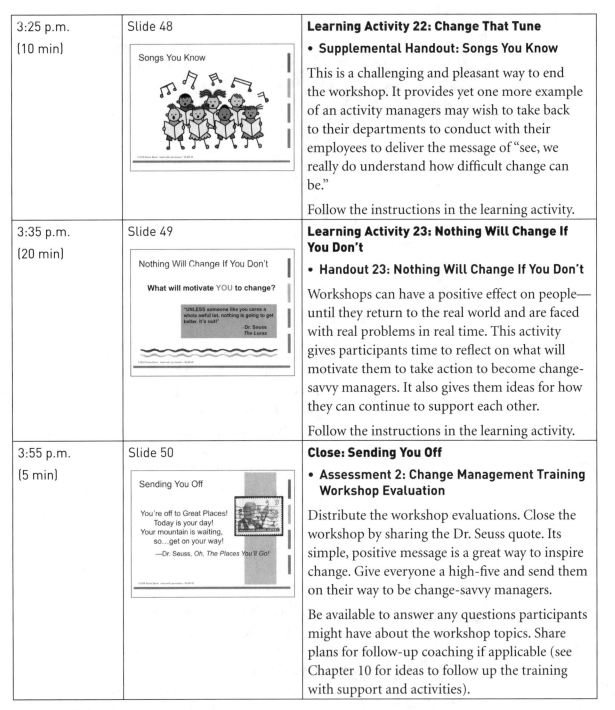	**Learning Activity 22: Change That Tune** • **Supplemental Handout: Songs You Know** This is a challenging and pleasant way to end the workshop. It provides yet one more example of an activity managers may wish to take back to their departments to conduct with their employees to deliver the message of "see, we really do understand how difficult change can be." Follow the instructions in the learning activity.
3:35 p.m. (20 min)	Slide 49	**Learning Activity 23: Nothing Will Change If You Don't** • **Handout 23: Nothing Will Change If You Don't** Workshops can have a positive effect on people—until they return to the real world and are faced with real problems in real time. This activity gives participants time to reflect on what will motivate them to take action to become change-savvy managers. It also gives them ideas for how they can continue to support each other. Follow the instructions in the learning activity.
3:55 p.m. (5 min)	Slide 50	**Close: Sending You Off** • **Assessment 2: Change Management Training Workshop Evaluation** Distribute the workshop evaluations. Close the workshop by sharing the Dr. Seuss quote. Its simple, positive message is a great way to inspire change. Give everyone a high-five and send them on their way to be change-savvy managers. Be available to answer any questions participants might have about the workshop topics. Share plans for follow-up coaching if applicable (see Chapter 10 for ideas to follow up the training with support and activities).

What to Do Next

- Determine the schedule for training classes; reserve location and catering you may wish to provide.

- Identify and invite participants.

- Inform participants about pre-work, such as Assessment 1: Rate Your Managing Change Skills (Handout 4), if you want it completed before the workshop begins.

- Review the workshop objectives, activities, and handouts to plan the content you will use.

- Prepare copies of the participant materials and any activity-related materials you may need. Refer to Chapter 14 for information about how to access and use the supplemental materials provided for this workshop.

- Ensure that you have printed the supplemental handouts required for Learning Activities 2, 7, 18, 20, and 22. These handouts are included with the corresponding learning activities in Chapter 11 and require a close hold by you until the appropriate time within the activity.

- Gather tactile items, such as Koosh balls, crayons, magnets, Play-Doh, or others, you wish to place on the tables for tactile learners. See Chapter 8 for other ideas to enhance the learning environment of your workshop.

- Prepare yourself both emotionally and physically. Confirm that you have addressed scheduling and personal concerns so that you can be fully present to facilitate the class.

- Get a good night's sleep before you facilitate your workshop so that you have the energy and focus to deliver an outstanding session for your participants.

Chapter 2

One-Day Change Management Training Workshop

What's in This Chapter

- Objectives of the one-day Change Management Workshop
- Summary chart for the flow of content and activities
- One-day program agenda

There are two approaches you can take to designing and delivering a one-day workshop. You can select one topic and focus only on that topic, or you can take a broader perspective and allow the participants to sample a range of topics. In fact many of the topics in this book could lend themselves to full-day discussions such as improving communication, gaining resiliency, problem solving, addressing resistance, working on teams, and so on. Managing change in an organization is one of the most critical roles for a manager. Change managers must think broadly, across the organization. Making that mindset change can be difficult for many new managers. So, given the nature of the change management role, we have chosen a more comprehensive approach in this workshop.

Leaders' attitudes and actions greatly influence an organization's culture. The Conference Board reported in its 2015 annual survey that "organizations must focus on behavioral change to make change more sustainable and become agile. It is about helping people embrace and adopt change by building personal competencies . . . It is about instilling personal responsibility and accountability for change at every level. . . .The focus should be on developing change leaders at all levels, not just reactive change managers" (Mitchell et al. 2015). The research was conducted with CEOs of global corporations. This is powerful information. When we also learn that recent research by Accenture shows that the business unit managers are the ones who ***play the most significant role in effectively implementing change*** in organizations, we have a compelling reason to provide as much knowledge and as many skills as possible (Parry 2015). It's all pretty heady stuff!

This one-day workshop is deliberately designed with a broad overview in mind. In one day participants can explore the many responsibilities required of them as change managers. The one-day session does not try to cram lots of content into the learner. Instead, the workshop allows participants the opportunity to sample multiple job requirements and experiences through activities, discussion, and handouts. It gives participants the chance to face how it might actually feel to be bombarded with many changes at the same time. Handouts are designed to be excellent sources of information after the workshop ends.

Well-designed workshops incorporate activities that engage participants, getting them out of their seats and actively participating in relevant and meaningful experiential activities, small group discussion, and practice. This workshop presents a good mix of activities, presentations, personal reflection, and small- and large-group discussions. Variety is key.

Here are some insider thoughts that will help you deliver a powerful game-changing one-day workshop:

- **A few activity times have been shaved.** You will see that timing on a few activities has been shaved. Although less time for personal reflection is available, we maintained the final action planning and commitment to interactive activities. We also limited the amount of discussion (as a last resort to fit into this timeframe). When a decision had to be made about whether to shorten an activity or remove a topic altogether, shaving 5 minutes off an activity usually won.

- **Several activities have been modified to learning content (handouts) only.** The handouts are excellent resources for participants to use after the workshop. In most cases it might be months before change managers really need the content. The first option is to not include them at all. However, we believe that it is better to give participants the resources letting them know they are available when they need them, than not giving them at all. If you are conducting a series of just-in-time workshops about change, you may decide to remove them and provide them at a later time. The agenda design assumes that this may be a one-time opportunity for some managers to learn about change. Recognizing the huge value in experiences, we've left in as many experiential learning activities as a very full day will hold.

- **Pre-work.** Most of the handouts stand alone, and you could provide them to participants to prepare for the workshop. I recommend that you ask participants to read Handouts 2, 3, 4, 5, 6 and 7. Quite honestly, we have had little success with participants actually completing pre-work unless threatened with not being able to attend. Using the pre-work option, however, can save 30-60 minutes in the session to allow time for more discussion and possibly reduce your feelings of anxiety and angst about facilitating this very full workshop. If you have a foolproof way to get everyone to read the content—go for it. In this case, participants will miss out on how change is changing and the fundamentals of change management. This workshop takes managers beyond the basics, so hopefully those who do not complete the reading will already have some knowledge about change management.

This chapter provides a comprehensive one-day workshop agenda focused on change management. Equipping managers with the skills and knowledge to navigate change is foundational to succeeding in today's complex changing world. Much of how we address change has changed (no double speak intended!) dramatically. Change is constant, complex, and happening at a dizzying pace. Success requires much more than what change management models offer. No longer is a step-by-step model enough. Things are changing all the time, everywhere, and overlapping in all areas. How can managers face everything that is flying at them at once? We suggest they focus on four key actions:

- Ensure the fundamentals are in place
- Enable excellent communication in all directions and at all times
- Confirm that all direct reports are change-ready with skills, mindset, knowledge, and attitude
- Build organizational capacity for continuous change in the future.

One-Day Workshop Objectives

By the end of the one-day workshop, participants will be able to

- Assess their change management areas of strength and areas requiring improvement
- Create a plan to determine organizational and departmental readiness
- Clarify the fundamentals of change management
- Lead a change management initiative in their department
- Manage change from an operational and an employee perspective
- Build change capacity for their organization
- Evaluate a change initiative from three result perspectives: effort, organization, and personal.

One-Day Workshop Overview

Assign pre-reading and exercises in Handouts 2, 3, 4, 5, 6, and 7.

TOPICS	TIMING
Workshop Opening: The Changing World of Change	
Welcome and Introduction	5 minutes
Learning Activity 1: Managers Navigate Constant, Complex Change	15 minutes
Learning Objectives	10 minutes
Workshop Guidelines	5 minutes
Assessment 1: Rate Your Managing Change Skills	15 minutes
Is Change a Sinking Ship?	10 minutes
Phase I: Assess the Situation	
Ensure the Fundamentals Are in Place	15 minutes
Learning Activity 5: Make Up Your Mind!	10 minutes
Learning Activity 6: Determine Organizational Readiness	20 minutes
BREAK	**15 minutes**
Learning Activity 7: Establish a Sense of Urgency	15 minutes
Phase II: Accept Leadership Accountability	
Learning Activity 9: What's Leadership Accountability?	15 minutes
Learning Activity 10: Optimize Communication	15 minutes
Learning Activity 11: Navigate Resistance to Change	30 minutes
Learning Activity 12: Work Is a Juggling Act	15 minutes
Tools to Manage Relationships	5 minutes
Learning Activity 16: Oceans of Respect for Good Role Models	25 minutes
LUNCH	**60 minutes**
Phase III: Attain Implementation Progress	
Involve and Engage Others	5 minutes
Full Speed Ahead to Generate Gains	10 minutes
Learning Activity 20: Smooth Sailing	45 minutes
Cross Your Arms, Fold Your Hands	5 minutes
Learning Activity 19: Test the Waters With Ideas for Change-Ready Employees	30 minutes
BREAK	**15 minutes**
Phase IV: Advance to Future Initiatives	
Learning Activity 21: Build Capacity for Continuous Change and My Next Steps	45 minutes
Learning Activity 23: Nothing Will Change If You Don't	20 minutes
Close: Sending You Off	5 minutes
TOTAL	**480 minutes (8 hours)**

One-Day Workshop Agenda

The one-day session is an overview of most of the topics. The handouts are detailed so that participants will find them useful as they refer back to them. Many quick "change" activities are included that managers will be able to use back on the job with their own employees.

Pre-reading: Handouts 2, 3, 4, 5, 6, and 7.

One Day: (8:00 a.m. to 4:00 p.m.)

TIMING	SLIDES	ACTIVITIES/NOTES/CONSIDERATIONS
8:00 a.m. (5 min)	Slide 1B 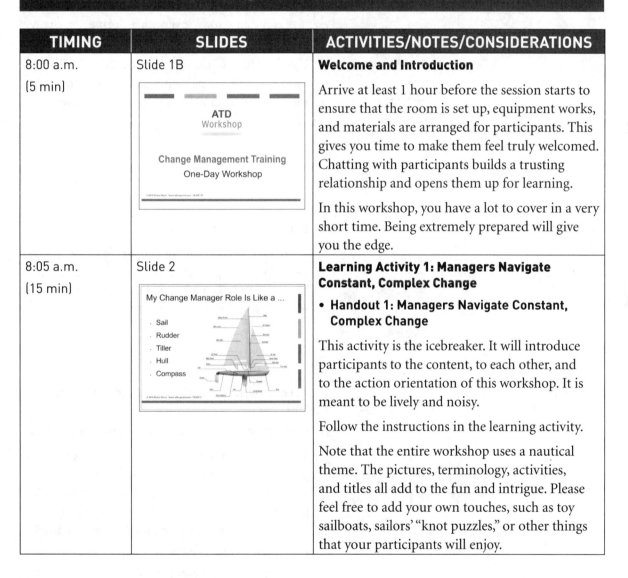	**Welcome and Introduction** Arrive at least 1 hour before the session starts to ensure that the room is set up, equipment works, and materials are arranged for participants. This gives you time to make them feel truly welcomed. Chatting with participants builds a trusting relationship and opens them up for learning. In this workshop, you have a lot to cover in a very short time. Being extremely prepared will give you the edge.
8:05 a.m. (15 min)	Slide 2	**Learning Activity 1: Managers Navigate Constant, Complex Change** • **Handout 1: Managers Navigate Constant, Complex Change** This activity is the icebreaker. It will introduce participants to the content, to each other, and to the action orientation of this workshop. It is meant to be lively and noisy. Follow the instructions in the learning activity. Note that the entire workshop uses a nautical theme. The pictures, terminology, activities, and titles all add to the fun and intrigue. Please feel free to add your own touches, such as toy sailboats, sailors' "knot puzzles," or other things that your participants will enjoy.

8:20 a.m. (10 min)	Slide 4 Learning Objectives · Assess your change management skills · Determine organizational readiness · Clarify change fundamentals · Lead a change management initiative · Manage operational and employee focus · Build organizational change capacity · Evaluate a change initiative three ways	**Learning Objectives** • **Handout 2: Change Management Training Objectives** • **Handout 3: A Manager's Model for Change** Review the global objectives on the slide and Handout 2. Explain that the session has many experiential activities to encourage participants to delve more deeply into the content. In addition, the detailed handouts allow them to continue to learn beyond the workshop. Ask if they are looking for specific information or solutions.
	Slide 5 Manager's Change Model	Use this slide to introduce the Manager's Change Model to give the participants the big picture of the content covered in the workshop (Handout 3).
8:30 a.m. (5 min)	Slide 6 Workshop Guidelines · Start & end on time · Ask questions · Offer ideas · Breaks · Get involved	**Workshop Guidelines** This slide lays out basic ground rules for the workshop. Ask participants what else they would like to include and add anything you think is pertinent.
8:35 a.m. (15 min)	Slide 7 Rate Your Skills · Complete the assessment · Respond to the questions · Pair with someone for feedback ABILITY	**Assessment 1: Rate Your Managing Change Skills** • **Handout 4: Rate Your Managing Change Skills** This assessment gives participants another picture of what is expected of them. They were asked to complete the assessment in Handout 4 before the workshop to introduce them to the topic. Pair them with someone to share feedback about the meaning of the assessment. If they did not complete the assessment beforehand, do not pause but suggest they complete it after the workshop.

8:50 a.m. (10 min)	**Slide 8** 	**Learning Content/Discussion** **Is Change a Sinking Ship?** • **Handout 5: Is Change a Sinking Ship?** • **Handout 6: It's Time to Change How We Change!** Handouts 5 and 6 were part of the pre-reading prior to the workshop. They explore the past record of managing change and how it has changed today. Both handouts are information dense, and you will want to read and digest them thoroughly prior to the workshop so that you can lead a quick but informative discussion. If you are not familiar with VUCA, get yourself up to speed quickly. You'll find interesting information with just a quick search on the Internet.
	Slide 9 	Use Slides 9 and 10 to highlight key points in Handouts 5 and 6.
	Slide 10 	

9:00 a.m. (15 min)	Slide 14	**Learning Content/Discussion**
	"The greatest danger in times of turbulence is not the turbulence; it is to act with yesterday's logic." —Peter Drucker	**Ensure the Fundamentals Are in Place** • **Handout 7a: Ensure the Fundamentals Are in Place** • **Handout 7b: Fundamental 1** • **Handout 7c: Fundamental 2** • **Handout 7d: Fundamental 3** • **Handout 7e: Fundamental 4** Handouts 7 were assigned as pre-reading to ensure that participants were grounded in the basics of change management principles. Quickly review the foundational elements of change management. Change is very different. It is no longer a single, spaced initiative; it is ongoing, constant, and complex. Given that this workshop is for managers, they have most likely learned the basics of using a model, developing a communication plan, ensuring systems are in place, and getting others involved. For those who are not familiar with the basics, this is a way to get a quick-and-dirty overview. It also serves as a refresher for those who may have forgotten the fundamentals. Be sure to substitute your organization's content, tools, and information as appropriate.
9:15 a.m. (10 min)		**Learning Activity 5: Make Up Your Mind!** This experiential learning activity clearly signals just how much fun this workshop is going to be. You will give the participants changing directions so that they get a sense of what it feels like when an organization has not planned well before moving into a change effort. Participants will first experience the dilemma and then discuss the content. The activity is short and requires you to be a good role player (all in fun). The content sets up the next activity and flows immediately into it. Follow the instructions in the learning activity.

9:25 a.m. (20 min)	Slide 15 Organizational Readiness Captains ensure a seaworthy boat: - Is the organization change-worthy? - What should you assess? - "5 in 5"	**Learning Activity 6: Determine Organizational Readiness** - **Handout 8: Determine Organizational Readiness** This activity discusses the importance of determining whether an organization is truly ready to take on a new change initiative. A sample organizational survey is included (Handout 8), but if you are conducting this workshop for one organization, I highly recommend that you customize it. Even better, have participants customize their own, no matter what organization employs them.
9:45 a.m. (15 min)	Slide 11 15-Minute Break	**BREAK** During the break, take time to meet and greet participants who may have arrived late.
10:00 a.m. (15 min)	Slide 17 Sense of Urgency **Two Methods Are Necessary:** - ½ increase energy, excitement - ½ reduce fear, anger, complacency - Index cards - 4 minutes	**Learning Activity 7: Establish a Sense of Urgency** - **Handout 9a: Establish a Sense of Urgency** - **Handout 9b: Deep Dive** - **Supplemental Handout: What Floats Your Boat?** - **Supplemental Resource: Ways to Establish a Sense of Urgency** This activity is a good mid-morning energizer because it incorporates something I created called a *lingo line*, where the participants facilitate the information flow for you. Follow the instructions in the learning activity but shorten preparation and discussion time a little.
	Slide 18 What Floats Your Boat? Ideas and actions you want to remember	Use this slide to wrap up this activity. Pass out the What Floats Your Boat? sheet, which is designed for them to capture ideas they want to remember when they return to work. Suggest they choose one idea they will do as a result of this exercise. Explain that throughout the workshop you will periodically remind them to capture their great ideas on this sheet.

10:15 a.m. (15 min)	Slide 19 What's Leadership Accountability? **On your index card, list:** · **One specific action that defines** *leadership accountability* LEAD	**Learning Activity 9: What's Leadership Accountability?** Use this lively activity to help you transition into phase two of the manager's change model: accept leadership accountability. When it comes to change, there are always questions about leadership and accountability, and so a few minutes spent here will help your participants focus on practical things they can do to demonstrate leadership accountability. Follow the instructions in the learning activity. Assure participants that there are no right or wrong answers.
10:30 a.m. (15 min)	Slide 21 Optimize Communication Or . . . What's a metaphor? "Like sitting in a dingy during a tsunami!" Got the picture?	**Learning Activity 10: Optimize Communication** • **Handout 10: Your Communication Plan** • **Handout 11: Optimize Your Communication Plan With Social Media** Move quickly through the handouts stating that they will be good references at a later time. Form the groups and begin the lively activity that gives participants experience with using metaphor as a powerful communication tool. Follow the instructions in the learning activity but tighten up the times.
	Slide 22 Your team has been hired for the important "Brussel Sprout Relaunch." · Create campaign slogan giving the sprout: – Its rightful splendor and pride – Its valuable place in the world · Draw a picture representing the slogan · 10 minutes	Ask them to work as teams to use metaphors to create a communication or marketing statement for a very unlikely candidate: the lowly brussels sprout. Expect fun.
	Slide 23 Common Metaphor Themes · Geography · Disasters · Community · Hurricane, storm · Family · Solar system · Growing · Animals · Sports · Body parts · Ocean, sea, water · Transportation · Racing · Heroics · Mountain climbing · Building · Trips or journeys · Working, jobs	Use this slide to list common metaphor themes to help the groups get started on their relaunch campaign.

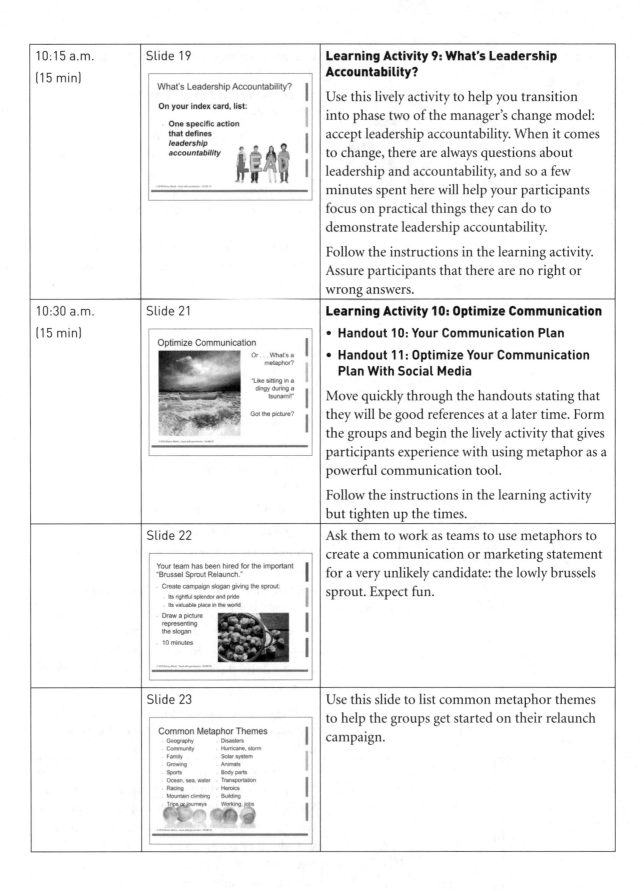

CHANGE MANAGEMENT training

	Slide 24	Social media is one of the newer tools in the communication toolkit. Use Handout 11 to help participants explore using social media to manage change more effectively. Ask them to share how they are already using social media to optimize their communication plans. Remind them to write the ideas they want to remember on their What Floats Your Boat? sheets.
	Slide 25	Close the activity by sharing Jimmy Dean's quote on leadership, which is, by the way, a great example of the power of just the right metaphor.
10:45 a.m. (30 min)	Slide 27	**Learning Activity 11: Navigate Resistance to Change** • **Handout 12: Navigate Resistance to Change** This practical activity results in participants tapping into the Internet to better understand resistance. They will learn ideas to keep their employees afloat. Follow the instructions in the learning activity except shorten the end by leading a discussion instead of having them design their own plan. Suggest that they design a plan for their employees once they complete the workshop.
11:15 a.m. (15 min)		**Learning Activity 12: Work Is a Juggling Act** Now, participants will get firsthand experience of how they, as managers, might be causing some of the resistance to change discussed in the previous activity. Practice this lively activity before the session with some colleagues. Follow the instructions in the learning activity.

11:30 a.m. (5 min)	Slide 28 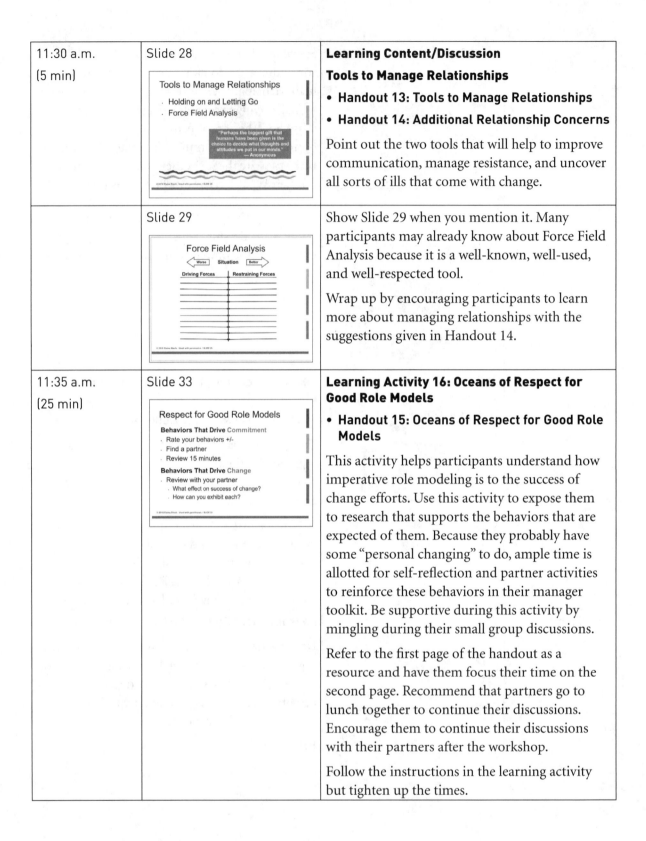	**Learning Content/Discussion** **Tools to Manage Relationships** • **Handout 13: Tools to Manage Relationships** • **Handout 14: Additional Relationship Concerns** Point out the two tools that will help to improve communication, manage resistance, and uncover all sorts of ills that come with change.
	Slide 29	Show Slide 29 when you mention it. Many participants may already know about Force Field Analysis because it is a well-known, well-used, and well-respected tool. Wrap up by encouraging participants to learn more about managing relationships with the suggestions given in Handout 14.
11:35 a.m. (25 min)	Slide 33	**Learning Activity 16: Oceans of Respect for Good Role Models** • **Handout 15: Oceans of Respect for Good Role Models** This activity helps participants understand how imperative role modeling is to the success of change efforts. Use this activity to expose them to research that supports the behaviors that are expected of them. Because they probably have some "personal changing" to do, ample time is allotted for self-reflection and partner activities to reinforce these behaviors in their manager toolkit. Be supportive during this activity by mingling during their small group discussions. Refer to the first page of the handout as a resource and have them focus their time on the second page. Recommend that partners go to lunch together to continue their discussions. Encourage them to continue their discussions with their partners after the workshop. Follow the instructions in the learning activity but tighten up the times.

44

12:00 p.m. (60 min)	Slide 40 60-Minute Lunch	**LUNCH**
1:00 p.m. (5 min)	Slide 34 Involve and Engage Others **Involve as Many as Possible** · Who? **Engage and Motivate** · What? **Develop Teams** · How? "Change is disturbing when it is done to us, exhilarating when it is done by us." —Rosabeth Moss Kanter	**Learning Content/Discussion** **Involve and Engage Others** • **Handout 16: Involve and Engage Others** Use this slide and handout to give participants lots of tips for involving and engaging others. Quickly go over the handout; if you are ahead of schedule, take a few minutes to obtain additional tips from the group to add to it.
1:05 p.m. (10 min)	Slide 36B Full Speed Ahead: Generate Gains · How do you create quick wins? · Large group brainstorm · What's the process? · Table group design	**Learning Content/Discussion** **Full Speed Ahead to Generate Gains** • **Handout 17: Full Speed Ahead to Generate Gains** Overview the handout and create a short discussion that draws upon what the participants already know about what is required to generate quick gains. If you have time, ask them to capture one idea on their What Floats Your Boat? sheets.
1:15 p.m. (45 min)	Slide 43 Smooth Sailing **Three Teams** · Engineering · Marketing · Financial	**Learning Activity 20: Smooth Sailing** **Supplemental Handouts:** • **Smooth Sailing Observer Sheet** • **Smooth Sailing Engineering Team Role** • **Smooth Sailing Marketing Team Role** • **Smooth Sailing Financial Team Role** • **Smooth Sailing Post-Leadership Meeting Debrief** This activity helps participants use everything they have learned in the workshop to analyze and solve problems that are exaggerated but realistic. It is a busy, fun, and chaotic activity. Its placement in the afternoon is intentional to act as an energizer. Follow the instructions in the learning activity, tightening up the timing a bit.

	Slide 44	To wrap up the activity, use this slide, which provides an example of a paper boat design that actually floats. Debrief the activity using the discussion questions provided in the learning activity.

2:00 p.m. (5 min)		**Cross Your Arms, Fold Your Hands**

These two quick activities bring participants back to why change can be difficult.

First, tell participants to cross their arms, look at how they are crossed, and then cross them with the *opposite* arm on top. Keep talking with them about how it feels, why, how they ended up with these feelings—any topic that keeps their arms folded the wrong way as long as possible. Soon you will see people separating their arms. For some, crossing their arms in a different way will be so uncomfortable that they can barely listen to you. Make the point that if they are that uncomfortable with such a little thing as crossing their arms, imagine how their employees must feel with the larger changes foisted upon them.

Second, make the same point by asking participants to fold their hands and then refold them with the *opposite* thumb on top. How long are they able to do this?

Let them know that these are both good activities they can take back to their people to help them understand their teams' discomfort and difficulty with change. |

2:05 p.m. (30 min)	Slide 39B Test the Waters Foster Change-Ready Employees Brainstorming topics: Content employees need Informal learning events Suggestions for attitude or mindset adjustments "You can't stop the waves, but you can learn to surf." —Jon Kabat-Zinn	**Learning Activity 19: Test the Waters With Ideas for Change-Ready Employees** • **Handout 18: Foster Change-Ready Employees** Be prepared to overview the highlights of the handout in 5 minutes. You will ***not*** follow the instructions in the learning activity, but create a different activity. Divide the group into three teams. Each will spend 10 minutes brainstorming its assigned topic on a flipchart and then present back to the larger group in less than 4 minutes. Here are the three topics with some examples for each: • Content employees need (resiliency) • Informal learning events (coaching, mentoring) • Suggestions for attitude or mindset adjustments (offer opportunity to lead a team, shadow a leader). To close the activity, suggest that they take pictures of the flipcharts with their smartphones during the break.
2:35 p.m. (15 min)	Slide 45 15-Minute Break	**BREAK**
2:50 p.m. (45 min)	Slide 46 Build Capacity for Continuous Change **What ideas do you need?** · If you need suggestions, review those in the handout for · Practical operational mechanisms · Successful change culture · Complete the statement with what *you* need (your own or from the list) · Write it on an index card	**Learning Activity 21: Build Capacity for Continuous Change and My Next Steps** • **Handout 21: Build Capacity for Continuous Change** • **Handout 22: Action Planning: My Next Steps** • **Handout 24: Additional Reading for Your Continued Development** This activity enables participants to explore ideas that build capacity for an organization's continuous change. Its "speed-dating" format helps them gather ideas from colleagues for specific ideas they want to pursue back at their workplace. Follow the instructions in the learning activity.

	Slide 47 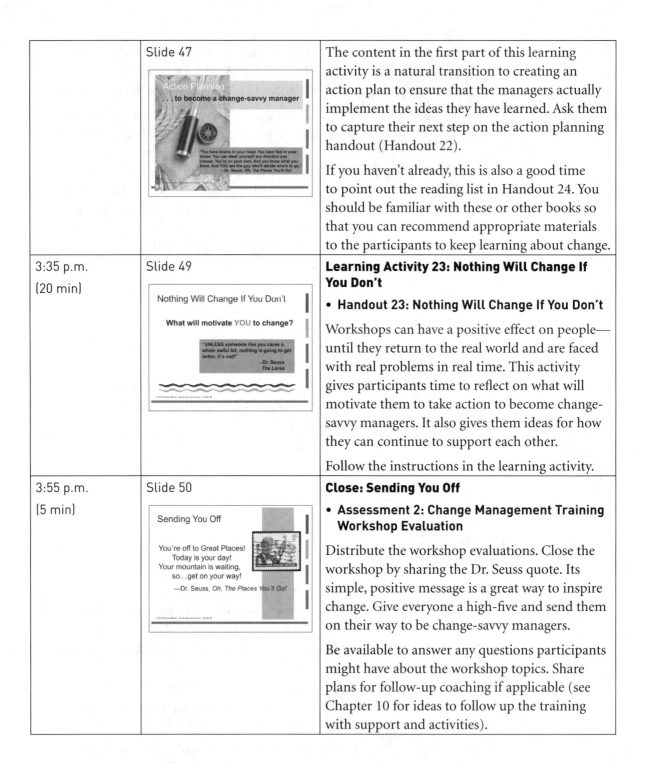	The content in the first part of this learning activity is a natural transition to creating an action plan to ensure that the managers actually implement the ideas they have learned. Ask them to capture their next step on the action planning handout (Handout 22). If you haven't already, this is also a good time to point out the reading list in Handout 24. You should be familiar with these or other books so that you can recommend appropriate materials to the participants to keep learning about change.
3:35 p.m. (20 min)	Slide 49	**Learning Activity 23: Nothing Will Change If You Don't** • **Handout 23: Nothing Will Change If You Don't** Workshops can have a positive effect on people—until they return to the real world and are faced with real problems in real time. This activity gives participants time to reflect on what will motivate them to take action to become change-savvy managers. It also gives them ideas for how they can continue to support each other. Follow the instructions in the learning activity.
3:55 p.m. (5 min)	Slide 50	**Close: Sending You Off** • **Assessment 2: Change Management Training Workshop Evaluation** Distribute the workshop evaluations. Close the workshop by sharing the Dr. Seuss quote. Its simple, positive message is a great way to inspire change. Give everyone a high-five and send them on their way to be change-savvy managers. Be available to answer any questions participants might have about the workshop topics. Share plans for follow-up coaching if applicable (see Chapter 10 for ideas to follow up the training with support and activities).

What to Do Next

- Determine the schedule for training classes; reserve location and catering you may wish to provide.

- Identify and invite participants.

- Inform participants about pre-work or reading. We recommend that participants read and complete the activities in Handouts 2, 3, 4, 5, 6, and 7.

- Review the workshop objectives, activities, and handouts to plan the content you will use.

- Prepare copies of the participant materials and any activity-related materials you may need. Refer to Chapter 14 for information about how to access and use the supplemental materials provided for this workshop.

- Ensure that you have printed the supplemental handouts required for Learning Activities 7 and 20. These handouts are included with the corresponding learning activities in Chapter 11 and require a close hold by you until the appropriate time within the activity.

- Gather tactile items, such as Koosh balls, crayons, magnets, Play-Doh, or others, you wish to place on the tables for tactile learners. See Chapter 8 for other ideas to enhance the learning environment of your workshop.

- Prepare yourself both emotionally and physically. Confirm that you have addressed scheduling and personal concerns so that you can be fully present to facilitate the class.

- Get a good night's sleep before you facilitate your workshop so that you have the energy and focus to deliver an outstanding session for your participants.

References

Mitchell, M., et al. (2015). *The Conference Board CEO Challenge: 2015.* New York: The Conference Board.

Parry, W. (2015). *Big Change, Best Path: Successfully Managing Organizational Change.* London: Kogan Page.

Chapter 3
Half-Day Change Management Training Workshop

What's in This Chapter

- Objectives of the half-day Change Management Workshop
- Summary chart for the flow of content and activities
- Half-day program agenda

We know that our organizations have been struggling to navigate the turbulent waters of constant, complex change. Bill Pasmore (2015), in his book *Leading Continuous Change,* likens the change organizations face to "riding a roller coaster: sudden drops, jarring turns, anxious climbs into the unknown." It's a challenge to adapt to change on a daily basis. It's even more of a challenge to deliver meaningful content in a half-day workshop about change. Many of the topics in this book could lend themselves to full-day discussions, such as improving communication, gaining resiliency, problem solving, addressing resistance, working on teams, and so on.

To help you deliver an effective and engaging workshop on this complex and vast topic in just four short hours, we have designed a "pseudo-flipped" approach to provide as much content as possible and yet give participants an opportunity to practice the skills and receive feedback. The concept of flipped learning emerged in K-12 education but has now made inroads into the workplace learning world. Flipped learning is an approach to learning in which direct instruction moves from the group space to the individual learning space so that the group space can be transformed into a dynamic, interactive learning environment. This workshop is "flipped" in the sense that it moves some of the content learning to the participants before the workshop begins. It is "pseudo" because unlike in most flipped learning where individuals learn by video instruction, we do not have videos to accompany the book—yet! Rather, this workshop uses reading assignments, partner activities, and opportunities for self-reflection to introduce participants to the content.

Managing change in an organization is one of the most critical roles for a manager. Change managers must think broadly, across the organization. Making that mindset change can be difficult for many new managers. Flipping the learning will help to ensure that we don't short change the participants.

Leaders' attitudes and actions greatly influence an organization's culture. The Conference Board reported in its 2015 annual survey that "organizations must focus on behavioral change to make change more sustainable and become agile. It is about helping people embrace and adopt change by building personal competencies . . . It is about instilling personal responsibility and accountability for change at every level. . . .The focus should be on developing change leaders at all levels, not just reactive change managers" (Mitchell et al. 2015). The research was conducted with CEOs of global corporations. This is powerful information. When we also learn that recent research by Accenture shows that business unit managers *play the most significant role in effectively implementing change* in organizations, we have a compelling reason to provide as much knowledge and as many skills as possible to managers (Parry 2015). It's all pretty heady stuff!

The Design. This half-day pseudo-flipped workshop is designed with a broad overview in mind. In a half day participants can experience the challenges of managing change. During the half-day session we do not try to cram lots of content into the learner. Instead, the workshop allows participants to create, design, experience, reflect, and produce tools and options for those they lead. It gives participants the chance to face how it might actually feel to be bombarded with many changes at the same time. Handouts are designed to be excellent sources of information before, during, and after the workshop ends.

The bottom line is that participants will benefit almost as much as they would with the complete two-day workshop.

Pre-Work. Prior to the workshop, participants must complete a lengthy reading assignment and several personal reflection activities as listed here. You will need to provide a complete set of handouts to each participant at least 21 days prior to the session.

- **Pre-reading** includes reading all handouts.

- **Pre-work** includes completing the activities in three handouts: Handout 4: Rate Your Managing Change Skills; Handout 8: Determine Organizational Readiness (completed for their departments); and Handout 15: Oceans of Respect for Good Role Models (including one of the choices in the deep-dive section).

- **Partner assignments** start at least 14 days prior to the session. Introduce the partners and give them these assignments:

  1. Call at least once to learn more about each other by answering these questions:
     - What kind of change are you involved in?
     - How much experience have you had?
     - What are your strengths and what do you need to work on?
     - What did you learn by completing the three work assignments?
     - How do you think I can be most helpful to you?
  2. Email the three assignments to each other.

Much of how we address change has changed (no doublespeak intended!) dramatically. Change is constant, complex, and happening at a dizzying pace. Success requires much more than what change management models offer. No longer is a step-by-step model enough. Things are changing all the time, everywhere, and overlapping in all areas. How can managers face everything that is flying at them at once? We suggest they focus on four key actions:

- Ensure the fundamentals are in place

- Enable excellent communication in all directions and at all times

- Confirm that all direct reports are change-ready with skills, mindset, knowledge, and attitude

- Build organizational capacity for continuous change in the future.

Half-Day Workshop Objectives

Due to the flipped design of the half-day workshop, participants will be able to do the same things as those who attended a full-day workshop and almost as many as those who attended a two-day workshop. It does require preparation and dedication by participants. By the end of the half-day workshop, participants will be able to

- Assess their change management areas of strength and areas requiring improvement

- Create a plan to determine organizational and departmental readiness

- Clarify the fundamentals of change management
- Lead a change management initiative in their department
- Manage change from an operational and an employee perspective
- Build change capacity for their organization
- Evaluate a change initiative from three result perspectives: effort, organization, and personal.

Half-Day Workshop Overview

TOPICS	TIMING
Workshop Opening: The Changing World of Change	
Welcome, Introductions, and Objectives	15 minutes
Q&A: Is Change a Sinking Ship?	10 minutes
Q&A: Change Fundamentals	5 minutes
Phase I: Assess the Situation	
Partner Activity: Organizational/Departmental Readiness	20 minutes
Phase II: Accept Leadership Accountability	
Learning Activity 9: What's Leadership Accountability?	15 minutes
Learning Activity 10: Optimize Communication	15 minutes
Partner Activity/Learning Activity 11: Navigate Resistance to Change	20 minutes
Learning Activity 12: Work Is a Juggling Act	15 minutes
BREAK	**15 minutes**
Phase III: Attain Implementation Progress	
Partner Activity: Oceans of Respect for Good Role Models	20 minutes
Q&A: Implementation Progress	5 minutes
Learning Activity 20: Smooth Sailing	35 minutes
Cross Your Arms, Fold Your Hands	5 minutes
Brainstorm: Foster Change-Ready Employees	20 minutes
Phase IV: Advance to Future Initiatives	
Partner Activity: My Next Steps	20 minutes
Close: Sending You Off	5 minutes
TOTAL	**240 minutes (4 hours)**

Half-Day Workshop Agenda

Half Day: (8:00 a.m. to 12:00 p.m.)

TIMING	SLIDES	ACTIVITIES/NOTES/CONSIDERATIONS
8:00 a.m. (15 min)	Slide 1C ATD Workshop Change Management Training Half-Day Workshop	**Welcome, Introductions, and Objectives** • **Supplemental Handout: What Floats Your Boat? (in Learning Activity 7)** Arrive at least 1 hour before the session starts to ensure that the room is set up, equipment works, and materials are arranged for participants. This gives you time to make the participants feel truly welcomed. Chatting with them builds a trusting relationship and opens them up for learning. You have a lot to cover in a very short time. Being extremely prepared will give you the edge you need to conduct a successful workshop.
	Slide 4 Learning Objectives - Assess your change management skills - Determine organizational readiness - Clarify change fundamentals - Lead a change management initiative - Manage operational and employee focus - Build organizational change capacity - Evaluate a change initiative three ways	Briefly review the workshop objectives with the participants. Let them know that you will not be reviewing any of what they read in the pre-reading assignments, but you will ask if anyone has questions as the workshop progresses. If you cannot answer the questions in the time allotted, follow up during one of the activities. Let them know that for most activities they will work together with their partners assigned from the pre-work portion of the workshop. As an icebreaker to help everyone get to know each other, ask everyone to introduce their assigned partners to the group.
	Slide 5 Manager's Change Model	Use this slide to remind participants of the Manager's Change Model introduced in their reading assignments. Point out that the workshop will follow the four change management phases, with at least one activity per phase.

	Slide 18	Encourage them to use their What Floats Your Boat? sheets to capture ideas they wish to implement when they return to their workplace.
	What Floats Your Boat? Ideas and actions you want to remember	
8:15 a.m. (10 min)	Slide 8 **Is Change a Sinking Ship?** **It's a VUCA world** · Volatile · Uncertain · Complex · Ambiguous . . . or a sunken treasure?	**Learning Content/Q&A** **Is Change a Sinking Ship?** • **Handout 5: Is Change a Sinking Ship?** • **Handout 6: It's Time to Change How We Change!** Handouts 5 and 6 were part of the pre-reading prior to the workshop. They explore the past record of managing change and how it has changed today. Both handouts are information dense, and you will want to read and digest them thoroughly prior to the workshop so that you can lead a quick but informative discussion. If you are not familiar with VUCA, get yourself up to speed quickly. You'll find interesting information with just a quick search on the Internet.
	Slide 9 **Change Can Be a Sunken Treasure** · Fundamentals are important— but not everything · Inform employees— but listen more · Build organizational change capacity— but create change-ready employees too	Use Slides 9 and 10 to highlight key points in Handouts 5 and 6 and ask if they had comments based on their pre-reading assignment.
	Slide 10 **Time To Change How We Change!** **Expand change capability** · Create change-ready employees · Create change-savvy managers	

8:25 a.m. (5 min)	Slide 14	**Learning Content/Q&A** **Change Fundamentals** • **Handout 7a: Ensure the Fundamentals Are in Place** • **Handout 7b: Fundamental 1** • **Handout 7c: Fundamental 2** • **Handout 7d: Fundamental 3** • **Handout 7e: Fundamental 4** Handouts 7 were assigned as pre-reading to ensure that participants were grounded in the basics of change management principles. Ask what questions they have about the fundamentals. Share the quote from legendary writer, educator, and management thinker Peter Drucker.
8:30 a.m. (20 min)	Slide 15	**Partner Activity** **Organizational/Departmental Readiness** • **Handout 8: Determine Organizational Readiness** The assessment in Handout 8 was part of their assigned pre-work. Ask partners to share the assessment results with each other and discuss how they would refine the assessment so that it is customized to meet their organization's unique needs.
8:50 a.m. (15 min)	Slide 19	**Learning Activity 9: What's Leadership Accountability?** When it comes to change, there are always questions about leadership and accountability, and so a few minutes spent here will help your participants focus on practical things they can do to demonstrate leadership accountability. Follow the instructions in the learning activity. Assure participants that there are no right or wrong answers. Use the final 2 minutes to ask partners to discuss what leadership accountability means to them.

9:05 a.m. (15 min)	Slide 21 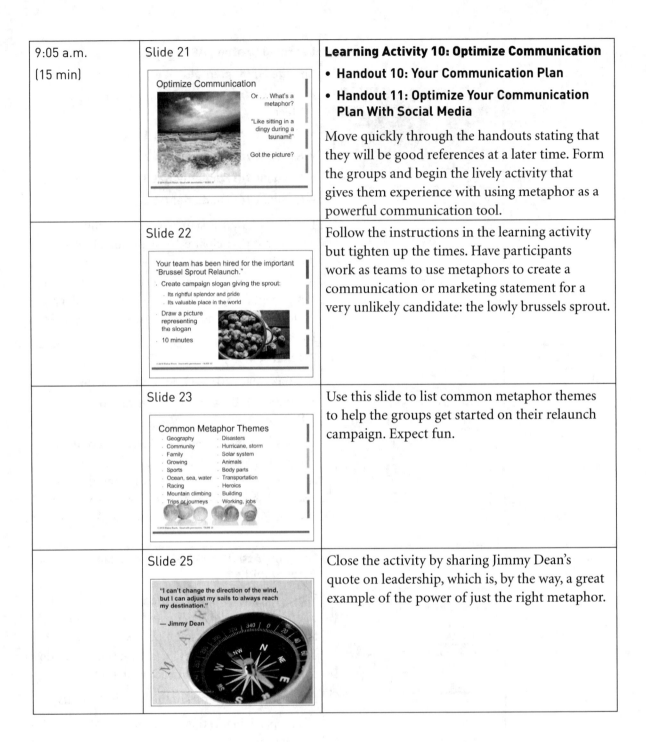	**Learning Activity 10: Optimize Communication** • **Handout 10: Your Communication Plan** • **Handout 11: Optimize Your Communication Plan With Social Media** Move quickly through the handouts stating that they will be good references at a later time. Form the groups and begin the lively activity that gives them experience with using metaphor as a powerful communication tool.
	Slide 22	Follow the instructions in the learning activity but tighten up the times. Have participants work as teams to use metaphors to create a communication or marketing statement for a very unlikely candidate: the lowly brussels sprout.
	Slide 23	Use this slide to list common metaphor themes to help the groups get started on their relaunch campaign. Expect fun.
	Slide 25	Close the activity by sharing Jimmy Dean's quote on leadership, which is, by the way, a great example of the power of just the right metaphor.

9:20 a.m. (20 min)	Slide 27 Navigate Resistance to Change What would you tell your boss? (5-7 minutes) Search on: Kanter ten reasons people resist change	**Partner Activity/Learning Activity 11: Navigate Resistance to Change** • **Handout 12: Navigate Resistance to Change** This practical activity results in participants tapping into the Internet to better understand resistance. They will learn ideas to keep their employees afloat. Follow the instructions in the learning activity except shorten the end by leading a discussion instead of having them design their own plan. Suggest that they design a plan for their employees once they complete the workshop.
9:40 a.m. (15 min)		**Learning Activity 12: Work Is a Juggling Act** Now participants will get firsthand experience of how they, as managers, might be causing some of the resistance to change. Practice this lively activity before the session with some colleagues because it can be a little tricky. Follow the instructions in the learning activity.
9:55 a.m. (15 min)	Slide 26 15-Minute Break	**BREAK**

10:10 a.m. (20 min)	Slide 33
	
	 Respect for Good Role Models
	
	 Behaviors That Drive Commitment
	 · Rate your behaviors +/-
	 · Find a partner
	 · Review 15 minutes
	
	 Behaviors That Drive Change
	 · Review with your partner
	    · What effect on success of change?
	    · How can you exhibit each?
		Partner Activity
		
		 Oceans of Respect for Good Role Models
		
		 • **Handout 15: Oceans of Respect for Good Role Models**
		
		 This handout was part of the participants' pre-work, so they should be familiar with the content. It exposed them to research that supports the behaviors that are expected of them. They probably have some "personal changing" they need to do.
		
		 Ask them to work with their partners. Refer to the first page as a resource and have them focus the majority of their time on the second page. Be supportive during this activity, ensuring you are mingling during their partner discussions. Encourage them to continue their discussions with their partners after the workshop.

10:30 a.m. (5 min)	Slide 34 Involve and Engage Others **Involve as Many as Possible** · Who? **Engage and Motivate** · What? **Develop Teams** · How? "Change is disturbing when it is done to us, exhilarating when it is done by us." —Rosabeth Moss Kanter	**Learning Content/Q&A** **Implementation Progress** • **Handout 16: Involve and Engage Others** • **Handout 17: Full Speed Ahead to Generate Gains** Ask what questions they have about engaging others and generating gains, two key skills in the third phase of the Manager's Change Model: attaining implementation progress. If time prevents you from responding to all questions, list the questions and get back to participants following the workshop.
	Slide 36C Full Speed Ahead: Generate Gains · How do you create quick wins? · What's the process?	

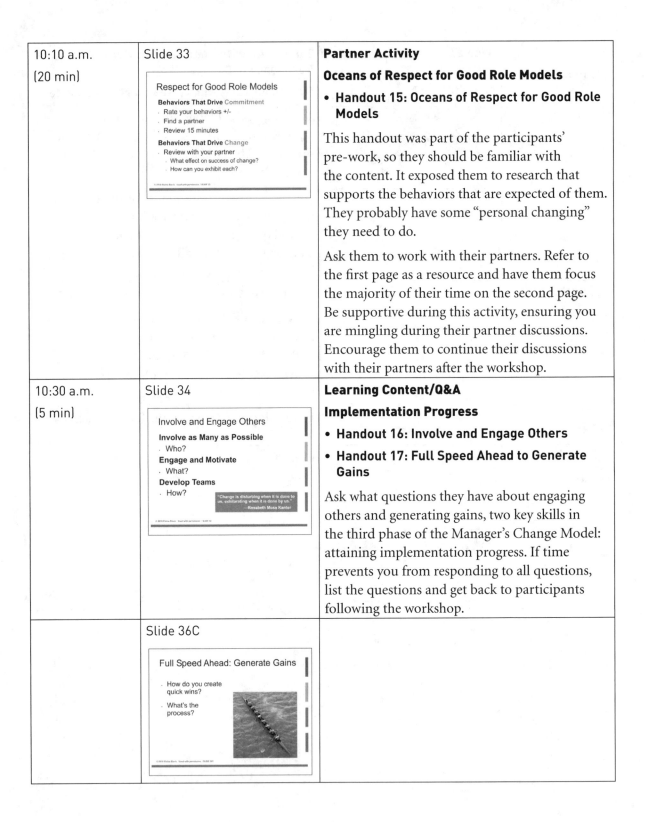

10:35 a.m. (35 min)	Slide 43 	**Learning Activity 20: Smooth Sailing** **Supplemental Handouts:** • **Smooth Sailing Observer Sheet** • **Smooth Sailing Engineering Team Role** • **Smooth Sailing Marketing Team Role** • **Smooth Sailing Financial Team Role** • **Smooth Sailing Post-Leadership Meeting Debrief** This activity helps participants use everything they have learned in the workshop to analyze and solve problems that are exaggerated but realistic. It is busy, fun, and chaotic. It may be difficult to get them to stop learning! Follow the instructions in the learning activity, tightening up the timing a bit. Be sure partners are on the same teams.
	Slide 44 	To wrap up the activity, use this slide, which provides an example of a paper boat design that actually floats. Debrief the activity selecting only a couple of the most pertinent discussion questions provided in the learning activity.

11:10 a.m. (5 min)		**Cross Your Arms, Fold Your Hands** These two quick activities bring participants back to why change can be difficult. First, tell participants to cross their arms, look at how they are crossed, and then cross them with the *opposite* arm on top. Keep talking with them about how it feels, why, how they ended up with these feelings—any topic that keeps their arms folded the wrong way as long as possible. Soon you will see people separating their arms. For some, crossing their arms in a different way will be so uncomfortable that they can barely listen to you. Make the point that if they are that uncomfortable with such a little thing as crossing their arms, imagine how their employees must feel with the larger changes foisted on them. Second, make the same point by asking participants to fold their hands and then refold them with the *opposite* thumb on top. How long are they able to do this? Let them know that these are both good activities they can take back to their people to help them understand their teams' discomfort and difficulty with change.
11:15 a.m. (20 min)	Slide 39C 	**Learning Content/Brainstorm** **Foster Change-Ready Employees** • **Handout 18: Foster Change-Ready Employees** Lead a brainstorm with the group and post ideas generated on a flipchart as you facilitate. Ask two questions: 1. What content do employees need? (for example, resiliency) 2. How can you best provide development? (for example, coaching, mentoring, or shadow a leader) Suggest that they take pictures of the flipcharts with their smartphones during the break.

11:35 a.m. (20 min)	Slide 47 	**Partner Activity** **My Next Steps** • **Handout 21: Build Capacity for Continuous Change** • **Handout 22: Action Planning: My Next Steps** • **Handout 23: Nothing Will Change If You Don't** Review Handout 21 with the participants as a group. Ask participants to work together with their partners to create an action plan (Handout 22) to help ensure that they implement the ideas they have learned in the workshop. Remind them to refer to the partner discussions they had and what they learned about each other prior to the workshop.
	Slide 49 	Workshops can have a positive effect on people—until they return to the real world and are faced with real problems in real time. Have partners work together to complete Handout 23, which will give them an opportunity to reflect on what will motivate them to take action to become a change-savvy manager. It also gives them ideas for how they can continue to support each other. Encourage them to schedule a follow-up time with their partners.
11:55 a.m. (5 min)	Slide 50 	**Close: Sending You Off** • **Assessment 2: Change Management Training Workshop Evaluation** Distribute the workshop evaluations. Close the workshop by sharing the Dr. Seuss quote. Its simple, positive message is a great way to inspire change. Give everyone a high-five and send them on their way to be change-savvy managers. Be available to answer any questions participants might have about the workshop topics. Share plans for follow-up coaching if applicable (see Chapter 10 for ideas to follow up the training with support and activities).

What to Do Next

- Determine the schedule for training classes; reserve location and catering you may wish to provide.

- Identify and invite participants.

- For this half-day pseudo-flipped session to work, all participants must complete the reading and pre-work assignments. Send the instructions and resources for the assignments to arrive at least 21 days prior to the workshop session.

- Introduce partners to each other at least 14 days prior to the session.

- Review the workshop objectives, activities, and handouts to plan the content you will use.

- Prepare copies of the participant materials and any activity-related materials you may need. Refer to Chapter 14 for information about how to access and use the supplemental materials provided for this workshop.

- Ensure that you have printed the supplemental handouts required for Learning Activities 7 and 20. These handouts are included with the corresponding learning activities in Chapter 11 and require a close hold by you until the appropriate time within the activity.

- Gather tactile items such as Koosh balls, crayons, magnets, Play-Doh, or other items you wish to place on the tables for tactile learners. See Chapter 8 for other ideas to enhance the learning environment of your workshop.

- Prepare yourself both emotionally and physically. Confirm that you have addressed scheduling and personal concerns so that you can be fully present to facilitate the workshop.

- Get a good night's sleep before you facilitate your workshop so that you have the energy and focus to deliver an outstanding session for your participants.

References

Mitchell, M., et al. (2015). *The Conference Board CEO Challenge: 2015*. New York: The Conference Board.

Parry, W. (2015). *Big Change, Best Path: Successfully Managing Organizational Change*. London: Kogan Page.

Pasmore, W. (2015). *Leading Continuous Change*. San Francisco: Berrett-Koehler.

Chapter 4

Customizing the Change Management Training Workshops

What's in This Chapter

- Ideas for creating new change management skills workshops
- Creative approaches for developing lunch-and-learn seminars
- Suggestions for theme-based workshops

Many organizations find it difficult to have employees away from the workplace for an entire day or two, even for professional and skill development. As a result, you may need to adjust and adapt your workshop to the scheduling needs of the organization. Additionally, organizations often prefer to select the content and topics to match the needs of the employees attending the training. Your training needs analysis will help you prioritize and select the content and activities of highest value for your participants. For more on needs analysis, see Chapter 5 in this volume.

The materials in this ATD Workshop Series volume are designed to meet a variety of training needs. They cover a range of topics related to change management skills training and can be offered in many timeframes and formats. Although lengthy immersion in a learning environment can enhance and increase the depth of learning experiences, the challenges of the workplace sometimes demand that training be done in short, small doses.

By using the expertly designed learning content and activities provided here as a foundation, you can modify and adapt the learning experience by customizing the content and activities, customizing the format, and customizing delivery with technology.

Customizing the Content and Activities

Your level of expertise with training facilitation and change management skills will determine how much customization you may want to do. If you are new to both training and the topic, you'll want to stick as closely as possible to the workshop as designed.

If you are a new trainer but an expert in change management, use the outline and materials as designed but feel free to include relevant materials you have developed. If you are internal, take advantage of any actual documents your organization uses. In Learning Activity 4, for example, be sure to incorporate your change management model and the jargon your organization uses. The more actual content learners see the better it will be.

Finally, if you are an expert facilitator, feel free to adapt the agenda and materials as you see necessary. Add new materials that you have developed to augment the learning. Or you can simply incorporate the learning activities, assessments, handouts, and tools into your own agenda.

As you become more confident with both the topic and facilitation, you will be able to introduce more of your own personal style into the workshop. You will also be better able to tailor the workshop to specific organizational needs and business imperatives.

Explore the variations in the learning activities. Many of the learning activities describe ideas for variations to a given activity. Try some of these alternatives to see which ones resonate with your facilitation style and your participants' preferences.

What we know about the topic of change management is changing at a rapid pace—similar to the VUCA world our organizations are adapting to. Stay on top of the research and new books in the field (approximately one new change book enters the market weekly). Be sure that you read those that are steeped in rigorous research. You can trust organizations such as the Center for Creative Leadership, Zenger Folkman, DDI, Blanchard, Bersin, The Conference Board, and others.

Customizing the Workshop Format

Use the content from the two-day workshop (Chapter 1) to adapt the workshop format to build a series of 90- to 120-minute workshops, lunchtime seminars, or thematic workshops.

Change Management Skills Series

To address the need to provide learning in shorter segments, Table 4-1 breaks down the content into a series of nine 90- to 120-minute workshops. These workshops can be offered on a daily, weekly, biweekly, or monthly basis, depending on the scheduling needs of the organization. Note that the segments require some additional connections to make them a good session. Exploring the topics through additional debriefing questions or adding your organization's documents and examples will make them extremely valuable.

Use the Manager's Change Model as a road map to help participants recognize the specific area they are addressing at each session.

Table 4-1. Change Management Skills Workshop Series

SESSION	90- TO 120-MINUTE WORKSHOP TOPICS	ACTIVITIES AND RESOURCES
1	• Managers Navigate Constant, Complex Change • A Manager's Model for Change • Rate Your Managing Change Skills • What's Leadership Accountability?	• Learning Activities 1, 9 • Handouts 3, 4
2	• Is Change a Sinking Ship? • It's Time to Change How We Change!	• Learning Activity 3 • Handouts 5, 6
3	• Ensure the Fundamentals Are in Place	• Learning Activity 4 • Handouts 7
4	• Your Communication Plan • Optimize Communication With Social Media • Make Up Your Mind! • Involve and Engage Others	• Learning Activities 5, 10 • Handouts 10, 11, 16
5	• Navigate Resistance to Change • Work Is a Juggling Act • Tools to Manage Relationships • Additional Relationship Concerns	• Learning Activities 11, 12, 13 • Handouts 12, 13, 14

Table 4-1, *continued*

SESSION	90- TO 120-MINUTE WORKSHOP TOPICS	ACTIVITIES AND RESOURCES
6	• Determine Organizational/Departmental Readiness • Establish a Sense of Urgency • Full Speed Ahead to Generate Gains • Institutionalize Changes • Evaluate the Change Results	• Learning Activities 6, 7, 17 • Handouts 8, 9a-9b, 17, 20, 21 • Supplemental Handout: What Floats Your Boat?
7	• Oceans of Respect for Good Role Models • Smooth Sailing	• Learning Activities 16, 20 • Handout 15 • Supplemental Handouts: Smooth Sailing (5 sheets)
8	• Build Capacity for Continuous Change • Foster Change-Ready Employees • Cross Your Arms, Fold Your Hands	• Learning Activities 19, 21 • Handouts 18, 21, 22, 24
9	• Select Change Books to Review • Action Planning: My Next Steps	• Handouts 22, 24

Small Bites—Lunch-and-Learn Seminars

Sometimes small means big impact. Table 4-2 shows topics that could be delivered effectively in one-hour sessions. The key to doing these bite-sized chunks successfully is to have a clear design with the right amount of content. Trying to cram in too much content can make a seminar seem shallow and rushed. Ask yourself one key question when creating a session of this size: What is the one key concept I would like the participants to remember after this workshop?

Table 4-2. Lunch-and-Learn Seminars

TOPICS FOR ONE-HOUR LUNCHTIME SEMINARS	ACTIVITIES AND RESOURCES
• Is Change a Sinking Ship?	• Learning Activity 3 • Handouts 5, 6
• Time to Change How We Change!	• Handout 6
• It's a Manager's Change Model—Fill in the Blanks	• Handout 3
• The Fundamentals: Approaches, Tools, and Models	• Learning Activity 4 • Handouts 2, 3, 7a, 7b
• The Fundamentals: Creating a Compelling Story	• Handouts 7c, 9a

TOPICS FOR ONE-HOUR LUNCHTIME SEMINARS	ACTIVITIES AND RESOURCES
• The Fundamentals: How to Communicate With the Workforce	• Learning Activity 10 • Handouts 7c, 10, 11
• The Fundamentals: Make Change Stick	• Handouts 7d, 9a, 9b
• Change: How Do You Involve Others?	• Handouts 7e, 16
• Rate Your Managing Change Skills • Create an Action Plan to Improve	• Handouts 4, 22
• What the Heck Is Leadership Accountability?	• Learning Activity 9
• Create a Communication Plan • Optimize Your Communication With Social Media	• Learning Activity 10 • Handouts 10, 11
• Navigate Resistance to Change • Tools to Manage Relationships	• Learning Activities 11, 13 • Handouts 12, 13, 14
• The Many Ways to Determine Organizational Readiness	• Learning Activity 6 • Handout 8
• Institutionalize Change • How We Evaluate Change	• Handouts 19, 20
• Respect for Good Role Models	• Learning Activity 16 • Handout 15
• Smooth Sailing Role Play	• Learning Activity 20 • Supplemental Handouts: Smooth Sailing (5 sheets)
• Build Change Capacity for Our Organization	• Handout 21
• How Do We Prepare Our Workforce? • Foster Change-Ready Employees	• Learning Activity 19 • Handout 18
• Reading List • Book Discussion (Ask people to read one of the books in Handout 24 and come prepared to discuss it.)	• Handout 24

Theme-Based Workshops

Change management is a hot topic right now. Organizations want to know how to do it better. Most managers are expected to know something about change, change processes, change models, and the other mechanics of change. Generally they do not have time to go outside the organization in search of more knowledge. These theme-based workshops can provide skills and knowledge for your workforce (Table 4-3).

Table 4-3. Theme-Based Workshops

THEME	WORKSHOP TOPICS	ACTIVITIES AND RESOURCES
Ensure the Fundamentals Are in Place	• The Myths of Managing Change • Models, Approaches, and Tools • Creating a Compelling Story • Communicating With the Workforce • Confirm Systems Are in Place • Gain Support and Involvement • Measuring Organizational Readiness • It's Time to Change How We Change	• Learning Activities 3, 4, 6 • Handouts 2, 3, 5, 6, 7a-7e, 8, 9a-9b • Supplemental Handout: What Floats Your Boat?
Enable Excellent Communication During Change	• Promote Communication • How to Design a Communication Plan • Optimize Communication With Social Media • Involve and Engage Others • Navigate Resistance to Change	• Learning Activities 10, 11 • Handouts 10, 11
Prepare a Change-Ready Workforce	• Build Resiliency • Understand Resistance • Find Opportunities to Develop • Be a Better Team Player • Coaching and Mentoring Skills • Learn to Be a Good Role Model	• Learning Activities 11, 13, 16 • Handouts 12, 13, 14, 15, 16
Grow Change-Savvy Managers	• A Manager's Model for Change • Rate Your Managing Change Skills • Is My Department Ready for Change? • Be a Good Role Model • Learn Leadership Accountability • Build Trust With the Workforce • Learn to Inspire and Motivate • Be Courageous • Incorporate 360-Degree Feedback	• Learning Activities 6, 9 • Handouts 3, 4, 8, 15, 16

CHANGE MANAGEMENT training

THEME	WORKSHOP TOPICS	ACTIVITIES AND RESOURCES
Build Organizational Capacity for Continuous Change in the Future	• Evaluate the Organization's Change Capacity • Change in a VUCA World • Guarantee Leadership Accountability • Navigate Resistance to Change • Manage Relationships • Develop a Sense of Urgency • Institutionalize Changes Quickly • Evaluate Our Change Efforts	• Learning Activities 6, 7, 9, 11, 13 • Handouts 5, 6, 8, 9a-9b, 12, 13, 14, 19, 20 • Supplemental Handout: What Floats Your Boat?
Change From Start to Finish	• Gather and Analyze Data • Establish a Sense of Urgency • Determine Organizational Readiness • Select Teams • Create a Compelling Vision • Design the Implementation Plan • Select Appropriate Metrics • Conduct a Risk Assessment • Clarify the Change Agent's Role • Generate Short-Term Gains • Institutionalize the Change	• Learning Activities 4, 6, 7, 17 • Handouts 3, 4, 7a-7e, 8, 9a-9b, 16, 17, 19 • Supplemental Handout: What Floats Your Boat?

Customizing Delivery With Technology

Learning technologies can play an important role in adapting workshops to fit your organization. They have the potential to enhance learners' abilities to understand and apply workshop concepts. Examples include webinars, wikis, email groups, online surveys, and teleconferencing, to name just a few. Learn more about how to use technology to maximize learning in Chapter 7 of this book.

The Bare Minimum

With any of these customization options, always keep in mind the essentials of training design (Chapter 6) and delivery (Chapter 8). At a bare minimum, remember these basics:

- **Prepare, prepare, prepare.** Ready the room, the handouts, the equipment, and you. Familiarize yourself with the content, materials, and equipment. Practice can only make you a better facilitator. The more comfortable you feel, the more open and relaxed you will be for your participants. Many things can go wrong: Equipment can fail, the hotel can double-book your room, your Internet connection may not work, or 10 more participants may show up, as you well know. You simply cannot control it all. You can, however, control 100 percent of how much you prepare.

- **Start with a bang.** The beginning of your session is crucial to the dynamics of the workshop. How participants respond to you can set the mood for the remainder of the workshop. Get to the classroom *at least* an hour before the session begins. Be ready to welcome and greet the participants. Have everything ready so that you are available to learn something about them and their needs. Ask them simple questions to build rapport. After introducing yourself, introduce participants to each other or provide an activity in which participants can meet each other. The more time they spend getting to know you and each other, the more all of you will benefit when the session begins. Once the session starts, conduct an opening icebreaker that introduces the topic, ensures participants learn more about each other, and sets the stage for the rest of the seminar by letting participants know that this will be an active learning session. Try a provocative opening to get their attention.

- **Don't lecture without interaction.** Your learners like to have fun and participate in interactive learning opportunities. Be sure to vary the learning and teaching methods to maintain engagement. Yes, there will be times when you need to deliver information, but be sure to include participants by asking questions, posing critical incidents, incorporating a survey question, or using the dozens of other ways to engage your participants in the learning.

- **End strong.** Providing time for participants to reflect and create an action plan at the end of a module or the session will help establish learning. Don't skip this opportunity to encourage participants to take action on something they have learned. Several of the activities in the workshop provide an opportunity to plan for next steps. Stress the importance of implementing what they learned upon returning to the workplace.

What to Do Next

- When customizing a workshop it is important to have a clear understanding of the learning objectives. Conduct a needs analysis to identify the gap between what the organization needs and what the employees are able to do and then determine how best to bridge the gap. At a minimum, identify who wants the training, how the results will be defined, why the training is being requested now, and what the budget is. Chapter 5 provides more guidance on identifying training needs.

- Modify or add your own content to an existing agenda from Chapters 1-3 or create your own agenda using the learning support documents included in this book. There is no one way to flow change management content, but you must ensure that the topics build on one another and that you solidly connect the concepts and ideas together to leverage the most of the learning opportunity.

- Make sure to incorporate interactive practice activities into the design of the workshop.

- Compile and review all learning activities, handouts, and slides you will use for the session.

- Add your own slides or your own touches to the slides provided.

- Build a detailed plan for preparing for this session, including scheduling and room reservations, invitations, supply list, teaching notes, and time estimates.

SECTION II

ESSENTIALS OF EFFECTIVE CHANGE MANAGEMENT TRAINING

Chapter 5

Identifying Needs for Change Management Training

What's in This Chapter

- Discovering the purpose of needs analysis

- Introducing some data-gathering methods

- Determining the bare minimum needed to deliver training

Ideally, you should always carry out a needs analysis before designing and creating a workshop to address a performance gap. The cost of *not* identifying and carefully considering the performance requirement can be high: wasted training dollars, unhappy staff going to boring or useless sessions, increased disengagement of employees, and so forth. But the world of training is rarely ideal, and the existence of this book, which essentially provides a workshop in a box, is testament to that. This chapter describes the essential theory and techniques for a complete needs analysis to provide the fundamentals of the process and explain how it fits into designing learning. However, because the decision to train may already be out of your hands, the last part of this chapter provides a bare-bones list of things you need to know to train effectively even if someone just handed you this book and told you to put on a workshop.

Why Needs Analysis?

In short, as a trainer, learning professional, performance consultant, or whatever job title you hold, your role is to ensure that the employees of your organization know how to do the work that will make the organization succeed. That means you must first identify the skills, knowledge, and abilities that the employees need for optimal performance and then determine where these are lacking in the employee population to bridge that gap. However, the most important reason for needs assessment is that it is not your learning experience. You may deliver it, but the learning belongs to the learner. Making decisions for learners about what performance they need without working with them is inappropriate. If you are an experienced facilitator, you have a large repository of PowerPoint decks at your disposal. Resist the urge while talking with your customers to listen for words that allow you just to grab what you already have. Be open to the possibilities. A training needs analysis helps you do this (see Figure 5-1). Methods to identify this information include strategic needs analysis, structured interviews, focus groups, and surveys.

Strategic Needs Analysis

An analysis of future directions usually identifies emerging issues and trends with a major potential effect on a business and its customers over a two- to three-year period. The analysis helps a business develop goals and programs that proactively anticipate and position the organization to influence the future.

Figure 5-1. Introducing the ADDIE Model

A needs analysis is the first step in the classic instructional design model called ADDIE, which is named after its steps: analysis, design, development, implementation, and evaluation. Roughly speaking, the tasks involved in ADDIE are

1. **Analysis:** Gather data about organizational and individual needs as well as the gap between the goals the organization means to accomplish and the skills and knowledge needed to accomplish those goals.

2. **Design:** Identify and plan the topics and sequence of learning to accomplish the desired learning.

3. **Development:** Create the components of the learning event, such as learning activities and materials.

4. **Implementation:** Put on the learning event or launch the learning materials.

5. **Evaluation:** Gather data to determine the outcome of the learning to improve future iterations of the learning, enhance materials and facilitation, and justify budget decisions.

Instructional design models such as ADDIE are a systematic approach to developing learning and could also be viewed as a project management framework for the project phases involved in creating learning events.

A Note From Elaine: Special Considerations for Change Management

Gathering data for your change management workshop may be a bit different from the needs assessments you usually do. There is a list of knowledge and skills that the participants will require, but it isn't quite that simple. Change encompasses attitude more than almost any other topic.

Generally, we focus on skills and knowledge that we can list and test and to which we can apply logical measures. After all, isn't the purpose of training to provide participants with something that they can apply in the form of skills or knowledge back at the workplace? Yes, of course, but that's only half the story when addressing change. A needs assessment must also attend to the elements we can't see or measure so easily.

So while you are preparing the list of change management skills and knowledge, remember that to be completely successful you also need to pay attention to issues such as mindset, resistance, pride, values, beliefs, opinions, and attitudes.

To conduct such an analysis, organizations look at issues such as expected changes within the business (for example, technology and professional requirements) and expected changes outside the company (for example, the economy, demographics, politics, and the environment).

Results of an analysis provide a rationale for developing company and departmental goals and for making policy and budgetary decisions. From the analysis comes a summary of key change dynamics that will affect the business.

These questions often are asked in strategic needs analysis:

- What information did previous organizational analyses impart?
- Are those issues and trends still relevant?
- Do the results point to what may need to be done differently in the future?
- How has the organization performed in achieving results?
- What is the present workforce like?
- How will it change or need to change?
- What does the organization know about future changes in customer needs?
- Are customer surveys conducted and, if so, what do they reveal?
- How might the organization have to change to serve customers better?

- Is the company's organizational structure working to achieve results?
- What are the strengths and limitations of the company?
- What are the opportunities for positive change?
- What do competitors do or say that might have implications for the organization?
- What are the most important opportunities for the future?
- What are the biggest problems?
- Is the organization in a competitive marketplace?
- How does the organization compare with competitors?

The results can be summarized in a SWOT analysis model (strengths, weaknesses, opportunities, threats—see Figure 5-2). Action plans are then developed to increase the strengths, overcome the weaknesses, plan for the opportunities, and decrease the threats.

Figure 5-2. SWOT Analysis Model

	STRENGTHS	WEAKNESSES
INTERNAL		
	OPPORTUNITIES	THREATS
EXTERNAL		

Structured Interviews

Start structured interviews as high up in the organization as you can go, with the CEO if possible. Make sure that you include input from human resource personnel and line or operations managers and supervisors. Managers and supervisors will want to tell you what they have seen and what they consider the most pressing issues in the organization.

A Note From Elaine: Using Social Media for Data Collection

Dr. Kella Price of Price Consulting Group obtains participants' Twitter usernames before her training sessions. If many participants do not have Twitter accounts she provides them with a tutorial prior to the session about how to get one. By using Twitter's online social networking, she is able to ask questions that help her tailor the content for a learning session.

She tweets each question individually, including the session hashtag in her tweets. She introduces each question with a message such as "I will facilitate next week's training. Pls help tailor training 2ur needs with 5 questions. B sure 2include Q# w/response. #hashtag." Consider asking questions such as these:

- Q1: What is your role in managing change? #hashtag
- Q2: What do you want to learn as a result of this workshop? #hashtag
- Q3: What skills do you want to gain from this workshop? #hashtag
- Q4: What is your biggest challenge as it relates to managing change? #hashtag
- Q5: How will you use the content in your work? #hashtag

A side benefit of using social media is that the responses stimulate discussion among participants before arriving in your training session.

Focus Groups

Focus groups can be set up to give people opportunities to brainstorm ideas about issues in the organization and to realize the potential of team involvement. One comment may spark another and so on. Focus groups should begin with questions that you prepare. It is important to record the responses and comments on a flipchart so everyone can see them. If that is not possible, you may simply take notes. Results of the sessions should be compiled.

Surveys

Surveys, whether paper or web based, gather information from a large or geographically dispersed group of employees. The advantages of surveys are speed of data collection, objectivity, repeatability, and ease of analysis.

Individual Learning Needs Analysis

While identifying organizational learning needs is critical to making the best use of an organization's training budget, analyzing individual learning needs is also important. Understanding the training group's current skills and knowledge can help to focus the training on those areas that require most work—this also helps to avoid going over what the individuals already know, thus wasting their time, or losing them by jumping in at too advanced a level. In addition, individual learning needs analysis can uncover unfavorable attitudes about training that trainers will be better able to address if they are prepared for them. For example, some learners may see the training as a waste of time, as an interruption to their normal work, or as a sign of potentially frightening organizational change.

Many of the same methods used to gather data for organizational learning needs are used for individual learning needs analysis. Analyzing employee learning needs should be carried out in a thoughtful, sensitive, and inclusive manner. Here are potential pitfalls to avoid:

- **Don't analyze needs you can't meet.** Training needs analysis raises expectations. It sends a message to employees that the organization expects them to be competent in particular areas.

- **Involve employees directly.** Sometimes employees don't see a value in participating in training. In assessing needs, trainers need to prepare employees to buy into the training. Asking useful questions and listening carefully to stated needs are excellent methods for accomplishing both of those goals. Ask these questions: "To what degree would you like to learn how to do [X] more effectively?" and "To what degree would you seriously consider participating in training to improve your competency in [X]?"

- **Make the identified needs an obvious part of your training design.** Participants should be able to see that they have influenced the content and emphasis of the training session. A good practice is briefly to summarize the local trends discovered in the training needs analysis when you introduce the goals of the session.

- **Don't think of training as a "magic bullet."** Sometimes a given employee needs coaching, counseling, or consulting, which is best carried out one on one and customized to the individual and the situation. Still other times, the problem is caused by equipment or processes that need upgrading, not people who need training.

The Bare Minimum

As noted, in an ideal world, you would have gathered all this data about the needs of the organization and the employees and determined that training was the right way to connect those dots. However, even if the decision to put on this workshop has already been made, you still need a bare minimum of information to be successful:

- **Who is your project sponsor (who wants to do this, provides the budget, and so on)?** In fact, if you don't have a project sponsor, *stop* the project. Lack of a project sponsor indicates that the project isn't important to the business. Optimally, the project sponsor should come from the business side of the organization. If the project sponsor is the head of training, then the mentality behind the training—"build it and they will come"—is likely wrong. Even compliance training should have a functional sponsor.

- **What does the sponsor want the learners to be able to do when they are done with training?** How does the sponsor define measures of success? Answering these critical questions brings clarity to the sponsor's expectations and thus to the workshop design.

- **What are the objectives of the training?** What, specifically, do you want participants to be able to *do* after the workshop? Build clear, specific, and measurable learning objectives and then develop learning activities that directly support them. A good resource for writing objectives is Bloom's Taxonomy; if you use it, aim to create Application-level or higher objectives. Knowledge- and Comprehension-level objectives have their place, but learning events need to go beyond these levels of learning to effectively change behaviors in the workplace.

- **Why does the sponsor want this right now?** Is something going on in the organization of which you should be aware?

- **What is the budget?** How much time and money will be invested in the training?

Key Points

- Needs analysis identifies the gap between what the organization needs and what the employees are able to do and then determines how best to bridge that gap.

- Methods of data gathering for needs analysis include strategic needs analysis, structured interviews, surveys, focus groups, and others.

- Sometimes, needs analysis is not an option, but some minimum information is necessary, including who wants the training, how the results will be defined, why the training is being requested now, and what the budget is.

What to Do Next

- If you have the option, carry out a needs analysis to determine if this training is really what your organization requires to succeed. If it isn't, prepare to argue against wasting time, money, and effort on training that will not support the organization's goals.

- If you don't have the option of a needs analysis, make sure that you seek out at least the bare minimum information to conduct effective training.

- Prepare learning objectives that are measurable, clear, and specific.

- If you have little training background, read the next chapter (Chapter 6) to learn about the theories and concepts that are at the root of training design. If you are an experienced trainer, skim Chapter 6 on design theory or go straight to Chapters 7 and 8 for tips on leveraging technology and delivering training, respectively.

Additional Resources

Biech, E., ed. (2008). *ASTD Handbook for Workplace Learning Professionals.* Alexandria, VA: ASTD Press.

Biech, E., ed. (2014). *ASTD Handbook: The Definitive Reference for Training & Development.* Alexandria, VA: ASTD Press.

Russo, C. "Be a Better Needs Analyst." ASTD *Infoline* no. 258502. Alexandria, VA: ASTD Press.

Tobey, D. (2005). *Needs Assessment Basics.* Alexandria, VA: ASTD Press.

Chapter 6

Understanding the Foundations of Training Design

What's in This Chapter

- Introducing adult learning theory

- Exploring multiple intelligences

- Incorporating whole brain learning

- Learning how theory enters into practice

Because this book provides fully designed workshops, you don't need to know all the details of designing a course—the design has already been done for you. However, understanding some of the principle design and learning theories that underpin these workshops is useful and helpful—especially if you are somewhat new to the field of workplace training and development. To effectively deliver training to learners requires a core understanding of how and why people learn. This gives you the flexibility to adapt a course to the unique learners in the room as needed.

When designing a workshop, paying attention to content flow is especially important. While there is no one right way to flow change management content, you must ensure that the topics build on one another and that you solidly connect the concepts and ideas together so you leverage the most of the learning opportunity. New skills require practice, so always include interactive practice sessions in the design of the workshop. Short but well-designed activities can have significant impact.

Basic Adult Learning Theory

The individual participant addressed in these workshops is typically an adult with learning needs that differ in many (but not all) ways from children. Much has been documented about how adults learn best. A key figure in adult education is Malcolm Knowles, who is often regarded as the father of adult learning. Knowles made several contributions to the field but is best known for popularizing the term *andragogy*, which refers to the art and science of teaching adults. Here are six assumptions about adult learners noted in *The Adult Learner: A Neglected Species* (Knowles 1984):

- Adults need to know why learning something is important before they learn it.
- Adults have a concept of self and do not like others imposing their will on them.
- Adults have a wealth of knowledge and experience and want that knowledge to be recognized.
- Adults open up to learning when they think that the learning will help them with real problems.
- Adults want to know how the learning will help them in their personal lives.
- Adults respond to internal motivations, such as the prospect of a promotion or an increase in salary.

Given these principles of adult learning, designing sessions that are highly interactive and engaging is critical (see sidebar for more tips). Forcing anyone to learn anything is impossible, so the goal of effective training design is to provide every opportunity and encouragement to the potential learner. Involvement of the learner is the key. As an old Chinese proverb says, "Tell me and I will forget. Show me and I may remember. Involve me and I will understand." The designs in this book use several methods to convey information and engage participants. By incorporating varied training media—such as presentation media, discussion sessions, small-group work, structured exercises, and self-assessments—these designs maximize active participant involvement and offer something for every learning style.

In addition to engaging the interest of the learner, interactive training allows you to tap into another source of learning content: the participants themselves. In a group-learning situation, a good learning environment encourages participants to share with others in the group so the entire group's cumulative knowledge can be used.

Tips for Adult Learning

To reach adult learners, incorporate these ideas into your next training session:

- Incorporate self-directed learning activities in the session design.
- Avoid overuse of lectures and "talking to"; emphasize discussion.
- Use interactive methods such as case studies, role playing, and so forth.
- Make the content and materials closely fit assessed needs.
- Allow plenty of time to "process" the learning activities.
- Promote inquiry into problems and affirm the experience of participants.
- Give participants a rationale for becoming involved and provide opportunities for success.
- Promote getting acquainted and interpersonal linkages.
- Diagnose and prioritize learning needs and preferences before and during the session.
- Use learning groups as "home bases" for participants.
- Include interpersonal feedback exercises and opportunities to experiment.
- Use subgroups to provide safety and readiness to engage in open interchange.
- Make all learner assessment self-directed.
- Provide activities that focus on cognitive, affective, and behavioral change.

More Theoretical Ideas Important to Learning

Research on how people learn and how the brain works occurs continuously. A few ideas that come up frequently in training design and delivery are multiple intelligences and whole brain learning.

Multiple Intelligences

Multiple intelligences reflect how people prefer to process information. Howard Gardner, from Harvard University, has been challenging the basic beliefs about intelligence since the early 1980s. Gardner initially described a list of seven intelligences. Later, he added three additional intelligences to his list, and he expects the list to continue to grow (Gardner 2011). The intelligences are

- **interpersonal:** aptitude for working with others
- **logical/mathematical:** aptitude for math, logic, and deduction

- **spatial/visual:** aptitude for picturing, seeing
- **musical:** aptitude for musical expression
- **linguistic/verbal:** aptitude for the written and spoken word
- **intrapersonal:** aptitude for working alone
- **bodily kinesthetic:** aptitude for being physical
- **emotional:** aptitude for identifying emotion
- **naturalist:** aptitude for being with nature
- **existential:** aptitude for understanding one's purpose.

How do multiple intelligences affect your learning? Gardner suggests that most people are comfortable in three or four of these intelligences and avoid the others. For example, if you are not comfortable working with other people, doing group case studies may interfere with your ability to process new material. Video-based instruction will not be good for people with lower spatial/visual aptitudes. People with strong bodily/kinesthetic aptitudes prefer to move around while they are learning.

Allowing your learners to use their own strengths and weaknesses helps them process and learn. Here's an example: Suppose you are debriefing one of the exercises in the material. The exercise has been highly interpersonal (team activity), linguistic (lots of talking), spatial/visual (the participants built an object), musical (music was playing), logical/mathematical (there were rules and structure), and kinesthetic (people moved around). You've honored all the processing styles except intrapersonal, so the people who process information in this manner probably need a return to their strength of working alone. Start the debriefing by asking people to quietly work on their own, writing down five observations of the activity. Then ask them to share as a group.

Whole Brain Learning

Ned Herrmann pioneered the concept of whole brain learning in the 1970s, developing the Herrmann Whole Brain Model, which divides the brain into four distinct types of thinking: analytical, sequential, interpersonal, and imaginative. Each individual tends to favor one type of thinking over another, and this thinking preference evolves continually throughout a person's life. In fact, the brain changes all the time with new input and new ways of thinking—a feature that is known as *plasticity*.

Although each person has a preferred thinking style, he or she may prefer it to varying degrees. To identify a person's thinking preference, Herrmann developed the Herrmann Brain Dominance Instrument in 1979. Learning about your own thinking and learning preferences can motivate you to learn new ways to learn and think. For trainers and facilitators, learning about your own preferences can help you identify where you may be neglecting other styles or preferences in your training design and delivery. As Ann Herrmann-Nehdi, daughter of Ned Herrmann and researcher in her own right, notes in the *ASTD Handbook for Workplace Learning Professionals,* "Effective learning is whole brained—designing, delivering, and evaluating the learning to best meet the varying needs of diverse learners" (2008, p. 215).

Herrmann-Nehdi continues, "Our knowledge of the brain and its inherent uniqueness shows that each individual is a unique learner with learning experiences, preferences, and avoidances that will be different from those of other learners. This means that learning designs must somehow factor in the uniqueness of the individual learner" (2008, p. 221). That is to say that effective facilitation must provide a blend of learning activities that addresses various thinking processes from analytical to sequential to interpersonal to imaginative. Because each individual has a unique combination of varying preferences for different types of learning, such a blend can engage most learners even when they are not directly learning in their preferred style. Engaging varied thinking styles ensures *whole brain learning,* rather than a narrow focus on one or two thinking styles.

Here are some tips for incorporating whole brain learning into your facilitation:

- Identify your own thinking preferences to avoid getting too one-sided in your presentation. Deliberately include styles you don't typically prefer.

- Recognize that your learners have unique brains that have continually changed as a result of a lifetime of experiences, learning, and ways of thinking.

- Address those variations in learning and thinking preferences by identifying different ways to deliver learning, including facts, case studies, metaphors, brainstorming, simulations, quizzes, outlines, procedures, group learning, role plays, and so on to engage their whole brains.

- Avoid diminishing learners' motivation to learn.

- Avoid overwhelming the brain or causing stress. Stick to need-to-know rather than nice-to-know.

Theory Into Practice

These theories (and more that are not addressed here) affect the way the content of the workshops are put together. Some examples of training features that derive from these theories include handouts, research references, and presentation media to read; quiet time to write notes and reflect; opportunities for listening and talking; and exercises for practicing skills.

The workshop activities and materials for the programs in this book have taken these theories to heart in their design, providing content, activities, and tools that will appeal to and engage many learning and thinking styles. Additional ways to translate learning and design theory into practice include the following:

Establishing a Framework

For learners to understand the goals of training and how material relates to real work situations, a framework can be helpful. When presenting the training in the context of a framework, trainers should provide an overview of why the organization has decided to undertake the training and why it is important. This explanation should also highlight what the trainer hopes to accomplish and how the skills learned in this training will be useful back on the job.

Objectives and goals of the programs and learning activities are described in this workbook; share those objectives with the learners when discussing the purposes of specific exercises. Handouts will also help provide a framework for participants.

Identifying Behaviors

Within any training goal are many behaviors. For example, listening and giving clear directions are necessary behaviors for good customer service. Customer service does not improve simply because employees are told to do so—participants need to understand the reasons and see the relevant parts of the equation. For these reasons, facilitators should identify and discuss relevant behaviors throughout the program.

Training helps people identify the behaviors that are important, so that those behaviors can be targeted for improvement. Learning activities enable participants to analyze different skills and behaviors and to separate the parts from the whole. The learning activities in this book, with their clearly stated objectives, have been carefully crafted to take these considerations into account.

Practicing

Practice is crucial for learning because learning takes place by doing and by seeing. In the training designs included in this workbook, practice occurs in written exercises, verbal exercises, and role playing. Role playing helps participants actually practice the behaviors that are being addressed. Role-play exercises bring skills and behaviors to life for those acting out particular roles and for those observing the scenarios.

Learning a new skill takes a lot of practice. Some participants learn skills more quickly than others. Some people's attitudes might prevent them from being open to trying new behaviors. Your job is to facilitate the session to the best of your ability, taking different learning styles into account. The rest is up to the participants.

Providing Feedback

A key aspect of training is the feedback trainers give to participants. If delivered in a supportive and constructive manner, feedback helps learners develop a deeper understanding of the content you are presenting and the behaviors they are practicing. Feedback in role plays is especially powerful because this is where "the rubber hits the road." In role plays, observers can see if people are able to practice the behaviors that have been discussed, or whether habitual responses will prevail.

Making It Relevant

Throughout the program you will discuss how to use skills and new behaviors on the job. These discussions will help answer the question "So what?" Exercises and action plans help participants bring new skills back to actual work situations. This is also important in addressing the adult need for relevancy in learning.

The Bare Minimum

- **Keep the focus on self-reflection.** Be purposeful in designing content that encourages participants to analyze their own behaviors instead of what others do wrong.
- **Build practice into the design.** Provide your participants with hands-on, engaging opportunities to practice the correct skills.

Key Points

- Adults have specific learning needs that must be addressed in training to make it successful.
- People also have different intelligences; that is, different areas in which they are more comfortable and competent. Addressing different intelligences in the workshop keeps more people engaged in more ways.
- People take in new information in different ways; addressing a variety of different thinking styles can help everyone learn more effectively.
- Bring theory into practice by creating a framework, identifying behaviors, practicing, providing feedback, and making the learning relevant.

What to Do Next

- Look through the training materials to identify how they address the learning theories presented in this book. If you make modifications to the material, consider whether those modifications leave out an intelligence or a thinking style. Can you address more intelligences without making the material cumbersome?

- Read the next chapter to identify how to incorporate technology into the workshop to make it more effective.

Additional Resources

Biech, E., ed. (2008). *ASTD Handbook for Workplace Learning Professionals*. Alexandria, VA: ASTD Press.

Biech, E., ed. (2014). *ASTD Handbook: The Definitive Reference for Training & Development*, 2nd edition. Alexandria, VA: ASTD Press.

Gardner, H. (2006). *Multiple Intelligences: New Horizons in Theory and Practice*. New York: Basic Books.

Gardner, H. (2011). *Frames of Mind: The Theory of Multiple Intelligences*. New York: Basic Books.

Herrmann, N. (1988). *Creative Brain*. Lake Lure, NC: Brain Books.

Herrmann, N., and A. Herrmann-Nehdi. (2015). *Whole Brain Business Book*, 2nd edition. San Francisco: McGraw-Hill.

Herrmann-Nehdi, A. (2008). "The Learner: What We Need to Know." In E. Biech, ed., *ASTD Handbook for Workplace Learning Professionals*. Alexandria, VA: ASTD Press.

Jones, J.E., W.L. Bearley, and D.C. Watsabaugh. (1996). *The New Fieldbook for Trainers: Tips, Tools, and Techniques*. Amherst, MA: HRD Press.

Knowles, M.S. (1984). *The Adult Learner: A Neglected Species*. Houston, TX: Gulf Publishing.

Russell, L. (1999). *The Accelerated Learning Fieldbook: Making the Instructional Process Fast, Flexible, and Fun*. San Francisco: Jossey-Bass/Pfeiffer.

Chapter 7

Leveraging Technology to Maximize and Support Design and Delivery

What's in This Chapter

- Recognizing the importance of technology tools
- Determining when to use learning technologies
- Identifying types of learning technologies
- Enhancing learner engagement
- Deepening learner understanding
- Increasing learning application

The workshops offered in this book are designed to be facilitated in person. Even so, learning technologies can and should play a role in adapting workshops to fit your organization, reinforce learning, and measure effectiveness. Technology is an important learning component, but it can also become an expensive distraction. The key is whether and how well technology enhances learners' abilities to understand and apply workshop concepts.

Your use of technology should also align with your organization's culture and readiness. For example, using webinars and wikis in a high-tech environment where employees are familiar with these tools may be logical and welcome, but you might need to introduce these tools more slowly at another company where email is the primary technology used for communication (see Figure 7-1 for some dos and don'ts of recording webinars).

The most important factor to consider when deciding whether to use learning technologies is how they can best support your workshop's learning objectives. This is particularly critical (and not at all straightforward) when delivering these workshops' soft skills training because personal and interpersonal habits and skills tend to require participants to challenge their beliefs and shift their mindsets. This deeper level of self-reflection, though tougher to do in a virtual setting, can be done if you select the right tool and use it at the right time in the learning process.

In the previous chapter, you learned about the adult learning theories and learning styles that underpin the workshops in this volume. Keep these in mind as you assess and weigh opportunities to use learning technologies. In this chapter, you will explore where technology can augment learning transfer and application in your workshop. Please note that the information has been kept general for two reasons. First, each organization has access to specific and limited technologies, and you should learn about them and creatively use what you have. Second, recommendations for specific technologies are likely to become obsolete quickly; so instead, focus on the types of learning technologies that might best augment in-person workshops.

Figure 7-1. Dos and Don'ts of Recording Webinars

To increase your chances of a successful webinar, consider and incorporate these tips.

Do
- Introduce yourself and the topic.
- Keep recorded webinars short—ideally 20 minutes or less.
- Use a conversational voice to increase interest.
- Use adequate numbers of slides so that you do not stay on one slide for more than 30 or 45 seconds.
- Address simple, focused topics with five or fewer key points.
- Use pictures and minimal text on slides.

Don't
- Use your computer's microphone to record; instead, invest in a good headset.
- Use a recorded webinar that has poor audio quality; instead, re-record if needed.
- Use too much text or small fonts.
- Assume that participants are just watching the webinar; you have to keep their interest or they will get distracted.
- Try to cover a complex topic using a recorded webinar; the webinar should focus on one topic with a few main points.

Why Consider Learning Technologies?

You have decided to provide in-person workshops and will use the agendas offered in this book to plan and conduct the training. Learning technologies can be essential tools in your tool kit. Most behavior change does not occur in the classroom. The workshop is important, but it must be supported by strong pre- and post-course reinforcement. To learn something, learners need

A Note From Elaine: m-Learning

Learning in the palm of your hand. What could be better? m-Learning is still relatively new, so it is not widely used. For our purpose here, we are thinking about content that might be displayed on a smartphone or tablet for learning.

Any content you might wish to provide in this format should have the following features:

- It is concise—probably less than 5 minutes long.
- It encourages a response from the learner.
- It is straightforward and easy to understand because the user will not likely be in a distraction-free environment.
- It offers support or knowledge required just in time, such as an updated policy, a job aid, or a short communication skill.

m-Learning could be perfect for managing change. You could follow up with a series of mini-modules that act as reminders for some of the new skills presented in your workshop. You could also follow up with "next steps." For example, you have discussed "fostering change-ready employees" and you could follow up with a list of skills based on the workshop activity.

If you know that several of the participants will be involved in initiating an upcoming change initiative, you could share a short checklist with them to remind them of what to do. The beauty of each of these examples is that once you have designed them, you can use them over and over.

m-Learning allows you to pair a tiny but critical (either timeframe or importance) data point with a skill check, giving you a quick connection with your learners. This connection accomplishes several goals. It provides the learner with content, allows the learner to provide you with an update, and it keeps the relationship between the two of you alive.

One last thought: Design for the tiniest screen your participants may be using.

many points of contact with the new skills and concepts, such as presentation, reflection, discussion, practice, feedback, and exploration. Moreover, most of your participants are very busy and unable to attend multiple in-person pre- or post-course sessions. So to ensure learning transfer, you can augment in-person activities with technology-based engagement. The good news is that you can use technology in many ways to enhance learning, even of soft skills.

Opportunities to Use Learning Technologies

Whether you have many or few technology resources upon which to draw for learning, start by asking yourself this question: For this topic or series, how can I best use technology to increase learner engagement, understanding, and application? You will use these criteria to discover and evaluate potential ways technology might provide value in the learning process, including

- when designing the training
- before the training
- during the training
- after the training
- while building a learner community.

Note that this chapter offers ways to use technology to enhance traditional learning workshops (blended learning). It is important that you consult with a technology partner if you are considering a technology-driven training program—such as a workplace simulation or self-directed online learning. That said, the content found in this training series could be adapted for use in an online learning platform. For more information on how to use the online tools and downloads, see Chapter 14.

When Designing Training

The ATD Workshop Series offers fully designed training you can use with minimal preparation and solid facilitation skills. Even so, you will be creating a learning implementation plan that is an important part of the design process.

To increase engagement: You have to know your audience members to engage them, because engagement is a choice driven by interest, challenge, and relevance of the topic. Use learning technologies to ensure that you understand where your audience is coming from and the learning approaches they will most value. Email groups, online surveys, teleconferencing, and web meetings with polling can help you ascertain their wants and needs before you solidify your training plan.

To deepen understanding: When in the planning stage, make sure that you have not tried to cram too much presentation into the learning process and that you have planned sufficient time and attention to engaging participants. Flowcharting or mind-mapping software can help you visualize and communicate your learning plan and ensure that you allow for maximum engagement and practice.

To increase application: Increasing retention and application requires buy-in from sponsors and managers to ensure that what is learned is welcomed and applied on the job. Use email groups, online surveys, teleconferencing, and web meetings with polling to communicate with sponsors and managers about what they want out of the training and to identify ways to apply the learning back on the job. Having this information is also valuable in developing the training plan.

Before Training

You want to prime your participants' minds for the topic you will be presenting during the workshop. Pre-work does not have to be something arduous and unwelcome. In fact, a great pre-work assignment can help maximize precious time in the classroom and allow you to focus on the topics that require thorough discussion.

To increase engagement: Tap into the most fascinating aspects of the workshop topic and introduce these through video clips, blog posts, and online resources (see Figure 7-2 about the legal

Figure 7-2. Copyright Beware

Copyright law is a sticky, complex area that is beyond the scope of this book to address in detail. For legal advice, consult your legal department.

However, it's very important to note a few things about copyright, fair use, and intellectual property:

- Just because you found an image, article, music, or video online doesn't mean that you can use it in training without permission. Make sure you obtain permission from the copyright owner before you use it (sometimes the copyright owner is not obvious and you will need to do some research).

- Fair use is pretty limited. Although most fair use allows an educational exception, that does *not* include corporate or organizational training. Other exceptions relate to how much material relative to the original was used, the nature of the original work (creative work generally has more protection), and the effect on the market for the original (Swindling and Partridge 2008). Once again, your best bet is to get written permission.

- Just because something doesn't have a copyright notice on it doesn't mean that it isn't copyright protected. All original material is protected under copyright law as soon as it is published or created.

Don't despair. Plenty of online sources of images, videos, text, and so forth exist that you can use for free or for a minimal fee. Just search on the terms "copyright free" or "open source." Another place to look is Wikimedia Commons, which has millions of freely usable media files. For more information about how copyright law affects your use of materials in this volume, please see Chapter 14 on how to use the online materials and downloads.

use of video clips, images, and so forth). Avoid boring participants with long "how-to" articles or book chapters before the workshop. In fact, do the opposite and ensure that the pre-work is interesting, provocative (even controversial), and brief. You might select a blog post or video clip that offers a counterpoint to the training or something that inspires your participants to think about the topic before attending training.

To deepen understanding: If you know that the workshop topic will be challenging to some of your participants, prepare and share a brief recorded webinar, video clip, or article that introduces the topic. For example, if your managers tend to tell versus coach, try sharing one or two external resources that discuss the value of service-oriented coaching conversations.

To increase application: You can improve the chances that your participants will apply what they learn by ensuring they identify real-world work challenges in which they can apply their new skills. Start with a one- or two-question pre-workshop survey (using Survey Monkey or similar) that requires they identify these opportunities and then use the responses to enhance your in-workshop discussions. If your organization has an internal social network or ways to create collaboration groups, use the pre-work questions to begin an online discussion of the topic. The conversations will help your participants think about the topic and will help you prepare for a great workshop (and will give you a beneficial "heads-up" on potential areas of conflict or disagreement).

During Training

Learning technologies can help make your workshops more interesting and can help enhance understanding of the material. Beware, however, that you always want to have a "Plan B" in case of technology glitches or breakdowns. Another critical point to make here is that technology does not change how people learn. Learning and performance drive the technology choice, not the other way around.

To increase engagement: The perennial favorite technology for spicing up a workshop is the use of a great video. Boring videos don't help! If you can find short video clips that reinforce your most important points, please do so. In addition to adding contrast to the workshop flow, having other "experts" say what you want participants to hear is helpful. Another way to increase engagement is to use some kind of audience-response system or electronic polling. Although this might not be practical for small groups (the technology can be a bit pricey), some less expensive alternatives use texting schemas you might want to check out. Your participants will love seeing their collective responses instantly populate your PowerPoint charts. (For more on PowerPoint, see Figure 7-3 and Chapter 8.)

To deepen understanding: Videos can also help improve understanding. If your participants have access to computers during the workshop, consider short technology-based games and short simulations that reinforce the points. You can also ask participants to fill out worksheets and surveys online during the class. Share animated models, flowcharts, or mind maps to help explain key concepts or how they connect together.

To increase application: Learning simulations and practice sessions help prepare participants to apply new skills. You can do these in person, and you can use technology to facilitate practices. This depends a lot on the topic.

Figure 7-3. PowerPoint or Prezi or Other?

Although PowerPoint is the most common presentation software, other platforms you might want to consider include Prezi, GoAnimate, Google Docs, mind-mapping programs, or others. Here are a few key considerations that will help you choose:

- Aside from the in-class workshop, where will you want to share the presentation?
- If you will be sharing the presentation with others, consider whether new software will be required.
- Which presentation platform is best for the content you are presenting, or does it matter?
- What are the costs and resources required for each platform?
- Which platform will partner well with technology tools you will use to reinforce the learning?
- What might be the advantage of using two or more platforms throughout the learning process?

After Training

Your participants are busy, and the new skills and concepts they learned in the workshop will become a distant memory without follow-up. Just as you did before the training, you can and should use learning technologies to augment the learning that occurs during the workshop.

To increase engagement: Learners engage when they perceive something as interesting, relevant right now, or challenging. Use tools such as video, blogs, social networks, chat, websites, and email to increase interest in the topic and to provide challenge.

To deepen understanding: Use post-workshop surveys and polling tools to assess understanding so you can address any gap. Add to the participants' understanding of the topic by posting materials on a SharePoint site or through blog posts that you push to their email inboxes using an RSS feed.

To increase application: Provide a just-in-time online resource where participants find quick reference sheets and get application tips using a group site, social network, or SharePoint site. Request or require that participants report how they have used new skills through an online project management collaboration site, wiki, or email group.

While Building a Learning Community

Creating an ongoing network of learners is extremely valuable, especially for soft skills. The in-person workshop is just the beginning of the learning journey and so keeping learners engaged is helpful. In addition, you want to create a safe place where learners can discuss challenges, provide encouragement, and share their best practices. Learning technologies are particularly useful for building community among learners and teams.

To increase engagement: Busy people value community but often can't make the time to attend follow-up sessions or network with peers. They might, however, be able to take 10 minutes to check in on an internal social network, group site, or blog to learn from and share with others. If your organization does not have social networking or collaboration software, you might need to get creative. Talk to your technology department about the tools you do have—whether they are SharePoint, blog software, internal messaging, a wiki-type project management collaboration tool, or other. You can even use email groups to connect learners. Look for ways you can create pull (they choose when to engage) and push (they get updates), such as using RSS feeds.

To deepen understanding: After the workshop, use web meetings, teleconferencing, and messaging to connect learning partners or mentors and facilitate their sharing real-time application stories. Periodically facilitate online discussion groups to reinforce the learning and bring participants back together.

To increase application: Use a collaborative online project site or social network to set expectations about post-workshop peer discussions and reinforce engagement. Poll participants and assign sub-teams to lead a portion of each web meeting.

The Bare Minimum

- **Know what resources you have available.** Many organizations have widely varying resources; don't assume that you know everything that is available.

- **Stretch yourself.** Be willing to try something new; develop your skills to use technology in innovative ways to facilitate learning.

- **Know your participants.** They may be far ahead of you in their skills with technology or they may be far behind. If you plan to use learning technologies, do your best to assess their skill level before designing the workshop.

- **Be prepared for challenges.** No matter the skill level of the group, technology glitches are unavoidable. Be sure to cultivate good working relationships with technology support staff.

Key Points

- Most behavior change does not happen in a classroom but through multiple points of reinforcement. Learning technologies are an efficient way to augment learning.

- You can use learning technologies your organization already has if you are creative and partner with your technology team.

- Use learning technologies throughout the learning process to increase engagement, understanding, and application.

What to Do Next

- **Highlight the portions of this chapter that seem most relevant to your learning plan.** Meet with your technology team and get its input on the most applicable tools you might use.

- **Create a plan for how you will use learning technologies to reinforce your workshop.** Ensure that you select only those tools and activities that will enhance the overall learning objectives and be mindful of your organization's culture and comfort level with technology.

- **Test, test, test!** Practice using technology tools to ensure they will deliver what you hope.

- **Read the next chapter to learn ways you can improve your facilitation skills.** Many of these skills will also be useful when using learning technologies, especially collaboration tools.

Additional Resources

Bozarth, J. (2014). "Effective Social Media for Learning." In E. Biech, ed., *ASTD Handbook: The Definitive Reference for Training & Development,* 2nd edition. Alexandria, VA: ASTD Press.

Chen, J. (2012). *50 Digital Team-Building Games: Fast, Fun Meeting Openers, Group Activities and Adventures Using Social Media, Smart Phones, GPS, Tablets, and More.* Hoboken, NJ: Wiley.

Halls, J. (2012). *Rapid Video Development for Trainers: How to Create Learning Videos Fast and Affordably.* Alexandria, VA: ASTD Press.

Kapp, K. (2013). *The Gamification of Learning and Instruction Fieldbook: Ideas Into Practice.* San Francisco: Wiley.

Palloff, R.M., and K. Pratt. (2009). *Building Online Learning Communities: Effective Strategies for the Virtual Classroom.* San Francisco: Jossey-Bass.

Quinn, C. (2014). "M-Thinking: There's an App for That." In E. Biech, ed., *ASTD Handbook: The Definitive Reference for Training & Development,* 2nd edition. Alexandria, VA: ASTD Press.

Swindling, L.B., and M.V.B. Partridge. (2008). "Intellectual Property: Protect What Is Yours and Avoid Taking What Belongs to Someone Else." In E. Biech, *ASTD Handbook for Workplace Learning Professionals.* Alexandria, VA: ASTD Press.

Toth, T. (2006). *Technology for Trainers.* Alexandria, VA: ASTD Press.

Udell, C. (2012). *Learning Everywhere: How Mobile Content Strategies Are Transforming Training.* Nashville, TN: Rockbench Publishing.

Chapter 8

Delivering Your Change Management Workshop: Be a Great Facilitator

What's in This Chapter

- Defining the facilitator's role

- Creating an effective learning environment

- Preparing participant materials

- Using program preparation checklists

- Starting and ending on a strong note

- Managing participant behaviors

Let's get one thing clear from the get-go: Facilitating a workshop—facilitating learning—is *not* lecturing. The title of ATD's bestselling book says it all: *Telling Ain't Training* (Stolovitch and Keeps 2011). A facilitator is the person who helps learners open themselves to new learning and makes the process easier. The role requires that you avoid projecting yourself as a subject matter expert (SME) and that you prepare activities that foster learning through "hands-on" experience and interaction.

Before you can help someone else learn, you must understand the roles you will embody when you deliver training: trainer, facilitator, and learner. When a workshop begins, you are the trainer, bringing to the learning event a plan, structure, experience, and objectives. This is only possible because you have a strong, repeatable logistics process. As you ask the learners to prioritize the learning objectives, you slowly release control, inviting them to become partners in their own learning. As you move from the trainer role into the facilitator role, the objectives are the contract between the learners and the facilitator. All great facilitators also have a third role in the classroom—the role of learner. If you are open, you can learn many new things when you are in class. If you believe you must be the expert as a learning facilitator, you will not be very effective.

To be most successful as a learning facilitator, consider this checklist:

- [ ] Identify the beliefs that limit your ability to learn and, therefore, to teach.
- [ ] Learning is a gift for you and from you to others.
- [ ] Choose carefully what you call yourself and what you call your outcomes.
- [ ] Clarify your purpose to better honor your roles at a learning event.
- [ ] If you can't teach with passion, don't do it.

This last point is especially important. Not everyone is destined to be a great facilitator and teacher, but you can still have enormous impact if you are passionate about the topic, about the process, and about helping people improve their working lives. If you are serious about becoming a great facilitator, Chapter 12 provides a comprehensive assessment instrument to help you manage your personal development and increase the effectiveness of your training (see Assessment 3). You can use this instrument for self-assessment, end-of-course feedback, observer feedback, or as a professional growth tracker.

With these points firmly in mind—facilitating is not lecturing and passion can get you past many facilitator deficiencies—let's look at some other important aspects of facilitating, starting with how to create an engaging and effective learning environment.

The Learning Environment

Colors, seating, tools, environmental considerations (such as temperature, ventilation, lighting), and your attitude, dress, preparation, and passion all enhance—or detract from—an effective and positive learning environment. This section describes some ways to maximize learning through environmental factors.

Color. Research has shown that bland, neutral environments are so unlike the real world that learning achieved in these "sensory deprivation chambers" cannot be transferred to the job.

Color can be a powerful way to engage the limbic part of the brain and create long-term retention. It can align the right and left brains. Ways to incorporate color include artwork, plants, and pictures that help people feel comfortable and visually stimulated. Consider printing your handouts and assessments in color. The training support materials provided in this book are designed in color but can be printed in either color or grayscale (to reduce reproduction costs).

Room Setup. Because much learning requires both individual reflection and role playing, consider seating that promotes personal thought and group sharing. One way to accomplish this is to set up groups of three to five at round or square tables, with each chair positioned so the projection screen can easily be seen. Leave plenty of room for each person so that when he or she does need to reflect, there is a feeling of privacy. Keep in mind that comfortable chairs and places to write help people relax to learn. Figure 8-1 details more room configurations that you can use to accomplish specific tasks or purposes in training.

Tools of the Trade. Lots of flipcharts (one per table is optimal) with brightly colored markers create an interactive environment. Flipcharts are about as basic and low tech as tools get, but they are also low cost and do the trick. Consider putting colorful hard candy on the tables (include sugar-free options), with bright cups of markers, pencils, and pens. Gather pads of colorful sticky notes and "fidgets" (quiet toys such as chenille stems, Koosh balls, and others) to place on the table as well. For the right level of trust to exist, your learners must feel welcome.

Your Secret Weapon. Finally, the key to establishing the optimal learning environment is *you*. You set the tone by your attitude, the way you greet people, the clothes you wear, your passion, and your interest and care for the participants. You set the stage for learning with four conditions that only you as the facilitator can create to maximize learning:

1. **Confidentiality.** Establish the expectation that anything shared during the training program will remain confidential among participants and that as the facilitator you are committed to creating a safe environment. An important step in learning is first admitting ignorance, which has some inherent risk. Adult learners may resist admitting their learning needs because they fear the repercussions of showing their weaknesses. You can alleviate these concerns by assuring participants that the sole purpose of the training is to build their skills, and that no evaluations will take place. Your workshop must be a safe place to learn and take risks.

Figure 8-1. Seating Configurations

Select a room setup that will best support the needs of your learners:

- **Rounds.** Circular tables are particularly useful for small-group work when you have 16 to 24 participants.
- **U-Shaped.** This setup features three long rectangular tables set up to form a U, with you at the open end. It is good for overall group interaction and small-group work (two to three people). This setup also helps you establish rapport with your learners.
- **Classroom.** This setup is a traditional grade-school format characterized by rows of tables with all the participants facing forward toward the trainer. Avoid this setup as much as possible because you become the focal point rather than the learners, and your ability to interact with learners is extremely limited. Problems of visibility also occur when rows in the back are blocked by rows in the front.
- **Chevron.** Chevron setup features rows of tables as in the classroom setup but the tables are angled to form a V-shape. This opens up the room to allow you to interact more with the learners and accommodates a larger group of learners without sacrificing visibility. However, it shares many of the drawbacks of the classroom setup.
- **Hybrid or Fishbone.** This setup combines a U-shaped configuration with that of a chevron. It is useful when there are too many learners to form a good U and there is room enough to broaden the U to allow tables to be set up as chevrons in the center of the U. This hybrid approach allows for interaction and enables the trainer to move around.

Source: Drawn from McCain (2015).

2. **Freedom from distractions.** Work and personal demands cannot be ignored during training, but to maximize each participant's learning, and as a courtesy to others, outside demands should be minimized:

    a. Select a training site away from the workplace to help reduce distractions.

    b. Acknowledge that participants probably feel they shouldn't be away from work; remind them that the purpose of the training is to improve their work lives.

    c. Ask that mobile devices be turned off or set to silent alerts.

    d. Emphasize that because they are spending this time in training, trainees should immerse themselves in the learning experience and thereby maximize the value of their time, because far from being time "away from work responsibilities," it *is* a work responsibility.

3. **Personal responsibility for learning.** A facilitator can only create the *opportunity* for learning. Experiential learning requires that participants actively engage with and commit to learning—they cannot sit back and soak up information like sponges.

4. **Group participation.** Each participant brings relevant knowledge to the training program. Through discussion and sharing of information, a successful training session will

tap into the knowledge of each participant. Encourage all participants to accept responsibility for helping others learn.

Program Preparation Checklist

Preparation is power when it comes to facilitating a successful workshop, and a checklist is a powerful tool for effective preparation. This checklist of activities will help you prepare your workshop:

- ☐ Write down all location and workshop details when scheduling the workshop.
- ☐ Make travel reservations early (to save money, too), if applicable.
- ☐ Send a contract to the client to confirm details, or if you are an internal facilitator, develop guidelines and a workshop structure in conjunction with appropriate supervisors and managers.
- ☐ Specify room and equipment details in writing and then confirm by telephone.
- ☐ Define goals and expectations for the workshop.
- ☐ Get a list of participants, titles, roles, and responsibilities.
- ☐ Send participants a questionnaire that requires them to confirm their goals for the workshop.
- ☐ Send the client (or the participants, if you are an internal facilitator) an agenda for the workshop, with times for breaks and meals.
- ☐ Recommend that lunch or dinner be offered in-house, with nutritious food provided.
- ☐ Make a list of materials that you will need in the room (pads of paper, pens, pencils, markers, flipcharts, and so forth). Make sure to plan for some extras.
- ☐ Design the room layout (for example, rounds, U-shaped, classroom, chevron, or hybrid).
- ☐ Confirm whether you or your internal/external client will prepare copies of the workshop handouts. The workshop handouts should include all tools, training instruments, assessments, and worksheets. You may choose also to include copies of the presentation slides as part of the participant guide. All the supplemental materials you need to conduct the workshops in this book are available for download (see Chapter 14 for instructions).
- ☐ Find out if participants would like to receive pre-reading materials electronically before the session.
- ☐ Prepare assessments, tools, training instruments, and workshop materials at least one week before the workshop so that you have time to peruse and check them and assemble any equipment you may need (see the next two sections).

Participant Materials

Participant materials support participant learning throughout the workshop and provide continuing references after the workshop has ended. There are several kinds of participant materials. Here are some options:

Handouts

The development and "look" of your handouts are vital to help participants understand the information they convey. To compile the handouts properly, first gather all assessments, tools, training instruments, activities, and presentation slides and arrange them in the order they appear in the workshop. Then bind them together in some fashion. There are several options for compiling your material, ranging from inexpensive to deluxe. The kind of binding is your choice—materials can be stapled, spiral bound, or gathered in a ring binder—but remember that a professional look supports success. Your choice of binding will depend on your budget for the project. Because first appearances count, provide a cover with eye-catching colors and appropriate graphics.

Using the agendas in Chapters 1–3, select the presentation slides, learning activities, handouts, tools, and assessments appropriate to your workshop. If you choose to print out the presentation slides for your participants, consider printing no more than three slides per handout page to keep your content simple with sufficient white space for the participants to write their own notes. Use the learning objectives for each workshop to provide clarity for the participants at the outset. Remember to number the pages, to add graphics for interest (and humor), and to include tabs for easy reference if the packet of materials has multiple sections.

Some participants like to receive the handouts before the workshop begins. You may want to email participants to determine if they would like to receive the handouts electronically.

Presentation Slides

This ATD Workshop Series book includes presentation slides to support the two-day, one-day, and half-day agendas. They have been crafted to adhere to presentation best practices. If you choose to reorder or otherwise modify the slides, keep in mind these important concepts.

When you use PowerPoint software as a teaching tool, be judicious in the number of slides that you prepare. In a scientific lecture, slides are usually a necessity for explaining formulas or results, but a workshop relies on interaction so keep the slide information simple. Also, do not include more than five or six bullet points per slide. See more tips for effective PowerPoint slides in Figure 8-2.

A message can be conveyed quickly through the use of simple graphics. For example, an illustration of two people in conversation may highlight interpersonal communication, whereas a photo of a boardroom-style meeting may illustrate a group engaged in negotiation. Please note that any use of the images in the presentation slides provided with this book other than as part of your presentation is strictly prohibited by law.

When you use presentation slides ask yourself: What will a slide add to my presentation? Ensure that the answer that comes back is "it will enhance the message." If slides are simply used to make the workshop look more sophisticated or technical, the process may not achieve the desired results.

It can be frustrating when a facilitator shows a slide for every page that the participants have in front of them. The dynamics of the class are likely to disconnect. If the information you are teaching is in the handouts or workbook, work from those media alone and keep the workshop personally interactive.

Workbooks and Journals

A participant journal can be included in the binder with your handouts, or it may be a separate entity. Throughout the workshop participants can assess their progress and advance their development by entering details of their personal learning in the journal. The benefit of this journal to participants is that they can separate their personal discoveries and development from the main workshop handouts and use this journal as an action plan if desired.

Videos

If you show a video in your workshop, ensure that the skills it contains are up to date and that the video is less than 20 minutes long. Provide questions that will lead to a discussion of the information viewed. Short video clips can be effective learning tools.

Toys, Noisemakers, and Other Props

Experienced facilitators understand the value of gadgets and games that advance the learning, provide a break from learning, or both.

Figure 8-2. Tips for Effective PowerPoint Slides

Presentation slides can enhance your presentation. They can also detract from it by being too cluttered, monotonous, or hard to read. Here are some tips for clear, effective slides:

Fonts

- Use sans-serif fonts such as Arial, Calibri, or Helvetica; other fonts are blurry when viewed from 20 feet or more and are more easily read on LCD screens and in video/web presentations.

- Use the same sans-serif font for most (if not all) of the presentation.

- Use a font size no smaller than 24 points. (This will also help keep the number of bullets per slide down.)

- Consider using a 32-point font—this is the easiest for web/video transmission.

- Limit yourself to one font size per slide.

Colors

- Font colors should be black or dark blue for light backgrounds and white or yellow on dark backgrounds. Think high contrast for clarity and visual impact.

- Avoid using red or green. It doesn't project well, doesn't transfer well when used in a webinar, and causes issues for people who suffer color blindness.

Text and Paragraphs

- Align text left or right, not centered.

- Avoid cluttering a slide—use a single headline and a few bullet points.

- Use no more than six words to a line; avoid long sentences.

- Use sentence case—ALL CAPS ARE DIFFICULT TO READ AND CAN FEEL LIKE YELLING.

- Avoid abbreviations and acronyms.

- Limit use of punctuation marks.

Source: Developed by Cat Russo.

Adults love to play. When their minds are open they learn quickly and effectively. Something as simple as tossing a rubber ball from person to person as questions are asked about topics studied can liven up the workshop and help people remember what they've learned.

Case studies and lively exercises accelerate learning. Bells and whistles are forms of communication; use them when you pit two teams against each other or to indicate the end of an activity.

Facilitator Equipment and Materials

When all details for the workshop have been confirmed, it is time to prepare for the actual facilitation of the workshop at the site. You may know the site well because you are providing in-house facilitation. If, however, you are traveling off site to facilitate, important elements enter the planning. Here's a checklist of things to consider:

- ☐ Pack a data-storage device that contains your handouts and all relevant workshop materials. In the event that your printed materials do not reach the workshop location, you will have the electronic files to reprint on site.

- ☐ Pack the proper power cords, a spare battery for the laptop, and a bulb for the LCD or overhead projector in the event that these items are not available at the workshop location. This requires obtaining the make and model of all audiovisual and electronic equipment from the client or the training facility during your planning process.

- ☐ Bring an extension cord.

- ☐ Bring reference materials, books, article reprints, and ancillary content. Take advantage of all technology options, such as tablets or other readers to store reference materials. As a facilitator, you will occasionally need to refer to materials other than your own for additional information. Having the materials with you not only provides correct information about authors and articles, but it also positively reinforces participants' impressions of your knowledge, training, openness to learning, and preparedness.

- ☐ Bring flipcharts, painter's tape, and sticky notes.

- ☐ Pack toys and games for the workshop, a timer or bell, and extra marking pens.

- ☐ Bring duct tape. You may need it to tape extension cords to the floor as a safety precaution. The strength of duct tape also ensures that any flipchart pages hung on walls (with permission) will hold fast.

You can ship these items to the workshop in advance, but recognize that the shipment may not arrive in time, and that even if it does arrive on time, you may have to track it down at the venue. Also, take some time identifying backups or alternatives in case the materials, technology, and so on do not conform to plan. What are the worst-case scenarios? How could you manage such situations? Prepare to be flexible and creative.

A Strong Start: Introduction, Icebreakers, and Openers

The start of a session is a crucial time in the workshop dynamic. How the participants respond to you, the facilitator, can set the mood for the remainder of the workshop. To get things off on the right foot, get to the training room early, at least 30 to 60 minutes before the workshop. This gives you time not only to set up the room if that has not already been done, but also to test the environment, the seating plan, the equipment, and your place in the room. Find out where the restrooms are. When participants begin to arrive (and some of them come very early), be ready to welcome them. Don't be distracted with problems or issues; be free and available to your participants.

While they are settling in, engage them with simple questions:

- How was your commute?
- Have you traveled far for this workshop?
- Was it easy to find this room?
- May I help you with anything?

When the participants have arrived and settled, introduce yourself. Write a humorous introduction, if that's your style, because this will help you be more approachable. Talk more about what you want to accomplish in the workshop than about your accomplishments. If you have a short biographical piece included in the handouts or in the workbook, it may serve as your personal introduction.

At the conclusion of your introduction, provide an activity in which participants can meet each other (often called an icebreaker). Because participants sometimes come into a training session feeling inexperienced, skeptical, reluctant, or scared, using icebreaker activities to open training enables participants to interact in a fun and nonthreatening way and to warm up the group before approaching more serious content. Don't limit the time on this too much unless you have an extremely tight schedule. The more time participants spend getting to know each other at the beginning of the workshop, the more all of you will benefit as the session proceeds.

Feedback

Feedback is the quickest, surest way for you, the facilitator, to learn if the messages and instruction are reaching the participants and if the participants are absorbing the content. It is also important for you to evaluate the participants' rate of progress and learning. Answers to the questions you ask throughout the workshop will help you identify much of the progress, but these answers come from only a few of the participants at a time. They're not a global snapshot of the entire group's comprehension and skills mastery.

When you lead a workshop, the participants walk a fine line between retention and deflection of knowledge. Continuing evaluations ensure that learning is taking root. Three levels of questions—learning comprehension, skills mastery, and skills application—help you determine where the training may not be achieving the intended results.

- Learning comprehension checks that the participants understand and grasp the skills being taught (see Figure 8-3).

- Skills mastery means that the participants are able to demonstrate their newly acquired knowledge by some activity, such as teaching a portion of a module to their fellow participants or delivering their interpretation of topic specifics to the class (see Figure 8-4).

- Skills application is the real test. You may choose to substantiate this through role plays or group case studies. When the participants have the opportunity to verbally communicate the skills learned and to reach desired results through such application, then skills application is established (see Figure 8-5).

The questions in Figures 8-3 to 8-5 are designed for written answers so you can incorporate them into the takeaway workbook you create. The questions concerning skills mastery and skills application could be used as a job-based assignment if the workshop is longer than one day. Keep in mind that you will also reevaluate after each day of a multiday session.

Let's now look at other forms of in-class learning assessments: role plays, participant presentations, ball toss, and journaling.

Role Plays

Role plays are an effective tool for assessing learning comprehension. If two or more participants conduct a role play that reveals their understanding of the information, with an outcome that reflects that understanding, then it becomes a "live feed," instantaneous learning for all.

You must set up the role play carefully. It is often wise for you to be a part of the first role-play experience to show participants how it's done and to make them more comfortable with the activity. Ensure that you explain all the steps of the role play and the desired outcome. It is insightful to role-play a negative version first, followed by participant discussion; then role-play a positive aspect the second time. For example, if confrontational communication is the topic and the situation under discussion involves a line manager and his or her supervisor, first enact

Figure 8-3. Learning Comprehension Questions

Here are some questions that can be asked to determine each participant's level of *learning comprehension*:

- Give a brief overview of your learning in this workshop. Begin your phrases with "I have learned. . . ." This will assist you in focusing your responses.
- How/where will you apply this knowledge in your workplace?
- Did you acquire this knowledge through lectures/practice/discussion or a combination of all methods?
- Do you feel sufficiently confident to pass on this knowledge to your colleagues?
- Are there any areas that will require additional learning for you to feel sufficiently confident?

Figure 8-4. Skills Mastery Questions

Now let's look at some questions you can use to evaluate your participants' *skills mastery*:

- If you were asked to teach one skill in this workshop, which skill would it be?
- What would your three key message points be for that skill?
- Describe the steps you would take to instruct each message point (for example, lecture, group discussion, PowerPoint presentation, and so forth).
- What methods would you use to ensure that your participants comprehend your instruction?
- Would feedback from your participants, both positive and negative, affect the development of your skills mastery? If yes, illustrate your response and the changes you would make.

Figure 8-5. Skills Application Questions

And finally, let's consider some questions that identify participants' *ability to apply the skills* they've learned in the workshop:

- Please describe a situation at your workplace where you could employ one specific skill from this workshop.
- How would you introduce this skill to your colleagues?
- How would you set goals to measure the improvement in this skill?
- Describe the input and participation you would expect from your colleagues.
- How would you exemplify mastery of the skill?

the role play using the verbal and body language that is causing the negative result. Discuss this as a class to identify the specific language that needs improvement. Then enact the role play again, this time using positive language.

Frequently it is helpful for a participant who has been on the receiving end of negative communication in his or her workplace to adopt the role of deliverer. Walking in the other person's shoes leads to a quicker understanding of the transaction. This positive role play should also be followed by whole-group discussion of the elements that worked. Participants can be invited to write about the process and its results to give them a real-life example to take back to the workplace.

Participant Presentations

You might ask a participant to present a module of learning to the group. This allows you to observe the participants from a different perspective—both as a contributor to the conversation and as a presenter leading the discussion. Be ready to assist or to answer questions. For example, a participant may choose assertive communication as his or her module, and the specific issue on return to the workplace may be a request for promotion. The participant defines and delivers the steps required to ask for the promotion while the facilitator and other participants observe and evaluate the success of the approach and demonstration of confidence and assertiveness.

Ball Toss

A quick method for evaluating a class's knowledge of the material presented is to ask the participants to form a standing circle. The facilitator throws out a soft rubber ball to an individual and asks a question about the previous learning activity. When the catcher gives the right answer, he or she throws the ball to another participant who answers another question. The facilitator can step out of this circle and let the participants ask as well as answer questions to review the skills as a group. Candy for all as a reward for contributions is always enjoyed by the participants (consider keeping some sugar-free treats on hand as well).

Journaling

Keeping a journal is a quiet, introspective way for participants to get a grip on their learning. When you complete an activity, have everyone take five minutes to write a summary of the skill just learned and then ask them to share what they've written with a partner. Invite the partner to correct and improve the material if necessary or appropriate.

Responding to Questions

When participants are asking questions, they are engaged and interested. Your responses to questions will augment the learning atmosphere. The way in which you respond is extremely important. Answers that are evasive can disturb a class because they cast doubts on your credibility. Glib or curt answers are insulting. Lengthy responses break the rhythm of the class and often go off track. When dealing with questions, the value of effective communication is in hearing the question, answering the question asked, and moving on. Repeat questions so that all participants hear them. In addition, this can ensure that you have heard the question correctly.

However, don't rush to answer. Take time to let everyone absorb the information. When time is of the essence, don't be tempted to give long, complicated answers that embrace additional topics. Be courteous and clear. Check that your answer has been understood. When a question comes up that could possibly derail the session or that is beyond the scope of the topic, you can choose to record it on a "parking lot" list and then revisit it later at an assigned time. A parking lot can be as simple as a list on a flipchart. However, whenever possible, answer a question at the time it is asked. Consider answering with analogies when they are appropriate because these often help elucidate challenging concepts.

You arc likely aware that effective questions that prompt answers are open ended. Here are some that you might ask:

- What have you learned so far?
- How do you feel about this concept?
- How would you handle this situation?

Any question that begins with "what" or "how" promotes a more extensive answer. Do you also know, though, that questions that begin with "why"—as in "why do you think that way?"—can promote defensiveness? So what is a facilitator to do when asked a "why" question?

When a participant asks a confrontational or negative question, handle it with dignity and do not become aggressive. It's helpful to ask open-ended questions of the participant to try to clarify the original question. For example, ask, "What do you mean by . . . ?" or "Which part of the activity do you find challenging?" This form of open-ended questioning requires additional accountability from the participant. The reason for the confrontation may have arisen from confusion about the information or the need to hear his or her own thoughts aloud. When you are calm and patient, the altercation is more likely to be resolved. If the participant persists, you may wish to ask him or her to discuss the specifics in a private setting. More ideas for dealing with difficult participants are provided later in this chapter.

Some participants enjoy being questioned because it gives them an opportunity to show their knowledge. Others are reticent for fear of looking foolish if they don't know the answer. Because your participants have unique styles and personalities, always have a purpose for asking questions: Will these questions test the participants' knowledge? Are these questions appropriate? Are you asking them in the style that suits the participant?

Training Room and Participant Management

When everything is in place and ready for the session, it's time to review the "soft skills" portion of your responsibilities—that is, how you conduct the workshop and interact with participants. Here are some things to consider:

- **"Respect and respond" should be a facilitator's mantra.** At all times respect the participants and respond in a timely manner.
- **Learn participants' names at the beginning of the workshop.** Focus on each participant, give a firm handshake, and repeat the name in your greeting. Paying attention to the details they share during your greeting, and thereby getting to know them on a

personal level, makes learning names much easier. When you have time, survey the room and write down every name without looking at nametags or name tents on the tables.

- **Manage workshop program time.** This is vital because it ensures that the goals will be met in the time allotted.

- **Read the participants' body language.** This will help you know when to pause and ask questions or to give them a stretch break.

- **Answer questions fully and effectively.** If you don't know an answer, open the question up to the participants or offer to get back to the questioner. Make a note to remind yourself to do so.

- **Add a "parking lot" to the room**—a large sheet of paper taped to one of the walls (use your own artistic prowess to draw a vehicle of some sort). When questions arise that are out of step with the current activity, ask the participant to write the question on a sticky note and put it in the parking lot. When the current activity is completed, you can address the questions parked there.

- **Control unruly participants through assertiveness of vocal tone and message.** When appropriate, invite them to help you with tasks because frequently they just need to be more physically involved. If the unruliness gets out of hand, accompany the person out of the room to discuss the situation.

- **Be sure to monitor a participant who is slower to assimilate the information.** If time permits, give that person some one-on-one time with you.

- **Keep your energy high.** Inject humor wherever possible. Ensure the learning is taking root.

A Word About Dealing With Difficult Participants

Much of the preparation you do before a training session will help you minimize disruptive behavior in your training session. But, sadly, you are still likely at some point to have difficult participants in your training room. Beyond preparation, you may need some specific strategies to help you manage disruptions and keep the learning on track. Figure 8-6, drawn from McCain's second edition of *Facilitation Basics* (2015), identifies many of these behaviors and gives strategies for nipping them in the bud.

Figure 8-6. Managing Difficult Participants

THE PROBLEM	THE SOLUTION
Carrying on a Side Conversation	• Don't assume the talkers are being disrespectful; depersonalize the behavior by thinking: "Maybe they are unclear about a point in the material, or the material is not relevant to their needs." • Ask the talkers if they don't understand something. • Walk toward the talkers as you continue to make your point; this stops many conversations dead in their tracks.
Monopolizing the Discussion	• Some participants tend to take over the conversation; while the enthusiasm is great, you don't want to leave other learners out. • Tell the monopolizer that her comments are valuable and interesting and that you would like to open up the discussion to others in the group. Then call on another person by name. • Enlist the monopolizer to help you by being a gatekeeper and ensuring that no one monopolizes the conversation.
Complaining	• Don't assume someone who complains doesn't have a valid reason to do so. • Ask the rest of the group if they feel the same way. If they do, try to address the issue as appropriate. If they don't, talk to the individual in the hallway during the break.
Challenging Your Knowledge	• Determine if this person really knows more than you do, or is just trying to act as though he does. • If he does know more, try to enlist his help in the training. If he doesn't, ask him to provide expertise, and he will usually realize he can't and back down.
Daydreaming	• Use the person's name in an example to get her attention. • Switch to something more active. • If behavior affects more than just one person, try to find out if something work related is causing it and have a brief discussion about it.
Heckling	• Don't get upset or start volleying remarks. • Try giving the person learning-oriented attention: "John, you clearly have some background in this area; would you care to share your thoughts with the rest of the group?" • Get the attention off you by switching to a group-oriented activity.
Clowning Around	• Give the person attention in a learning-oriented way by calling on her to answer a question or be a team leader. • If a joke is intended to relieve tension in the room and others seem to be experiencing it, deal with the tension head on by bringing it up. • If it is just a joke, and it's funny and appropriate, laugh!

CHANGE MANAGEMENT training

THE PROBLEM	THE SOLUTION
Making an Insensitive Remark	• Remember that if the person truly didn't intend offense, you don't want to humiliate him. But you do need to ensure that the person and everyone else in the room know that you will not tolerate bigoted or otherwise inappropriate remarks. • Give the person a chance to retract what he said by asking if that is what he meant to say. If it wasn't, then move on. If it was, you need to let the person know that the comment is not in line with the values of your organization and it can't be allowed to continue. • If the person persists, speak to him in the hallway, or as a last resort, ask him to leave.
Doing Other Work	• Talk to the person at a break to find out if the workshop is meeting her needs. • If the person is truly under too much pressure, offer to have her come to another session.
Not Talking	• If you can tell the person is engaged because he is taking notes, maintaining eye contact, or leaning forward, let him alone. • Give the person opportunities to interact at a greater comfort level by participating in small groups or in pairs.
Withdrawing	• Talk to the person at break to find out if something is going on. Deal with the issue as appropriate. • If the person feels excluded, have her act as a team leader for a turn, or ensure that all members of teams are given opportunities to participate.
Missing the Point	• If someone misses the point, be sensitive in dealing with him. Try to find something to agree with in his point. • Try to identify what the person is having trouble grasping and clear up the point with an analogy or an example. • Never laugh at the person or otherwise humiliate him.
Playing With Technology	• Minimize distractions by setting specific ground rules for technology use in the training room. (See Chapter 7 for creative ways to use technology to enhance training.) • Direct a training-related question to the person. • If the behavior persists, talk to the person at break to determine if there is an issue with which you can help.

Source: McCain (2015).

When all else fails, you have a few last resorts, although you would clearly rather not get to that point. One option is to simply pull aside the individual who is disrupting the class and talk to her privately. Dick Grote (1998) suggests in "Dealing With Miscreants, Snivelers, and Adversaries" that you can often catch someone off guard by asking: "Is it personal?" The direct question will usually cause the individual to deny that it is personal. Next, you tell the person that the behavior is unacceptable and that you will speak to a supervisor or training sponsor if it continues. This often works.

However, if it does not work, you can ask to have the person removed or cancel the program and speak to the person's supervisor. Clearly, these options are not to be taken lightly, but realize that they are available when you are faced with truly recalcitrant behavior.

Follow up when you have faced a difficult situation. Take some time to reflect on the event and write down the details of what happened. If possible, get perspectives and feedback from participants who witnessed it. If outside perspectives are not an option, think about the event from the points of view of the disruptive individual and other participants and ask yourself: What went wrong? What went well? How could I manage the situation better next time?

An Unforgettable End

In Biech (2008), contributor Mel Silberman explains that

> [m]any training programs run out of steam in the end. In some cases, participants are marking time until the close is near. In other cases, facilitators are valiantly trying to cover what they haven't got to before time runs out. How unfortunate! What happens at the end needs to be "unforgettable." You want participants to remember what they've learned. You also want participants to think what they've learned has been special. (p. 315)

Silberman suggests considering four areas when preparing to end your workshop:

- How will participants review what you've taught them?
- How will participants assess what they have learned?
- What will participants do about what they have learned?
- How will participants celebrate their accomplishments?

For example, consider what you've learned in this chapter. You've developed a well-rounded picture of what it takes to create an optimal, effective learning environment, from creating an inviting and engaging space to preparing and gathering materials that will make you feel like an organizational champ. You're ready to get the training off to a productive start, to manage difficult participants and situations, and to pull it all together in a powerful way. Now review the bullet points that follow to determine what the next steps are and take pride in the preparation that will enable you to adapt and thrive in the training room.

The Bare Minimum

- **Keep things moving.** Create an engaging, interactive environment.

- **Pay attention to the energy in the room.** Be prepared to adjust the activities as needed. Build in content that can be delivered standing or through networking activities to get participants out of their seats when needed.

- **Have fun!** If you create an upbeat tone and enjoy yourself, the participants are likely to have fun as well.

Key Points

- Facilitation is not lecturing. It's providing learning activities and support to make learning easier for the participant.

- Facilitation is not about the facilitator—it's about the learner.

- An inviting space and a safe, collaborative environment are necessary for learning to occur.

- Good facilitation starts with passion and significant attention to preparation.

- A good start sets the tone for the whole training session.

- A strong ending helps learners to remember the training and carry lessons forward into their work.

What to Do Next

- Prepare, modify, and review the training agenda. Use one of the agendas in Section I as a starting point.

- Review the program preparation checklist and work through it step by step.

- Make a list of required participant materials and facilitator equipment and begin assembling them.

- Review all learning activities included in the agenda and start preparing for your delivery.

Additional Resources

Biech, E. (2006). *90 World-Class Activities by 90 World-Class Trainers*. San Francisco: John Wiley/Pfeiffer.

Biech, E. (2008). *10 Steps to Successful Training*. Alexandria, VA: ASTD Press.

Biech, E., ed. (2008). *ASTD Handbook for Workplace Learning Professionals*. Alexandria, VA: ASTD Press.

Biech, E., ed. (2014). *ASTD Handbook: The Definitive Reference for Training & Development*. Alexandria, VA: ASTD Press.

Biech, E. (2015). *Training and Development for Dummies*. Hoboken, NJ: Wiley.

Duarte, N. (2010). *Resonate: Present Visual Stories That Transform Audiences.* Hoboken, NJ: Wiley.

Grote, D. (1998). "Dealing With Miscreants, Snivelers, and Adversaries," *Training & Development,* 52(10), October.

McCain, D.V. (2015). *Facilitation Basics,* 2nd edition. Alexandria, VA: ATD Press.

Stolovitch, H.D., and E.J. Keeps. (2011). *Telling Ain't Training,* 2nd edition. Alexandria, VA: ASTD Press.

Thiagarajan, S. (2005). *Thiagi's Interactive Lectures: Power Up Your Training With Interactive Games and Exercises.* Alexandria, VA: ASTD Press.

Thiagarajan, S. (2006). *Thiagi's 100 Favorite Games.* San Francisco: John Wiley/Pfeiffer.

Chapter 9
Evaluating Workshop Results

What's in This Chapter

- Exploring the reasons to evaluate your program
- Introducing the levels of measurement and what they measure

---

Evaluation represents the last letter of the ADDIE cycle of instructional design (analysis, design, development, implementation, and evaluation). Although evaluation is placed at the end of the model, an argument could be made for including it far earlier, as early as the design and development phase and perhaps even in the analysis phase. Why? Because the goals of the training, or the learning objectives (see Chapter 5), provide insight into what the purpose of the evaluation should be. In fact, business goals, learning goals, and evaluation of those goals are useful subjects to address with organizational leaders or the training sponsor. Trainers often begin a program without thinking about how the program fits into a strategic plan or how it supports and promotes specific business goals, but these are critical to consider before implementing the program.

However, this chapter is not about that upfront evaluation of the program design and materials; it is about evaluating the program after it has been delivered and reporting the results back to the training sponsor. This form of evaluation allows you to determine whether the program objectives were achieved and whether the learning was applied on the job and had an impact on the business. Evaluation can also serve as the basis for future program and budget discussions with training sponsors.

Levels of Measurement

No discussion of measurement would be complete without an introduction to the concepts that underpin the field of evaluation. The following is a brief primer on a very large and detailed subject that can be somewhat overwhelming. If your organization is committed to measuring beyond Level 2, take some time to read the classics of evaluation.

In 1956–57, Donald Kirkpatrick, one of the leading experts in measuring training results, identified four levels of measurement and evaluation. These four levels build successively from the simplest (Level 1) to the most complex (Level 4) and are based on information gathered at previous levels. For that reason, determining upfront at what level to evaluate a program is important. A general rule of thumb is that the more important or fundamental the training is and the greater the investment in it, the higher the level of evaluation to use. The four basic levels of evaluation are

- **Level 1—Reaction:** Measures how participants react to the workshop.
- **Level 2—Learning:** Measures whether participants have learned and understood the content of the workshop.
- **Level 3—Behavior (also referred to as application):** Measures on-the-job changes that have occurred because of the learning.
- **Level 4—Results:** Measures the impact of training on the bottom line.

These four levels correspond with the evaluation methods described below.

Level 1: Measuring Participant Reactions

One of the most common ways trainers measure participants' reactions is by administering end-of-session evaluation forms, often called "smile sheets" (for a sample, see Assessment 2). The main benefit of using smile sheets is that they are easy to create and administer. If you choose this method, consider the following suggestions, but first decide the purpose of evaluating. Do you want to know if the participants enjoyed the presentation? How they felt about the facilities? Or how they reacted to the content?

Here are a few suggestions for creating evaluation forms:

- Limit the form to one page.
- Make your questions brief.
- Leave adequate space for comments.

- Group types of questions into categories (for example, cluster questions about content, questions about the instructor, and questions about materials).

- Provide variety in types of questions (include multiple-choice, true-false, short-answer, and open-ended items).

- Include relevant decision makers in your questionnaire design.

- Plan how you will use and analyze the data and create a design that will facilitate your analysis.

- Use positively worded items (such as "I listen to others," instead of "I don't listen to others").

You can find additional tips for creating evaluation sheets and evaluating their results in the *Infoline* "Making Smile Sheets Count" by Nancy S. Kristiansen (2004).

Although evaluation sheets are used frequently, they have some inherent limitations. For example, participants cannot judge the *effectiveness* of training techniques. In addition, results can be overly influenced by the personality of the facilitator or participants' feelings about having to attend training. Be cautious of relying solely on Level 1 evaluations.

Level 2: Measuring the Extent to Which Participants Have Learned

If you want to determine the extent to which participants have understood the content of your workshop, testing is an option. Comparing pre-training and post-training test results indicates the amount of knowledge gained. Or you can give a quiz that tests conceptual information 30 to 60 days after the training to see if people remember the concepts. Because most adult learners do not generally like the idea of tests, you might want to refer to these evaluations as "assessments."

Another model of testing is criterion-referenced testing (CRT), which tests the learner's performance against a given standard, such as "greets the customer and offers assistance within one minute of entering the store" or "initiates the landing gear at the proper time and altitude." Such testing can be important in determining whether a learner can carry out the task, determining the efficacy of the training materials, and providing a foundation for further levels of evaluation. Coscarelli and Shrock (2008) describe a five-step method for developing CRTs that includes

1. Determining what to test (analysis)

2. Determining if the test measures what it purports to measure (validity)

3. Writing test items

4. Establishing a cut-off or mastery score

5. Showing that the test provides consistent results (reliability).

Level 3: Measuring the Results of Training Back on the Job

The next level of evaluation identifies whether the learning was actually used back on the job. It is important to recognize that application on the job is where learning begins to have real-world effects and that application is not solely up to the learner. Many elements affect transfer and application, including follow-up, manager support, and so forth. For example, consider a sales training attendee who attends training and learns a new, more efficient way to identify sales leads. However, upon returning to work, the attendee's manager does not allow the time for the attendee to practice applying those new skills in the workplace. Over time, the training is forgotten, and any value it may have had does not accrue.

Methods for collecting data regarding performance back on the job include reports by people who manage participants, reports from staff and peers, observations, quality monitors, and other quality and efficiency measures. In "The Four Levels of Evaluation," Kirkpatrick (2007) provides some guidelines for carrying out Level 3 evaluations:

- Use a control group, if practical.
- Allow time for behavior change to take place.
- Evaluate before and after the program, if possible.
- Interview learners, their immediate managers, and possibly their subordinates and anyone else who observes their work or behavior.
- Repeat the evaluation at appropriate times.

Level 4: Measuring the Organizational Impact of Training

Level 4 identifies how learning affects business measures. Consider an example related to management training. Let's say a manager attends management training and learns several new and valuable techniques to engage employees and help keep them on track. Upon return, the manager gets support in applying the new skills and behaviors. As time passes, the learning starts to have measurable results: Retention has increased, employees are demonstrably more engaged and are producing better-quality goods, and sales increase because the quality has increased. Retention, engagement, quality, and sales are all measurable business results improved as a result of the training.

Measuring such organizational impact requires working with leaders to create and implement a plan to collect the data you need. Possible methods include customer surveys, measurements of sales, studies of customer retention or turnover, employee satisfaction surveys, and other measurements of issues pertinent to the organization.

Robert Brinkerhoff, well-known author and researcher of evaluation methods, has suggested the following method to obtain information relevant to results:

- Send out questionnaires to people who have gone through training, asking: To what extent have you used your training in a way that has made a significant business impact? (This question can elicit information that will point to business benefits and ways to use other data to measure accomplishments.)
- When you get responses back, conduct interviews to get more information.

Return on Investment

Measuring return on investment (ROI)—sometimes referred to as Level 5 evaluation—is useful and can help "sell" training to leaders. ROI measures the monetary value of business benefits such as those noted in the discussion about Level 4 and compares them with the fully loaded costs of training to provide a percentage return on training investment. Hard numbers such as these can be helpful in discussions with organizational executives about conducting further training and raise the profile of training.

ROI was popularized by Jack Phillips. More in-depth information can be found in the *ASTD Handbook of Measuring and Evaluating Training* (Phillips 2010).

Reporting Results

An important and often under-considered component of both ROI and Level 4 evaluations is reporting results. Results from these types of evaluation studies have several different audiences, and it is important to take time to plan the layout of the evaluation report and the method of delivery with the audience in question. Consider the following factors in preparing communications:

- **Purpose:** The purposes for communicating program results depend on the specific program, the setting, and unique organizational needs.
- **Audience:** For each target audience, understand the audience and find out what information is needed and why. Take into account audience bias, and then tailor the communication to each group.

- **Timing:** Lay the groundwork for communication before program implementation. Avoid delivering a message, particularly a negative message, to an audience unprepared to hear the story and unaware of the methods that generated the results.

- **Reporting format:** The type of formal evaluation report depends on how much detailed information is presented to target audiences. Brief summaries may be sufficient for some communication efforts. In other cases, particularly those programs that require significant funding, more detail may be important.

The Bare Minimum

- If formal measurement techniques are not possible, consider using simple, interactive, informal measurement activities such as a quick pulse-check during the workshop.

- Empower the participants to create an action plan to capture the new skills and ideas they plan to use. Ultimately, the success of any training event will rest on lasting positive change in participants' behavior.

Key Points

- The four basic levels of evaluation cover reaction, learning, application, and organizational impact.

- A fifth level covers return on investment.

- Reporting results is as important as measuring them. Be strategic in crafting your results document, taking into consideration purpose, audience, timing, and format.

What to Do Next

- Identify the purpose and level of evaluation based on the learning objectives and learning goals.

- Prepare a training evaluation form, or use the one provided in Chapter 12.

- If required, develop plans for follow-up evaluations to determine skills mastery, on-the-job application, and business impact.

Additional Resources

Biech, E., ed. (2014). *ASTD Handbook: The Definitive Reference for Training & Development*, 2nd edition. Alexandria, VA: ASTD Press.

Brinkerhoff, R.O. (2006). *Telling Training's Story: Evaluation Made Simple, Credible, and Effective.* San Francisco: Berrett-Koehler.

Coscarelli, W., and S. Shrock. (2008). "Level 2: Learning—Five Essential Steps for Creating Your Tests and Two Cautionary Tales." In E. Biech, ed., *ASTD Handbook for Workplace Learning Professionals*. Alexandria, VA: ASTD Press.

Kirkpatrick, D.L. (2007). "The Four Levels of Evaluation." *Infoline* No. 0701, Alexandria, VA: ASTD Press.

Kirkpatrick, D., and J.D. Kirkpatrick. (2006). *Evaluating Training Programs: The Four Levels,* 3rd edition. San Francisco: Berrett-Koehler.

Kirkpatrick, D., and J.D. Kirkpatrick. (2007). *Implementing the Four Levels: A Practical Guide for Effective Evaluation of Training Programs.* San Francisco: Berrett-Koehler.

Kristiansen, N.S. (2004). "Making Smile Sheets Count." *Infoline* No. 0402, Alexandria, VA: ASTD Press.

Phillips, P.P., ed. (2010). *ASTD Handbook of Measuring and Evaluating Training.* Alexandria, VA: ASTD Press.

SECTION III
POST-WORKSHOP LEARNING

Chapter 10

Follow-Up for Change Management Training

What's in This Chapter

- The benefits of follow-up to your workshop

- Description of how follow-up extends from start to finish

- Dozens of ideas you can implement before, during, near the end, and after the workshop

---

Transitioning learners from "I tried it" to "I'll apply it" requires you to design follow-up activities and provide tools to both the participants and the managers who will continue to develop the participants after your workshop. If your participants are mostly managers (the audience for whom the workshop is intended), you may be working at a higher level in the organization. The facts don't change, however. For learning to transfer, the participants must be committed to implementing the skills, and their bosses must be willing to support the new skills. You support participants while they are in the workshop, but you also have a responsibility to follow up after the session.

Traditionally, organizations invest more than 90 percent of their resources in planning and delivering the formal training. Virtually nothing is invested in application support. Maximizing the transfer of learning to the workplace requires immediate follow-up as well as ongoing support.

The suggestions in this chapter can help provide this much-needed support; there are many ways to keep the learning alive. To ensure that what was learned is not "shelved" for implementation at another time but applied immediately, you can experiment with follow-up contact from you; follow-up sharing among participants, support groups, participant mentors, job aids; and management support and coaching.

Follow-up coaching starts before the workshop to ensure that each participant's manager gets involved. It is not really up to an organization's learning and development staff to develop employees; it is up to their direct managers. Wendy Axelrod (2011), author of *Make Talent Your Business*, suggests that if managers have an attitude of "making every day a development day," participants will return from a learning event to an environment in which follow-up will be expected.

One of the learning and development department's new roles is to help managers learn how to develop their employees. You can suggest that managers read *Help Them Grow, or Watch Them Go*, which offers rationale for development as well as ideas for how to make it happen (Kaye and Giulioni 2012).

The next sections of this chapter provide ideas for what you can do before, during, and after the workshop to help ensure that the change management skills are implemented and that your participants continue to grow and learn.

Before the Workshop Begins

Follow-up starts before the workshop begins. The one thing that a facilitator can do that will make the greatest difference is to meet with the participants' managers to ask questions, garner support, and share ideas for how the managers can support the participants once they return from the workshop. In the words of Stephen Covey, "start with the end in mind" and consider these ideas before your participants ever step into your classroom:

- **Meet with managers.** Meet the participants' managers to discuss what the managers expect from the workshop. Dana Robinson (2013) offers these examples of questions you can ask when exploring a manager's request for a training program:
  - What are the goals for your employees?
  - What are the measures you will use to determine success?
  - What must participants do more, better, or differently if your department or function is to be more effective in implementing change?
  - What have you observed your employees do that you believe needs to change?

- **Partner with stakeholders.** Work with managers and other stakeholders to help them determine how they can help the participants upon returning from the workshop and to ensure that you know what skills and knowledge are imperative for the group to learn. Ask questions to determine the linkage between the workshop and the performance results the manager seeks. At the very least leave them with a list of skills that you intend to discuss in the workshop so that they can reinforce participants when they see them implementing the skills or as *The New One Minute Manager* states, "catch them doing something right" (Blanchard and Johnson 2015).

- **Explain action plans.** Several activities in the workshop help participants create a plan for their future. Inform participants' managers about these plans, recommending that they discuss them with the participants upon returning. Consider providing workshop handouts and other content to the managers in advance to help them prepare for these vital conversations. Handouts 8, 9, 11, 12, 15, 18, 22, and 23 contain activities in which the participants identify how they can implement the concepts upon returning to the job.

- **Put support into words.** Collect messages of support from the participants' managers describing how they will support transfer of the skills after the workshop. Weave these messages into your workshop.

- **Personalize it.** Before the formal learning begins, ask participants to bring change challenges they have that they hope will be resolved by what they learn in the workshop. This commitment to learning something new helps to ensure that participants follow up with themselves.

During the Workshop

Set a good example during the workshop. Participants watch what you do, so if you stress the importance of listening until you understand or using metaphors as techniques for managing change, you need to model the skills as well. Try some of these ideas during the workshop that you can build on after the workshop:

- **Share successes.** Tell participants how past participant sessions have had a positive impact in the workplace.

- **Read messages of support from key people in the organization.** If you are an internal facilitator or working with just one organization you might include statements from participants' managers describing how they will support transfer after the workshop.

- **Observe the practice sessions.** Follow the rules in *The New One Minute Manager* to deliver helpful, timely feedback to the participants (Blanchard and Johnson 2015):

- If it was incorrect, correct the behavior. Describe what you observed, point out the expected behavior, and note what needs to change. Demonstrate the correct method or steps. Then have the participant perform the task correctly.

- If they did it well, praise the accurate behavior. Take advantage of people doing a great job to reinforce them.

- **Remember to use the debriefing questions.** It is only a start to learning when participants hear the "what" of your message. The most important part comes with the debriefing questions or the "so what" (so what does that mean or how does it relate?) and the "now what" (now what are you going to do or change or implement as a result?). Debriefing reduces the gap between talking and action and forces the learning to take an implementation focus.

- **Give the end of the workshop its due.** Don't get behind the schedule near the end. Be sure that participants have enough time to complete their action plans using Handouts 22 and 23. From a content perspective, action planning may not seem as important as the other modules, when in fact it may be the most important part. Once learners leave the workshop, they need to continue to implement what excited them during the workshop. Ensuring that participants have a plan and incentives to make a difference when they return to their workplace is one of your most important jobs.

- **Discover when participants will have an opportunity to implement what they are learning.** Tell them that they should watch for follow-up about this time. Prepare your follow-up so it is ready to send just in time. If you know that some of your participants will meet with employees to share information about a future change, for example, email information about the kinds of reactions to expect and reminders of how to address resistance about the same time.

At the Close of the Workshop

Many things come together at the end of your workshop. Be sure to allow enough time to discuss next steps. Learning Activity 23: Nothing Will Change If You Don't is not just a pleasant closing activity designed to keep participants in touch with each other. It should truly be billed as the participant's lifeline to support each other when things become difficult—as they will. Consider implementing some of these other ideas to support and ensure follow-up:

- **Create learning communities.** Ask participants to voluntarily opt into a continuing learning group. Create a wiki or a LinkedIn page to continue the learning. Participants can ask questions, share tips, give advice, or celebrate successes. You can seed the site with questions, links to videos, or short articles.

- **Commit to practice.** Ask participants to commit to trying one new skill within the week. Perhaps they could meet with one of their employees who has resisted a change and try to determine which of the five motivating factors is most important (Handout 9b). Ask them to publicly commit to their plans and have them text the entire group once they complete their actions.

- **Brainstorm barriers.** If it seems that participants will face major obstacles upon their return to the workplace, build in time to brainstorm a list of barriers they anticipate that may prevent them from implementing some of the skills discussed in the workshop. Form small groups to tackle each of the barriers and report out ideas to overcome them. Do the group a favor and have the lists compiled and emailed to them shortly after the session.

- **Support action plans.** Several activities in the workshop help participants plan for their future. After they complete these activities, recommend that they discuss them with their managers upon returning and ask for support in achieving their goals. Handouts 8, 9, 11, 12, 15, 18, 22, and 23 are good candidates for this action.

- **Organize peer practice groups.** Peer practice groups offer a great way for participants to support each other as they perfect their change-savvy manager competencies. They may be self-organizing, or you may wish to attend their first meeting to get them started and to provide resources and a suggested meeting format to ensure the peer groups are productive.

- **Encourage peer mentoring.** Near the end of the workshop, ask participants to partner with one other person whom they work most closely with (and ideally are in the same physical location). Call these partner/pairs *support buddies, accountability partners,* or *peer mentors,* depending on your audience. Ask them to sit together. Ask each individual to pick one topic from the workshop that they want to focus on individually in the coming month. Ask each partner to interview the other about strategies they will use to implement their chosen topic daily at work (and at home if applicable) for the next 30 days. Recommend that the partners schedule four weekly meetings with each other over the coming month to discuss their progress.

- **Send postcards to themselves.** At the close of the workshop, provide each participant with a postcard. Have participants address their postcards to themselves. On the other side of the postcard, have participants write two MVTs (most valuable tips) and two things they intend to implement from the workshop. Have the participants select a learning accountability partner and upon receipt of the postcard they will contact their partners to debrief. Mail the postcards out to arrive two to four weeks after the workshop.

After the Workshop

According to Cal Wick, most organizations still schedule facilitators in back-to-back workshops, allowing them no time to follow up and support prior program participants. A few enlightened organizations have begun to recognize that making time for ongoing support results in more learning implemented back on the job. The responsibility can be shared between the facilitators and the participants' managers. These ideas for follow-up activities after the workshop are simple but require deliberate and sustained effort to be effective.

Facilitator Actions. As facilitator, you are uniquely placed to support your participants' continued growth and learning. After all, you helped start them on this journey; these activities will help keep them on that path:

- Follow up your session by emailing a resource to participants. It could be something that came up during the session, an article that you think will be pertinent and helpful to participants, or a link to a YouTube presentation.

- Follow up your session with a quiz. Share responses with everyone and offer prizes for the best responses.

- About a week after the session, tweet to participants with a simple question that they can respond to. For example, you could ask them to identify a new skill they have tried and then rate how successful they think they were. You could use a 100 percent scale or a letter grade scale (A, B, C, D, F). Follow up to see what you can do to help.

- Drop off a copy of Bill Pasmore's *Leading Continuous Change* (2015) or an article from a recent journal to each participant. Ask them to read it over the next 10 days. Then begin to text questions to the group. If you've set up a Twitter account for your group, you can use that as well.

- Several months after the workshop, invite the participants to return for a review and celebration session where participants share their successes and review situations they needed additional knowledge or skills to complete. If possible invite one of the senior leaders to attend also.

- Facilitate a book club that meets over lunch once or twice each month to read and discuss change management and leadership books. Choose a book on a relevant topic such as resiliency or engagement or something addressing a current corporate concern. Assign the book as pre-reading and host the first meeting. You could also facilitate the discussion by creating an online discussion forum using a webinar or conference call format.

- Create short videos or podcasts about some of the topics presented in the workshop and send the link to participants. The easiest way to do this is to interview someone who is respected in your organization for change or innovations. It could be one of the participants who just had a breakthrough or a success.

- Reinforce the content using your workplace communication processes. Use your workplace employee newsletter, safety newsletter, intranet, or posters to reinforce key training concepts. A poster could say, "Let's change the way we change!" Provide tips, funny self-assessments, and other means for your employees to apply and refine what they've learned.

- Teach managers and participants how to use an After Action Report (AAR) to create a retrospective analysis on actions completed by the participant.

Manager Actions. Encourage the participants' supervisors to continue developing participants. You may share these ideas with each manager to ensure that they take on the responsibility and continue to develop their employees:

- Familiarize the manager with the skills taught in the workshop so they can correct or reinforce behaviors they observe. They can correct inaccurate behavior by describing what was observed and explaining the expected behavior. If the participant models something that was learned in the workshop, the supervisor should praise the accurate behavior.

- Encourage managers to find other ways for the participant to practice change management or leadership skills. Leading change teams is one of the best experiences. This gives employees an opportunity to experiment with new skills. Ensure that the manager meets regularly with the new change team leader to provide coaching along the way.

- Suggest that managers ask participants to review key concepts learned in training with others in the department once they return to the workplace.

- Encourage managers to discuss how the participant's newly acquired skills and knowledge are improving as they are being used on the job. Develop a simple checklist of items that were in the workshop so that the manager knows what to look for.

- Ensure that managers discuss any problems in transferring skills and knowledge from the workshop to the job. Managers can help remove barriers and enable the participant to practice new skills.

Additional Topics. There are hundreds of topics and nuances to topics that a change manager needs to continue to learn. The workshop was just a start. There is no learning stopping point as a change-savvy manager. Use a needs assessment to determine what topics you might want to deliver next. To help give you a head start, here are topics that the workshop touched on only briefly or not at all:

- Fostering change-ready employees
- Engaging employees

- Building organizational capacity for continuous change
- Helping others embrace change
- Practicing and modeling resiliency
- Problem solving
- Rapid prototyping
- Innovation
- Managing stress: yours and your employees
- Negotiation
- Strategic planning
- Creating transition plans
- Process improvement methods
- Statistical process control
- Tools to stimulate creative thinking
- Change as a business strategy
- Establishing visions and urgent messages
- Gathering data
- Change management and planning
- Creating engaged employees
- Building teams
- The role of a change agent
- The job of a change implementation team
- Public speaking
- Presenting to senior leaders
- Leadership skills
- Helping employees understand the emotional aspects of change
- Adapting to learning and employing new ways of thinking
- Ensuring balance

. . . and many others. The bottom line is that there will always be a need to continue to provide knowledge and skills in this changing world. Consider enlisting some of the participants to deliver these topics in the future.

The Bare Minimum

Remember that most learning occurs after the workshop when participants have a chance to try out the content in the real world. Stress to managers and participants how critical reinforcement is. You can do this in several ways:

- Give learners the support they need to implement ideas and concepts learned in the Change Management Workshops.

- Explain to managers how critical it is for them to be a part of the participants' continued growth.

- Encourage learners to continue learning by using other resources, mentoring, coaching, and growth opportunities such as those listed here.

What to Do Next

Many ideas are presented here. Decide which ones you will do based on these guidelines:

- **Determine what is and what is not in your control.** You can't force managers to do anything they don't want to do. And if it isn't in the budget, it probably isn't going to happen.

- **Maintain momentum.** Decide the best ways to get managers involved to maintain the momentum for their participants.

- **Be choosy.** You can't do everything. Decide which actions will yield the best results.

- **Select something that would be a stretch for you—yes you.** Remember, you are a lifelong learner too.

- **Stay connected.** Select follow-up activities that allow you to stay in touch with your learners.

References

Axelrod, W. (2011). *Make Talent Your Business: How Exceptional Managers Develop People While Getting Results.* San Francisco: Berrett-Koehler.

Biech, E., ed. (2014). *ASTD Handbook: The Definitive Reference for Training & Development.* Alexandria, VA: ASTD Press.

Biech, E., ed. (2015). *101 More Ways to Make Training Active.* New York: Wiley.

Biech, E. (2015). *Training and Development for Dummies.* New York: Wiley.

Blanchard, K., and S. Johnson. (2015). *The New One-Minute Manager.* New York: William Morrow.

Kaye, B., and J. W. Giulioni. (2012). *Help Them Grow or Watch Them Go: Career Conversations Employees Want.* San Francisco: Berrett-Koehler.

Pasmore, B. (2015). *Leading Continuous Change: Navigating Churn in the Real World.* San Francisco: Berrett-Koehler.

Robinson, D. (2013). *Training for Impact.* San Francisco: Pfeiffer.

SECTION IV

WORKSHOP SUPPORTING DOCUMENTS AND ONLINE SUPPORT

Chapter 11
Learning Activities

What's in This Chapter

- 23 activities for use in the workshop sessions
- Complete step-by-step instructions for conducting the learning activities
- Supplemental handouts that you hold until the appropriate time within the activity

---

To help you facilitate adult learning, we have designed learning activities to deploy regularly throughout the workshop. Their purpose is to challenge and engage learners by providing stimulation for different types of learners and helping them acquire new knowledge. Many of the activities in this workshop are experiential in nature—that is, learners experience something that helps them uncover the learning. Learners will go beyond the "what" did I learn to discuss the "so what" and "now what." In some cases the activities will showcase your learners and draw upon their experiences and expertise to share with the rest of the participants.

Each learning activity provides detailed information about learning objectives, materials required, timeframe, step-by-step instructions, and variations and debriefing questions if required. Follow the instructions in each learning activity to prepare your workshop agenda, identify and gather materials needed, and successfully guide learners through the activity. The experiences provided by the learning activities support the topics covered in the workshop. See Chapter 14 for complete instructions on how to download the workshop support materials. Note that Learning Activities 2, 7, 18, 20, and 22 each contain handouts or resource pages that the participant should not have access to until time specified in each activity's instructions.

Learning Activities Included in *Change Management Training*

Learning Activity 1: Managers Navigate Constant, Complex Change

Learning Activity 2: Quote Me

    Supplemental Resource: Quote Me Cards

Learning Activity 3: Is Change a Sinking Ship?

Learning Activity 4: Ensure the Fundamentals Are in Place

Learning Activity 5: Make Up Your Mind!

Learning Activity 6: Determine Organizational Readiness

Learning Activity 7: Establish a Sense of Urgency

    Supplemental Resource: Ways to Establish a Sense of Urgency

    Supplemental Handout: What Floats Your Boat?

Learning Activity 8: Snap, Snap, Change

Learning Activity 9: What's Leadership Accountability?

Learning Activity 10: Optimize Communication

Learning Activity 11: Navigate Resistance to Change

Learning Activity 12: Work Is a Juggling Act

Learning Activity 13: Tools to Manage Relationships

Learning Activity 14: A Different Perspective

Learning Activity 15: Angles, Tangles, and Dangles

Learning Activity 16: Oceans of Respect for Good Role Models

Learning Activity 17: Full Speed Ahead to Generate Gains

Learning Activity 18: Naval Slang Energizer

    Supplemental Resource: Answer Key for Naval Slang Energizer

    Supplemental Handout: Naval Slang

Learning Activity 19: Test the Waters With Ideas for Change-Ready Employees

Learning Activity 20: Smooth Sailing

    Supplemental Handout: Smooth Sailing Observer Sheet

    Supplemental Handout: Smooth Sailing Engineering Team Role

    Supplemental Handout: Smooth Sailing Marketing Team Role

    Supplemental Handout: Smooth Sailing Financial Team Role

    Supplemental Handout: Smooth Sailing Post-Leadership Meeting Debrief

Learning Activity 21: Build Capacity for Continuous Change and My Next Steps

Learning Activity 22: Change That Tune

    Supplemental Handout: Songs You Know

Learning Activity 23: Nothing Will Change If You Don't

Learning Activity 1: Managers Navigate Constant, Complex Change

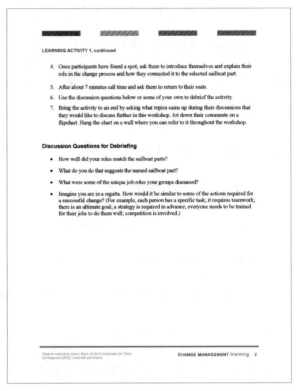

LEARNING ACTIVITY 1

Managers Navigate Constant, Complex Change

Objectives

Participants will be able to

- List several roles required of managers to support change
- Hear topics of interest from fellow participants.

Materials

- Handout 1: Managers Navigate Constant, Complex Change
- Pictures or words representing sail, rudder, tiller, hull, and compass taped to five different places in the room
- Flipchart

Time

20 minutes

Instructions

1. After you welcome everyone, ask them to turn to Handout 1. Briefly overview the introduction on the page. Connect the nautical theme to the "permanent whitewater" of change that organizations experience.

2. Show the slide naming the 5 sailboat parts and ask participants to read the descriptions in the handout to decide which description is most like the role they play in managing change.

3. Point out the 5 pictures or words around the room and ask participants to form small groups next to the part that is most like the role they play.

Learning Activity 1: Managers Navigate Constant, Complex Change, *continued*

LEARNING ACTIVITY 1, continued

4. Once participants have found a spot, ask them to introduce themselves and explain their role in the change process and how they connected it to the selected sailboat part.

5. After about 7 minutes call time and ask them to return to their seats.

6. Use the discussion questions below or some of your own to debrief the activity.

7. Bring the activity to an end by asking what topics came up during their discussions that they would like to discuss further in this workshop. Jot down their comments on a flipchart. Hang the chart on a wall where you can refer to it throughout the workshop.

Discussion Questions for Debriefing

- How well did your roles match the sailboat parts?
- What do you do that suggests the named sailboat part?
- What were some of the unique job roles your groups discussed?
- Imagine you are in a regatta. How would it be similar to some of the actions required for a successful change? (For example, each person has a specific task; it requires teamwork; there is an ultimate goal; a strategy is required in advance; everyone needs to be trained for their jobs to do them well; competition is involved.)

Learning Activity 2: Quote Me

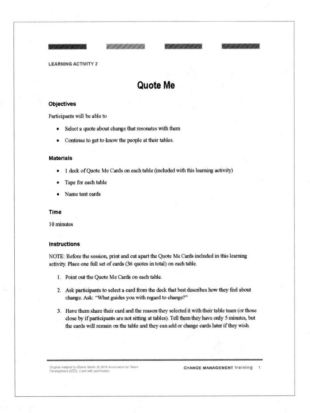

LEARNING ACTIVITY 2

Quote Me

Objectives

Participants will be able to

- Select a quote about change that resonates with them
- Continue to get to know the people at their tables.

Materials

- 1 deck of Quote Me Cards on each table (included with this learning activity)
- Tape for each table
- Name tent cards

Time

10 minutes

Instructions

NOTE: Before the session, print and cut apart the Quote Me Cards included in this learning activity. Place one full set of cards (36 quotes in total) on each table.

1. Point out the Quote Me Cards on each table.

2. Ask participants to select a card from the deck that best describes how they feel about change. Ask: "What guides you with regard to change?"

3. Have them share their card and the reason they selected it with their table team (or those close by if participants are not sitting at tables). Tell them they have only 5 minutes, but the cards will remain on the table and they can add or change cards later if they wish.

Learning Activity 2: Quote Me, *continued*

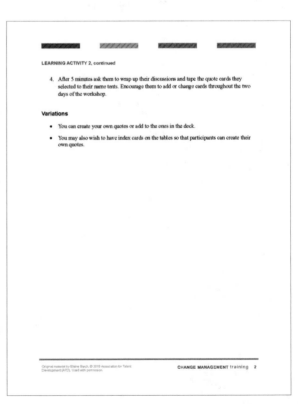

LEARNING ACTIVITY 2, continued

4. After 5 minutes ask them to wrap up their discussions and tape the quote cards they selected to their name tents. Encourage them to add or change cards throughout the two days of the workshop.

Variations

- You can create your own quotes or add to the ones in the deck.
- You may also wish to have index cards on the tables so that participants can create their own quotes.

Learning Activity 2, *Supplemental Resource*

Quote Me Cards

"Change is constant." -Benjamin Disraeli	"We must change to master change." -Lyndon B. Johnson
"If you want to truly understand something, try to change it. -Kurt Lewin	"High expectations are the key to everything." -Sam Walton
"When the drumbeat changes, the dance changes." -Hausa People	"Determine that the thing can and shall be done, and we shall find the way." -Abraham Lincoln
"Great ideas need landing gear as well as wings." -C.D. Jackson	"Change your thoughts and you change your world." -Norman Vincent Peale

CHANGE MANAGEMENT training   3

Learning Activity 2, *Supplemental Resource*

"Opportunities are never lost. The other fellow takes those you miss." -Anonymous	"The way I see it, if you want the rainbow, you must put up with the rain." -Dolly Parton
"If the window of opportunity appears, don't pull the shade down." -Tom Peters	"If there were none who were discontented with what they have, the world would never reach for anything better." -Florence Nightingale
"One change makes way for the next, giving us the opportunity to grow." -Vivian Buchan	"It is not because things are difficult that we do not dare; it is because we do not dare that things are difficult." -Seneca
"I never think of the future; it comes soon enough." -Albert Einstein	"The business graveyard is littered with companies that failed to recognize inevitable changes." -Anonymous
"Dig a well before you are thirsty." -Chinese Proverb	"Turbulence is life force. It is opportunity. Let's love turbulence and use it for a change." -Ramsay Clark

CHANGE MANAGEMENT training   4

Learning Activity 2, *Supplemental Resource*

"All birth is unwilling." -Pearl S. Buck	"Neither situations nor people can be altered by the interference of an outsider; it must come from within." -Phyllis Bottome
"You must do the thing you think You cannot do." -Eleanor Roosevelt	"Life is either a daring adventure or nothing." -Helen Keller
"Before you change your thinking, You have to change what goes into your mind." -Anonymous	"A habit cannot be tossed out the window; it must be coaxed down the stairs a step at a time." -Mark Twain
"Our stomachs quiver at the prospects of change. But today's leaders and managers have no choice." -Robert Waterman	"If in the last few years you haven't discarded a major opinion or acquired a new one, check your pulse. You may be dead." -Gelett Burgess
"Progress is not created by contented people." -Frank Tyger	"'Come to the edge,' he said. They said, 'We are afraid.' 'Come to the edge,' he said. They came. He pushed them. . . And they flew." -Guillaume Apollinaire

CHANGE MANAGEMENT training   5

Learning Activity 2, *Supplemental Resource*

"Why not go out on a limb? That's where the fruit is." -Will Rogers	"It is one thing to learn from the past; it is another to wallow in it." -Kenneth Auchincloss
"It is not the strongest of the species that survive, nor the most intelligent, but the one most responsive to change." -Charles Darwin	"We must become the change we want to see." -Mahatma Gandhi
"The difficulty lies not so much in developing new ideas, as in escaping from old ones." -David Meier	"We don't see things as they are. We see things as we are." -Anais Nin
"Change is scary causing us to use our power of fantasy to come up with scenarios of disaster." -Rose Dewolf	"If you don't like something, change it. If you can't change it, change your attitude." -Maya Angelou

CHANGE MANAGEMENT training   6

Learning Activity 3: Is Change a Sinking Ship?

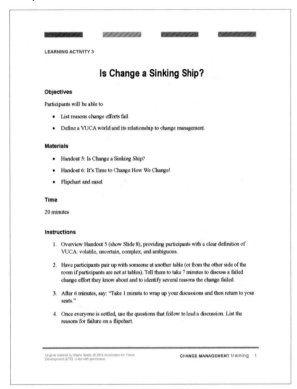

LEARNING ACTIVITY 3

Is Change a Sinking Ship?

Objectives

Participants will be able to

- List reasons change efforts fail
- Define a VUCA world and its relationship to change management.

Materials

- Handout 5: Is Change a Sinking Ship?
- Handout 6: It's Time to Change How We Change!
- Flipchart and easel

Time

20 minutes

Instructions

1. Overview Handout 5 (show Slide 8), providing participants with a clear definition of VUCA: volatile, uncertain, complex, and ambiguous.

2. Have participants pair up with someone at another table (or from the other side of the room if participants are not at tables). Tell them to take 7 minutes to discuss a failed change effort they know about and to identify several reasons the change failed.

3. After 6 minutes, say: "Take 1 minute to wrap up your discussions and then return to your seats."

4. Once everyone is settled, use the questions that follow to lead a discussion. List the reasons for failure on a flipchart.

Original material by Elaine Biech, © 2016 Association for Talent Development (ATD). Used with permission. CHANGE MANAGEMENT training   1

Learning Activity 3: Is Change a Sinking Ship?, *continued*

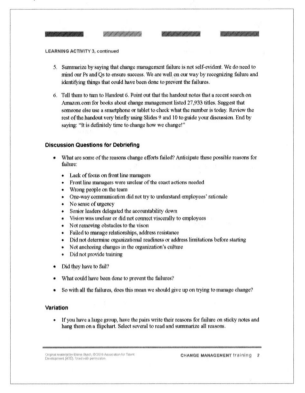

LEARNING ACTIVITY 3, continued

5. Summarize by saying that change management failure is not self-evident. We do need to mind our Ps and Qs to ensure success. We are well on our way by recognizing failure and identifying things that could have been done to prevent the failures.

6. Tell them to turn to Handout 6. Point out that the handout notes that a recent search on Amazon.com for books about change management listed 27,933 titles. Suggest that someone else use a smartphone or tablet to check what the number is today. Review the rest of the handout very briefly using Slides 9 and 10 to guide your discussion. End by saying: "It is definitely time to change how we change!"

Discussion Questions for Debriefing

- What are some of the reasons change efforts failed? Anticipate these possible reasons for failure:
  - Lack of focus on front line managers
  - Front line managers were unclear of the exact actions needed
  - Wrong people on the team
  - One-way communication did not try to understand employees' rationale
  - No sense of urgency
  - Senior leaders delegated the accountability down
  - Vision was unclear or did not connect viscerally to employees
  - Not removing obstacles to the vision
  - Failed to manage relationships, address resistance
  - Did not determine organizational readiness or address limitations before starting
  - Not anchoring changes in the organization's culture
  - Did not provide training

- Did they have to fail?

- What could have been done to prevent the failures?

- So with all the failures, does this mean we should give up on trying to manage change?

Variation

- If you have a large group, have the pairs write their reasons for failure on sticky notes and hang them on a flipchart. Select several to read and summarize all reasons.

Original material by Elaine Biech, © 2016 Association for Talent Development (ATD). Used with permission. CHANGE MANAGEMENT training   2

Learning Activity 4: Ensure the Fundamentals Are in Place

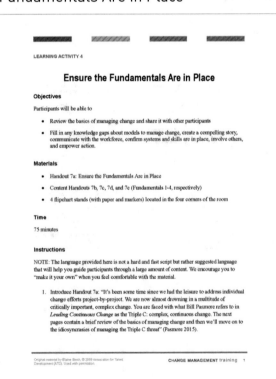

LEARNING ACTIVITY 4

Ensure the Fundamentals Are in Place

Objectives

Participants will be able to

- Review the basics of managing change and share it with other participants
- Fill in any knowledge gaps about models to manage change, create a compelling story, communicate with the workforce, confirm systems and skills are in place, involve others, and empower action.

Materials

- Handout 7a: Ensure the Fundamentals Are in Place
- Content Handouts 7b, 7c, 7d, and 7e (Fundamentals 1-4, respectively)
- 4 flipchart stands (with paper and markers) located in the four corners of the room

Time

75 minutes

Instructions

NOTE: The language provided here is not a hard and fast script but rather suggested language that will help you guide participants through a large amount of content. We encourage you to "make it your own" when you feel comfortable with the material.

1. Introduce Handout 7a: "It's been some time since we had the leisure to address individual change efforts project-by-project. We are now almost drowning in a multitude of critically important, complex change. You are faced with what Bill Pasmore refers to in *Leading Continuous Change* as the Triple C: complex, continuous change. The next pages contain a brief review of the basics of managing change and then we'll move on to the idiosyncrasies of managing the Triple C threat" (Pasmore 2015).

Original material by Elaine Biech, © 2016 Association for Talent Development (ATD). Used with permission. CHANGE MANAGEMENT training   1

Learning Activity 4: Ensure the Fundamentals Are in Place, *continued*

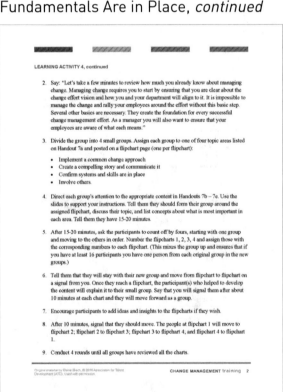

LEARNING ACTIVITY 4, continued

2. Say: "Let's take a few minutes to review how much you already know about managing change. Managing change requires you to start by ensuring that you are clear about the change effort vision and how you and your department will align to it. It is impossible to manage the change and rally your employees around the effort without this basic step. Several other basics are necessary. They create the foundation for every successful change management effort. As a manager you will also want to ensure that your employees are aware of what each means."

3. Divide the group into 4 small groups. Assign each group to one of four topic areas listed on Handout 7a and posted on a flipchart page (one per flipchart):
   - Implement a common change approach
   - Create a compelling story and communicate it
   - Confirm systems and skills are in place
   - Involve others.

4. Direct each group's attention to the appropriate content in Handouts 7b – 7e. Use the slides to support your instructions. Tell them they should form their group around the assigned flipchart, discuss their topic, and list concepts about what is most important in each area. Tell them they have 15-20 minutes.

5. After 15-20 minutes, ask the participants to count off by fours, starting with one group and moving to the others in order. Number the flipcharts 1, 2, 3, 4 and assign those with the corresponding numbers to each flipchart. (This mixes the group up and ensures that if you have at least 16 participants you have one person from each original group in the new groups.)

6. Tell them that they will stay with their new group and move from flipchart to flipchart on a signal from you. Once they reach a flipchart, the participant(s) who helped to develop the content will explain it to their small group. Say that you will signal them after about 10 minutes at each chart and they will move forward as a group.

7. Encourage participants to add ideas and insights to the flipcharts if they wish.

8. After 10 minutes, signal that they should move. The people at flipchart 1 will move to flipchart 2; flipchart 2 to flipchart 3; flipchart 3 to flipchart 4; and flipchart 4 to flipchart 1.

9. Conduct 4 rounds until all groups have reviewed all the charts.

Original material by Elaine Biech, © 2016 Association for Talent Development (ATD). Used with permission. CHANGE MANAGEMENT training   2

CHANGE MANAGEMENT training

Learning Activity 4: Ensure the Fundamentals Are in Place, *continued*

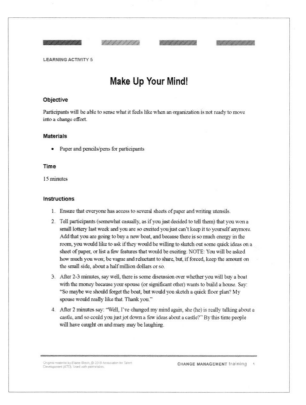

10. Ask everyone to take their seats and ask what questions they have.

11. Encourage them to take pictures of the flipchart pages with their smartphones for future reference.

12. Summarize the activity with the Peter Drucker quote slide.

Variations

- If you have a small group (under 12), have them form 4 pairs or trios. Assign or let them choose one of the topics. Give them 15 minute to prepare a 10-minute presentation. Have each small team present its information.

- Another approach for a small group is to assign three of the topics to three groups and you can take the fourth and review it with everyone at the same time.

- Participants may self-select their flipchart topics, but for this option to work best there must be at least four people in each group.

- Be sure to substitute your corporate materials with those in the handouts. For example, you can substitute Handout 7a with the change management model your organization uses or Handout 7b with an actual communication plan that has been implemented.

- NOTE: If you happen to be behind schedule at this point in the workshop, this activity could easily be tightened up if you have experienced managers who understand your organization's process.

Reference

Pasmore, B. (2015). *Leading Continuous Change: Navigating Churn in the Real World*. San Francisco: Berrett-Koehler.

CHANGE MANAGEMENT training **3**

Learning Activity 5: Make Up Your Mind!

Make Up Your Mind!

Objective

Participants will be able to sense what it feels like when an organization is not ready to move into a change effort.

Materials

- Paper and pencils/pens for participants

Time

15 minutes

Instructions

1. Ensure that everyone has access to several sheets of paper and writing utensils.

2. Tell participants (somewhat casually, as if you just decided to tell them) that you won a small lottery last week and you are so excited you just can't keep it to yourself anymore. Add that you are going to buy a new boat, and because there is so much energy in the room, you would like to ask if they would be willing to sketch out some quick ideas on a sheet of paper, or list a few features that would be exciting. NOTE: You will be asked how much you won; be vague and reluctant to share, but, if forced, keep the amount on the small side, about a half million dollars or so.

3. After 2-3 minutes, say well, there is some discussion over whether you will buy a boat with the money because your spouse (or significant other) wants to build a house. Say: "So maybe we should forget the boat, but could you sketch a quick floor plan? My spouse would really like that. Thank you."

4. After 2 minutes say: "Well, I've changed my mind again, she (he) is really talking about a castle, and so could you just jot down a few ideas about a castle?" By this time people will have caught on and many may be laughing.

CHANGE MANAGEMENT training **1**

Learning Activity 5: Make Up Your Mind!, *continued*

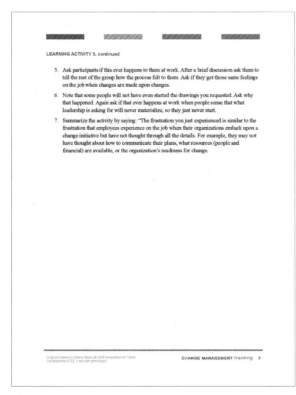

5. Ask participants if this ever happens to them at work. After a brief discussion ask them to tell the rest of the group how the process felt to them. Ask if they get those same feelings on the job when changes are made upon changes.

6. Note that some people will not have even started the drawings you requested. Ask why that happened. Again ask if that ever happens at work when people sense that what leadership is asking for will never materialize, so they just never start.

7. Summarize the activity by saying: "The frustration you just experienced is similar to the frustration that employees experience on the job when their organizations embark upon a change initiative but have not thought through all the details. For example, they may not have thought about how to communicate their plans, what resources (people and financial) are available, or the organization's readiness for change."

CHANGE MANAGEMENT training **2**

Learning Activity 6: Determine Organizational Readiness

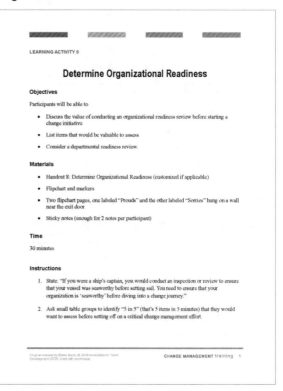

Determine Organizational Readiness

Objectives

Participants will be able to

- Discuss the value of conducting an organizational readiness review before starting a change initiative

- List items that would be valuable to assess

- Consider a departmental readiness review.

Materials

- Handout 8: Determine Organizational Readiness (customized if applicable)

- Flipchart and markers

- Two flipchart pages, one labeled "Prouds" and the other labeled "Sorries" hung on a wall near the exit door

- Sticky notes (enough for 2 notes per participant)

Time

30 minutes

Instructions

1. State: "If you were a ship's captain, you would conduct an inspection or review to ensure that your vessel was seaworthy before setting sail. You need to ensure that your organization is 'seaworthy' before diving into a change journey."

2. Ask small table groups to identify "5 in 5" (that's 5 items in 5 minutes) that they would want to assess before setting off on a critical change management effort.

CHANGE MANAGEMENT training **1**

Learning Activity 6: Determine Organizational Readiness, *continued*

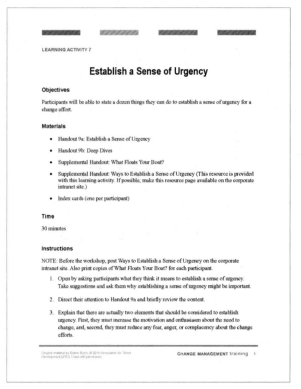

LEARNING ACTIVITY 6, continued

3. At about 5 minutes, ask the teams to wrap up what they are saying.

4. Lead a round robin discussion about their ideas, posting them on the flipchart as they are mentioned.

5. Tell groups to turn to the sample readiness assessment (Handout 8) and have them complete it for their organizations.

6. Lead a brief discussion about their organization's strengths and areas of need.

7. Ask participants what they think should happen if they find deficiencies (pause to remedy; consider the risk of moving forward; ponder other options).

8. Ask: "Can you see value in using the assessment for individual departments?" Lead a discussion in how they think it would be useful—especially in their own departments.

9. Tell participants that sometimes you need to go back into the organization's past to learn what worked and what didn't. Some authors call these "prouds" (what we've done well) and "sorries" (what we could have done better.) Ask: "What are some of your organizations proud and sorry moments?"

10. Ask participants to take two sticky notes. At the top of one they write "proud" and at the top of the other "sorry." Then have them write one thing they think their organization has done well with change efforts and write it on the "proud" note. Ask them to write one thing they think their organization could do better and write it on the "sorry" note. Then have them post their notes on the two separate flipchart pages that you have designated.

11. Wrap up with a brief comment about the importance of determining organizational readiness before taking on a change initiative.

Original material by Elaine Biech, © 2010 Association for Talent Development (ATD). Used with permission.   CHANGE MANAGEMENT training   2

Learning Activity 7: Establish a Sense of Urgency

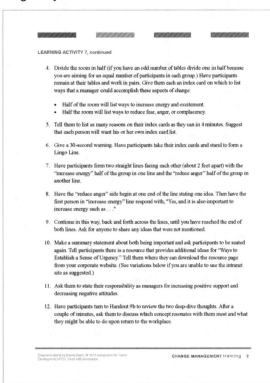

LEARNING ACTIVITY 7

Establish a Sense of Urgency

Objectives

Participants will be able to state a dozen things they can do to establish a sense of urgency for a change effort.

Materials

- Handout 9a: Establish a Sense of Urgency
- Handout 9b: Deep Dives
- Supplemental Handout: What Floats Your Boat?
- Supplemental Handout: Ways to Establish a Sense of Urgency (This resource is provided with this learning activity. If possible, make this resource page available on the corporate intranet site.)
- Index cards (one per participant)

Time

30 minutes

Instructions

NOTE: Before the workshop, post Ways to Establish a Sense of Urgency on the corporate intranet site. Also print copies of What Floats Your Boat? for each participant.

1. Open by asking participants what they think it means to establish a sense of urgency. Take suggestions and ask them why establishing a sense of urgency might be important.

2. Direct their attention to Handout 9a and briefly review the content.

3. Explain that there are actually two elements that should be considered to establish urgency. First, they must increase the motivation and enthusiasm about the need to change, and, second, they must reduce any fear, anger, or complacency about the change efforts.

Original material by Elaine Biech, © 2010 Association for Talent Development (ATD). Used with permission.   CHANGE MANAGEMENT training   1

Learning Activity 7: Establish a Sense of Urgency, *continued*

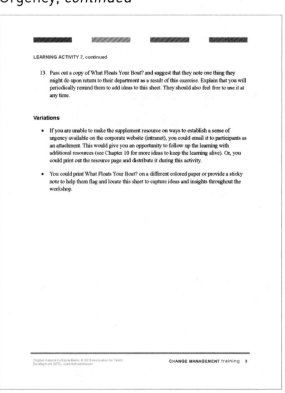

LEARNING ACTIVITY 7, continued

4. Divide the room in half (if you have an odd number of tables divide one in half because you are aiming for an equal number of participants in each group.) Have participants remain at their tables and work in pairs. Give them each an index card on which to list ways that a manager could accomplish these aspects of change:

- Half of the room will list ways to increase energy and excitement.
- Half the room will list ways to reduce fear, anger, or complacency.

5. Tell them to list as many reasons on their index cards as they can in 4 minutes. Suggest that each person will want his or her own index card list.

6. Give a 30-second warning. Have participants take their index cards and stand to form a Lingo Line.

7. Have participants form two straight lines facing each other (about 2 feet apart) with the "increase energy" half of the group in one line and the "reduce anger" half of the group in another line.

8. Have the "reduce anger" side begin at one end of the line stating one idea. Then have the first person in "increase energy" line respond with, "Yes, and it is also important to increase energy such as . . ."

9. Continue in this way, back and forth across the lines, until you have reached the end of both lines. Ask for anyone to share any ideas that were not mentioned.

10. Make a summary statement about both being important and ask participants to be seated again. Tell participants there is a resource that provides additional ideas for "Ways to Establish a Sense of Urgency." Tell them where they can download the resource page from your corporate website. (See variations below if you are unable to use the intranet site as suggested.)

11. Ask them to state their responsibility as managers for increasing positive support and decreasing negative attitudes.

12. Have participants turn to Handout 9b to review the two deep-dive thoughts. After a couple of minutes, ask them to discuss which concept resonates with them most and what they might be able to do upon return to the workplace.

Original material by Elaine Biech, © 2010 Association for Talent Development (ATD). Used with permission.   CHANGE MANAGEMENT training   2

Learning Activity 7: Establish a Sense of Urgency, *continued*

LEARNING ACTIVITY 7, continued

13. Pass out a copy of What Floats Your Boat? and suggest that they note one thing they might do upon return to their department as a result of this exercise. Explain that you will periodically remind them to add ideas to this sheet. They should also feel free to use it at any time.

Variations

- If you are unable to make the supplement resource on ways to establish a sense of urgency available on the corporate website (intranet), you could email it to participants as an attachment. This would give you an opportunity to follow up the learning with additional resources (see Chapter 10 for more ideas to keep the learning alive). Or, you could print out the resource page and distribute it during this activity.

- You could print What Floats Your Boat? on a different colored paper or provide a sticky note to help them flag and locate this sheet to capture ideas and insights throughout the workshop.

Original material by Elaine Biech, © 2010 Association for Talent Development (ATD). Used with permission.   CHANGE MANAGEMENT training   3

CHANGE MANAGEMENT training

Learning Activity 7, *Supplemental Resource*

Ways to Establish a Sense of Urgency

Many ways exist to help employees understand the compelling reasons for change. John Kotter is credited with introducing this concept.

Ways to heighten energy and motivation toward a need to change:

- Present data from outside sources, such as articles in business journals or industry magazines
- Share data that compares your organization to your competitor or others
- Invite employees speak with dissatisfied customers
- Hold town hall meetings with exciting messages
- Hire consultants to expose data and lead discussions about employee concerns
- Coach and mentor managers about what it takes to be change champions
- Show employees' how their personal performance is linked to the business performance
- Share information about trends developing in the market
- Communicate about corporate errors; don't hide them
- Share information that addresses future opportunities and the reward for pursuing them.

Reduce fear, anger, or complacency that may prevent change:

- Start by eliminating symbols of executive privilege
- Open lines of communication from top to bottom and bottom up
- Communicate integrity by encouraging constructive criticism
- Identify the root of the attitudes
- Explore any reasons for a lack of trust
- Increase communication with the workforce about their concerns
- Refer to engagement or employee satisfaction surveys to discover what needs to change
- Address difficult issues in meetings
- Celebrate successes to help focus on future challenges
- Change gripe sessions to solution-focused sessions
- Invite ideas and suggestions for improvement.

Learning Activity 7, *Supplemental Handout*

What Floats Your Boat?

Many ideas will be shared in this workshop by your facilitator and your colleagues. These ideas will stimulate your thoughts and what you can implement in your department. This sheet gives you a single place to capture your ideas.

List your personal ideas here.

Learning Activity 8: Snap, Snap, Change

Snap, Snap, Change

Objective

Participants will be able to relate how change creates stress in the organization.

Materials

- Chairs arranged in a relatively tight circle
- Flipchart and markers (optional)

Time

15 minutes

Instructions

1. Ask participants to arrange their chairs in a circle. Have everyone, including you, sit in a chair. Starting with you (you are number 1), number off, with each person taking a different number.

2. Explain that this is a follow-the-leader activity. Each participant must do as you do.

3. Pat the top of your legs using both of your hands, palms down, raise your hands and clap twice, then snap the fingers on your right hand and snap the fingers on your left hand. Repeat, setting the rhythm, pat, pat, clap, clap, snap, snap. Repeat several times.

4. Once the group has the rhythm, explain that while everyone continues with the rhythm, they will take turns saying their own numbers aloud when they snap their right fingers; when they snap their left fingers, they should call out the next person's number in order. The person who has number 2 must repeat this action, saying his/her number while snapping his/her right fingers and calling on the next person (3) while snapping his/her left fingers, and so on. The goal is for all members to maintain the rhythm and get all the way around the circle. You start, to model how it's done.

Learning Activity 8: Snap, Snap, Change, *continued*

5. Pause the activity and ask how they are doing. Easy, right?

6. Start the activity again, pat, pat, clap, clap, snap, snap. State that this time they will not go in order but will still try to maintain the rhythm and the activity as long as they can. Call out your number (1) and then another participant's number. Slowly begin to increase the speed of the activity without telling anyone. Go faster and faster until someone stops.

7. After everyone stops laughing, debrief the activity with the discussion questions below.

Discussion Questions for Debriefing

- What had to happen to make the activity successful? (Know the rules; listen; be prepared.)
- What changes were made throughout the activity and how did it affect your success? (Speed was distracting; some people were laughing; I couldn't focus.)
- How is this activity like the changes that happen in your work environment? (Get used to doing things one way and then it changes; can't always keep up.)
- What did you do when you felt you were not able to keep up with the rhythm due to a change? (Just stopped; didn't try anymore; tried to catch up but kept falling behind; wasn't ready when my number was called.)
- Did anyone feel stressed during the activity and, if so, why? (I wanted to do it right; did not want to let my team down; didn't want to look dumb.)
- How does this activity relate to changes on the job? (Post responses on a flipchart if you wish.)
- What would be helpful when things such as this happen on the job? (Post responses if you wish.)
- What is your responsibility as a change manager? (Post responses if you wish.)
- What are you taking away from this activity?

Variation

- You could change the pace to be faster, slower, then faster again.

Source: Credit for the original concept of this exercise goes to Sarah E. Hurst.

Learning Activity 9: What's Leadership Accountability?

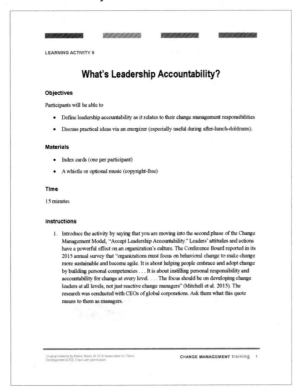

LEARNING ACTIVITY 9

What's Leadership Accountability?

Objectives

Participants will be able to

- Define leadership accountability as it relates to their change management responsibilities
- Discuss practical ideas via an energizer (especially useful during after-lunch-doldrums).

Materials

- Index cards (one per participant)
- A whistle or optional music (copyright-free)

Time

15 minutes

Instructions

1. Introduce the activity by saying that you are moving into the second phase of the Change Management Model, "Accept Leadership Accountability." Leaders' attitudes and actions have a powerful effect on an organization's culture. The Conference Board reported in its 2015 annual survey that "organizations must focus on behavioral change to make change more sustainable and become agile. It is about helping people embrace and adopt change by building personal competencies . . . It is about instilling personal responsibility and accountability for change at every level. . . . The focus should be on developing change leaders at all levels, not just reactive change managers" (Mitchell et al. 2015). The research was conducted with CEOs of global corporations. Ask them what this quote means to them as managers.

Original material by Elaine Biech, © 2016 Association for Talent Development (ATD). Used with permission   **CHANGE MANAGEMENT** training   1

Learning Activity 9: What's Leadership Accountability?, *continued*

LEARNING ACTIVITY 9, continued

2. Provide an index card to each person. Ask them to list one specific action that defines leadership accountability during change efforts for them—in other words, what do managers need to do to practice leadership accountability? Tell them to print or write clearly because others will need to be able to read their cards. It should be 5 to 20 words in length (so it can be read quickly and still be clearly understood).

3. After 2 minutes, ensure that everyone has one item on their index cards and ask participants to stand and bring their cards to the middle or back of the room (wherever there is space to move around). Have them hold their cards with the written side down. Tell them to walk around and exchange the cards with each other but not to read the ideas at this time. Just keep exchanging cards until they hear you whistle or clap (optional: you may use music if you wish.) After about 20 seconds, blow the whistle or stop the music.

4. Ask participants to pair up with the person nearest to them. Ask each pair to review the ideas they have on the two cards. Instruct them to distribute 7 points between these two ideas to reflect their relative usefulness. Any whole-number distribution will work, as long as it adds up to 7 (for example, 0 and 7; 1 and 6; 2 and 5; or 3 and 4.) They cannot use fractions. Direct them to write their scores on the back of each index card.

5. Once everyone has finished, repeat the process again. After 20 seconds, whistle (or stop the music or whatever), and have them again assign 7 points between the two ideas in a pair and write the numbers on the back of the index card. Tell them to ignore the earlier scores and score them against one another. Tell them that you will repeat this three more times.

6. After 5 rounds, have participants return to their seats and total the numbers on the card that they ended up with.

7. Count aloud backwards from 35. When a participant hears you say the total on the card in his or her hands, he or she should read the idea from the card. After reading the idea, everyone should cheer and applaud.

8. Continue on until you get the top 5 or 10 ideas or however many seems appropriate.

Original material by Elaine Biech, © 2016 Association for Talent Development (ATD). Used with permission   **CHANGE MANAGEMENT** training   2

Learning Activity 9: What's Leadership Accountability?, *continued*

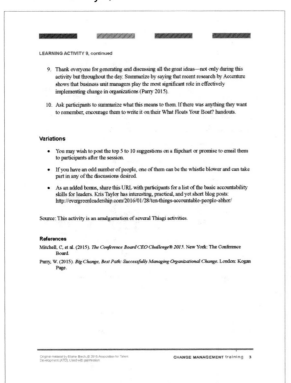

LEARNING ACTIVITY 9, continued

9. Thank everyone for generating and discussing all the great ideas—not only during this activity but throughout the day. Summarize by saying that recent research by Accenture shows that business unit managers play the most significant role in effectively implementing change in organizations (Parry 2015).

10. Ask participants to summarize what this means to them. If there was anything they want to remember, encourage them to write it on their What Floats Your Boat? handouts.

Variations

- You may wish to post the top 5 to 10 suggestions on a flipchart or promise to email them to participants after the session.
- If you have an odd number of people, one of them can be the whistle blower and can take part in any of the discussions desired.
- As an added bonus, share this URL with participants for a list of the basic accountability skills for leaders. Kris Taylor has interesting, practical, and yet short blog posts: http://evergreenleadership.com/2016/01/28/ten-things-accountable-people-abhor/

Source: This activity is an amalgamation of several Thiagi activities.

References

Mitchell, C., et al. (2015). *The Conference Board CEO Challenge® 2015.* New York: The Conference Board.

Parry, W. (2015). *Big Change, Best Path: Successfully Managing Organizational Change.* London: Kogan Page.

Original material by Elaine Biech, © 2016 Association for Talent Development (ATD). Used with permission   **CHANGE MANAGEMENT** training   3

Learning Activity 10: Optimize Communication

LEARNING ACTIVITY 10

Optimize Communication

Objectives

Participants will be able to

- State several elements of planned communication
- Discuss the purpose of a communication plan
- Experience creating a metaphor
- Implement social media as a communication tool.

Materials

- Handout 10: Your Communication Plan
- Handout 11: Optimize Your Communication Plan With Social Media
- One flipchart page for each team with colorful crayons or markers
- Optional: a bag of fresh Brussel sprouts for a prize

Time

25 minutes

Instructions

1. Ask: "What purpose does a communication plan serve?" Several reasons are noted on the Handout 10.

2. Ask what advice they would give leaders of change? Also, ask what have they incorporated in their communication plans that worked well? Briefly discuss their answers.

Original material by Elaine Biech, © 2016 Association for Talent Development (ATD). Used with permission   **CHANGE MANAGEMENT** training   1

Learning Activity 10: Optimize Communication, *continued*

LEARNING ACTIVITY 10, continued

3. Display Slide 21 and introduce the activity by saying: "We often discuss using analogies and metaphors for more effective communication, but what does that mean?" Explain that a metaphor, such as "like sitting in a dingy during a tsunami," is a powerful communication tool because it's direct and sparks instant understanding for a reader. An analogy, which is more of a logical argument, may need more elaboration to explain because it generally demonstrates how two things are alike. Pause and say: "But wait, this isn't an English writing class! Let's practice writing a metaphor instead."

4. Ask participants to form small groups of 3 to 5. This activity will help groups build a team and create some synergy. Suggest that they work with someone they have not worked with yet. Show Slide 22 that defines the task for this activity.

5. Tell them that their organization has been hired for the Brussel Sprout Relaunch. The lowly Brussel sprout has never gained the popularity or the recognition it deserves. They are to create a campaign that raises the Brussel sprout to its rightful splendor and ensures that it receives all the dignity it deserves as the most magnificent vegetable in the world. Their task is to first create and present a metaphor for the launch and to draw a picture that represents the metaphor. To get them started, display Slide 23, which lists several common metaphor themes:

- Geography, community
- Family
- Growing
- Sports
- Ocean, sea, water
- Racing
- Mountain climbing
- Trips or journeys
- Disasters: hurricane, storm
- Solar system
- Animals
- Body parts
- Transportation
- Heroics
- Building
- Working, jobs

6. Note that there are some communication plan tips on the second page of Handout 10. To introduce some multimedia into the activity, you could let them consult online resources on their smartphones or tablets to obtain competitors' information about the lowly Brussel sprout. Tell them they have 10 minutes for planning and design, after which they will deliver a one-minute marketing presentation to tell the compelling story of the Brussel sprout using a metaphor.

Learning Activity 10: Optimize Communication, *continued*

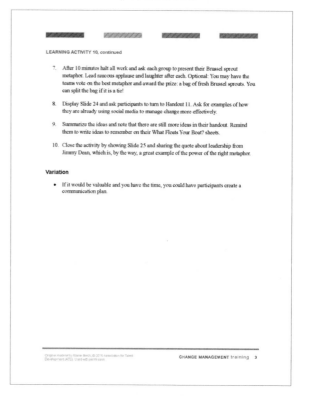

LEARNING ACTIVITY 10, continued

7. After 10 minutes halt all work and ask each group to present their Brussel sprout metaphor. Lead raucous applause and laughter after each. Optional: You may have the teams vote on the best metaphor and award the prize: a bag of fresh Brussel sprouts. You can split the bag if it is a tie!

8. Display Slide 24 and ask participants to turn to Handout 11. Ask for examples of how they are already using social media to manage change more effectively.

9. Summarize the ideas and note that there are still more ideas in their handout. Remind them to write ideas to remember on their What Floats Your Boat? sheets.

10. Close the activity by showing Slide 25 and sharing the quote about leadership from Jimmy Dean, which is, by the way, a great example of the power of the right metaphor.

Variation

- If it would be valuable and you have the time, you could have participants create a communication plan.

Learning Activity 11: Navigate Resistance to Change

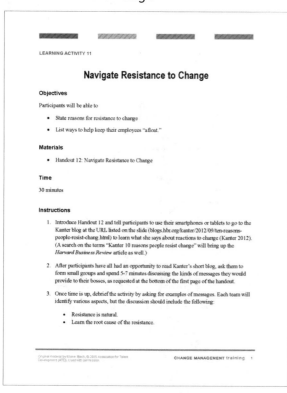

LEARNING ACTIVITY 11

Navigate Resistance to Change

Objectives

Participants will be able to

- State reasons for resistance to change
- List ways to help keep their employees "afloat."

Materials

- Handout 12: Navigate Resistance to Change

Time

30 minutes

Instructions

1. Introduce Handout 12 and tell participants to use their smartphones or tablets to go to the Kanter blog at the URL listed on the slide (blogs.hbr.org/kanter/2012/09/ten-reasons-people-resist-chang.html) to learn what she says about reactions to change (Kanter 2012). (A search on the terms "Kanter 10 reasons people resist change" will bring up the *Harvard Business Review* article as well.)

2. After participants have all had an opportunity to read Kanter's short blog, ask them to form small groups and spend 5-7 minutes discussing the kinds of messages they would provide to their bosses, as requested at the bottom of the first page of the handout.

3. Once time is up, debrief the activity by asking for examples of messages. Each team will identify various aspects, but the discussion should include the following:

- Resistance is natural.
- Learn the root cause of the resistance.

Learning Activity 11: Navigate Resistance to Change, *continued*

LEARNING ACTIVITY 11, continued

- Give ownership of the change when possible.
- Allow choices.
- Create certainty where they can with clear timelines and simple steps.
- Be transparent.
- Keep change to a minimum.
- Celebrate the past.
- Provide abundant information, education, training, mentors, and other support systems.
- Allow some to focus exclusively on change, adding rewards and recognition.
- Enlarge the circle of stakeholders to include everyone who is affected.
- Heal the past.
- When something painful must occur, be honest, transparent, fast, and fair.

This should take about 7 minutes.

4. Ask them to turn to the second page of Handout 12. Overview the concept that employees may see resistance as a kind of life raft—the last thing they can hang onto before sinking. Ask participants whether they think that is possible.

5. Invite them to respond to as many of the questions at the bottom of this handout page as they wish. This is a personal introspective activity for each manager. Allow about 5 minutes to complete.

6. Ask: "What are some of your ideas for how you can help your employees stay afloat? Suggest they note ideas on their What Floats Your Boat? sheets.

Variations

- If time allows, participants could discuss a real example from their experience.

- If participants do not have access to the Internet during the session, suggest that they review the blog when they return to the workplace.

Reference

Kanter, R.M. (2012). "Ten Reasons People Resist Change." *Harvard Business Review*, September 25.

Learning Activity 12: Work Is a Juggling Act

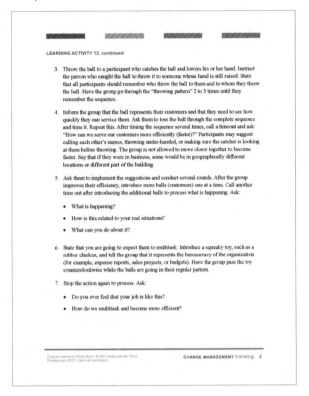

LEARNING ACTIVITY 12

Work Is a Juggling Act

Objective

Participants will be able to experience and discuss reasons employees feel pressure on the job when a change initiative is introduced.

Materials

- Demonstration items hidden in a box:
  - Three tennis or Nerf balls
  - One squeaky toy
  - One plastic glass filled with water
  - One hard-boiled egg
- Watch, timer, or app on your smartphone

Time

15 minutes

Instructions

1. Have the demonstration items in a box. Ask participants to form a circle with a diameter of 10 to 15 feet in a location where there is room to toss a ball.

2. Ask all participants to raise their right hands. Tell them that you are going to throw the ball to someone who will lower his/her hand and throw it to someone else. State that they will continue this until everyone's hands are lowered.

Learning Activity 12: Work Is a Juggling Act, *continued*

LEARNING ACTIVITY 12, continued

3. Throw the ball to a participant who catches the ball and lowers his or her hand. Instruct the person who caught the ball to throw it to someone whose hand is still raised. State that all participants should remember who threw the ball to them and to whom they threw the ball. Have the group go through the "throwing pattern" 2 to 3 times until they remember the sequence.

4. Inform the group that the ball represents their customers and that they need to see how quickly they can service them. Ask them to toss the ball through the complete sequence and time it. Repeat this. After timing the sequence several times, call a timeout and ask: "How can we serve our customers more efficiently (faster)?" Participants may suggest calling each other's names, throwing under-handed, or making sure the catcher is looking at them before throwing. The group is not allowed to move closer together to become faster. Say that if they were in business, some would be geographically different locations or different part of the building.

5. Ask them to implement the suggestions and conduct several rounds. After the group improves their efficiency, introduce more balls (customers) one at a time. Call another time out after introducing the additional balls to process what is happening. Ask:

   - What is happening?
   - How is this related to your real situations?
   - What can you do about it?

6. State that you are going to expect them to multitask. Introduce a squeaky toy, such as a rubber chicken, and tell the group that it represents the bureaucracy of the organization (for example, expense reports, sales projects, or budgets). Have the group pass the toy counterclockwise while the balls are going in their regular pattern.

7. Stop the action again to process. Ask:

   - Do you ever feel that your job is like this?
   - How do we multitask and become more efficient?

Learning Activity 12: Work Is a Juggling Act, *continued*

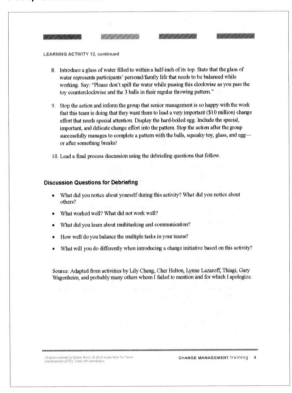

LEARNING ACTIVITY 12, continued

8. Introduce a glass of water filled to within a half-inch of its top. State that the glass of water represents participants' personal/family life that needs to be balanced while working. Say: "Please don't spill the water while passing this clockwise as you pass the toy counterclockwise and the 3 balls in their regular throwing pattern."

9. Stop the action and inform the group that senior management is so happy with the work that this team is doing that they want them to lead a very important ($10 million) change effort that needs special attention. Display the hard-boiled egg. Include the special, important, and delicate change effort into the pattern. Stop the action after the group successfully manages to complete a pattern with the balls, squeaky toy, glass, and egg—or after something breaks!

10. Lead a final process discussion using the debriefing questions that follow.

Discussion Questions for Debriefing

- What did you notice about yourself during this activity? What did you notice about others?
- What worked well? What did not work well?
- What did you learn about multitasking and communication?
- How well do you balance the multiple tasks in your teams?
- What will you do differently when introducing a change initiative based on this activity?

Source: Adapted from activities by Lily Cheng, Cher Holton, Lynne Lazaroff, Thiagi, Gary Wagenheim, and probably many others whom I failed to mention and for which I apologize.

Learning Activity 13: Tools to Manage Relationships

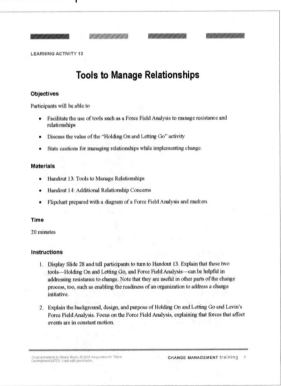

LEARNING ACTIVITY 13

Tools to Manage Relationships

Objectives

Participants will be able to

- Facilitate the use of tools such as a Force Field Analysis to manage resistance and relationships
- Discuss the value of the "Holding On and Letting Go" activity
- State cautions for managing relationships while implementing change.

Materials

- Handout 13: Tools to Manage Relationships
- Handout 14: Additional Relationship Concerns
- Flipchart prepared with a diagram of a Force Field Analysis and markers

Time

20 minutes

Instructions

1. Display Slide 28 and tell participants to turn to Handout 13. Explain that these two tools—Holding On and Letting Go, and Force Field Analysis—can be helpful in addressing resistance to change. Note that they are useful in other parts of the change process, too, such as enabling the readiness of an organization to address a change initiative.

2. Explain the background, design, and purpose of Holding On and Letting Go and Levin's Force Field Analysis. Focus on the Force Field Analysis, explaining that forces that affect events are in constant motion.

Learning Activity 13: Tools to Manage Relationships, *continued*

3. Explain the diagram (Slide 29) and suggest that they think of the center line as the status quo—or the way the situation exists today. Various forces have an impact on the status quo pushing from opposite sides to hold it firmly in place. For change to happen, the status quo must be upset. Tell them to imagine that the driving forces (the left-hand column) are favorable to the intended change and that the restraining forces (the right-hand column) are those that prevent change. The key is to identify both kinds of forces and then to strengthen the driving forces and weaken the restraining forces.

4. Ask: "What is the goal? Which direction do you want the center line to move?" The line should move to the right because it means that the driving forces are stronger than the restraining forces and you are getting closer to your goal.

5. Use a flipchart and post an example. Write "Clean out the garage" on the objective line. Fill in the right-hand column first and ask for suggestions, saying "What might be preventing (restraining) you from cleaning out the garage?" Expect responses such as "No time," "Don't know what to do with everything," and "Currently know where to find everything." Write these suggestions—one per line—in the right-hand column.

6. Next ask for suggestions for the left-hand column, "What could be the driving forces that would encourage you to clean the garage?" Expect things such as "My spouse would be happy," "We could have a party in the garage," "I'd feel a sense of accomplishment," and "I might find things that have been lost." Write these suggestions—one per line—in the left-hand column.

7. Next, move to the bottom of the page and ask "How can we strengthen the driving (left-hand column) forces?" Note these at the bottom of the flipchart.

8. Remind them that for change to happen, they need to either strengthen the driving forces or weaken the restraining forces. Ask: "How can we weaken or eliminate the restraining (right-hand column) forces?" Note these at the bottom of the flipchart.

9. Point out that if the driving forces can be strengthened and the restraining forces can be weakened, the center line (situation) moves toward the right—that is, toward the goal.

10. Ask them to think of a personal need—something they would like to change. Make suggestions such as lose weight, return to school, start a regular savings plan, take a trip to another country, and so on. Ask if this tool might be useful.

Learning Activity 13: Tools to Manage Relationships, *continued*

11. Now say that although we are discussing this tool as it relates to resistance, let's consider how it could be used for the entire change initiative (if there is a current one). Process the activity with the following questions:

   - What are some of the restraining forces?
   - What are some of the driving forces?
   - What can you do to weaken the restraining forces?
   - What can you do to strengthen the driving forces?
   - What do you think you can do to get to the goal?

12. Wrap up this activity by encouraging participants to learn more about managing relationships with the suggestions given in Handout 14.

Variations

- If time permits have participants circle ideas on Handout 14 and transfer personalized versions of their circled ideas to their What Floats Your Boat? sheets.
- If you want them to practice using a Force Field Analysis, have them select a personal goal and use the tool to explore it individually or in pairs.
- If the group is familiar with Force Field Analysis, you could leave out the group example and go directly from Step 4 to Step 10 (skipping Steps 5-9).

Learning Activity 14: A Different Perspective

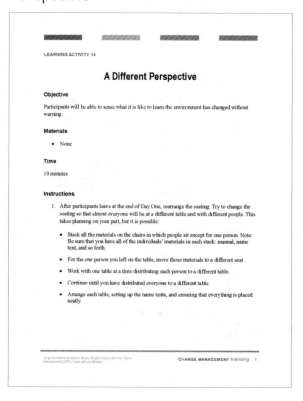

A Different Perspective

Objective

Participants will be able to sense what it is like to learn the environment has changed without warning.

Materials

- None

Time

10 minutes

Instructions

1. After participants leave at the end of Day One, rearrange the seating. Try to change the seating so that almost everyone will be at a different table and with different people. This takes planning on your part, but it is possible:

   - Stack all the materials on the chairs in which people sit except for one person. Note: Be sure that you have all of the individuals' materials in each stack: manual, name tent, and so forth.
   - For the one person you left on the table, move those materials to a different seat.
   - Work with one table at a time distributing each person to a different table.
   - Continue until you have distributed everyone to a different table.
   - Arrange each table, setting up the name tents, and ensuring that everything is placed neatly.

Learning Activity 14: A Different Perspective, *continued*

2. At the beginning of Day Two's session, ignore the fact that everyone was moved to a different location. Ask participants how their evening was. Ask a few questions based on earlier content. Announce any administrative items: registration information, new materials on the tables, changes in the schedule, and so forth.

3. Finally ask: "How did you feel about sitting in a different seat?"

4. You should expect to hear:

   - It was expected but still a shock.
   - Sitting in the same seat is habitual; there is comfort and familiarity in patterns and routines.
   - Emotional reaction: some good, some negative.

5. Lead a discussion about the lessons learned and how this relates to the resistance to change they experience as managers.

6. Then ask: "What would have made the change easier?" Here are suggestions you might hear:

   - A warning before it occurred
   - Being a part of the design
   - Being able to select our own location.

7. Wrap up by saying that you hope this helps them appreciate feelings of resistance.

8. It is up to you whether you will allow them to return to their original seats. Decide what will result in the most learning.

Variation

- If your workshop does not occur over two consecutive days, ask participants to take their materials but leave their name tent cards. Before the second day, use a similar process as listed above to move participants to a different seat.

Learning Activity 15: Angles, Tangles, and Dangles

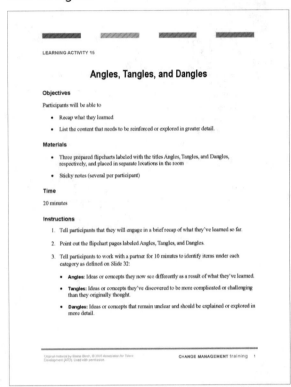

LEARNING ACTIVITY 15

Angles, Tangles, and Dangles

Objectives

Participants will be able to

- Recap what they learned
- List the content that needs to be reinforced or explored in greater detail.

Materials

- Three prepared flipcharts labeled with the titles Angles, Tangles, and Dangles, respectively, and placed in separate locations in the room
- Sticky notes (several per participant)

Time

20 minutes

Instructions

1. Tell participants that they will engage in a brief recap of what they've learned so far.

2. Point out the flipchart pages labeled Angles, Tangles, and Dangles.

3. Tell participants to work with a partner for 10 minutes to identify items under each category as defined on Slide 32:

   - **Angles:** Ideas or concepts they now see differently as a result of what they've learned.
   - **Tangles:** Ideas or concepts they've discovered to be more complicated or challenging than they originally thought.
   - **Dangles:** Ideas or concepts that remain unclear and should be explained or explored in more detail.

Original material by Elaine Biech, © 2016 Association for Talent Development (ATD). Used with permission.   CHANGE MANAGEMENT training   1

Learning Activity 15: Angles, Tangles, and Dangles, *continued*

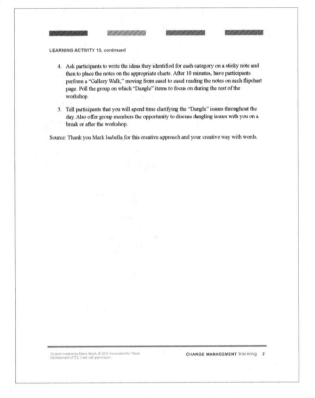

LEARNING ACTIVITY 15, continued

4. Ask participants to write the ideas they identified for each category on a sticky note and then to place the notes on the appropriate charts. After 10 minutes, have participants perform a "Gallery Walk," moving from easel to easel reading the notes on each flipchart page. Poll the group on which "Dangle" items to focus on during the rest of the workshop.

5. Tell participants that you will spend time clarifying the "Dangle" issues throughout the day. Also offer group members the opportunity to discuss dangling issues with you on a break or after the workshop.

Source: Thank you Mark Isabella for this creative approach and your creative way with words.

Original material by Elaine Biech, © 2016 Association for Talent Development (ATD). Used with permission.   CHANGE MANAGEMENT training   2

Learning Activity 16: Oceans of Respect for Good Role Models

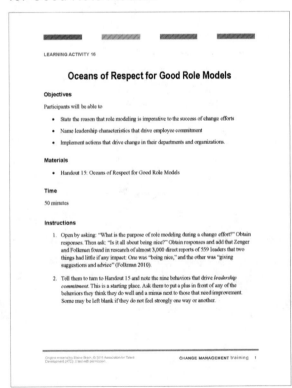

LEARNING ACTIVITY 16

Oceans of Respect for Good Role Models

Objectives

Participants will be able to

- State the reason that role modeling is imperative to the success of change efforts
- Name leadership characteristics that drive employee commitment
- Implement actions that drive change in their departments and organizations.

Materials

- Handout 15: Oceans of Respect for Good Role Models

Time

50 minutes

Instructions

1. Open by asking: "What is the purpose of role modeling during a change effort?" Obtain responses. Then ask: "Is it all about being nice?" Obtain responses and add that Zenger and Folkman found in research of almost 3,000 direct reports of 559 leaders that two things had little if any impact: One was "being nice," and the other was "giving suggestions and advice" (Folkman 2010).

2. Tell them to turn to Handout 15 and note the nine behaviors that drive *leadership commitment.* This is a starting place. Ask them to put a plus in front of any of the behaviors they think they do well and a minus next to those that need improvement. Some may be left blank if they do not feel strongly one way or another.

Original material by Elaine Biech, © 2016 Association for Talent Development (ATD). Used with permission.   CHANGE MANAGEMENT training   1

Learning Activity 16: Oceans of Respect for Good Role Models, *continued*

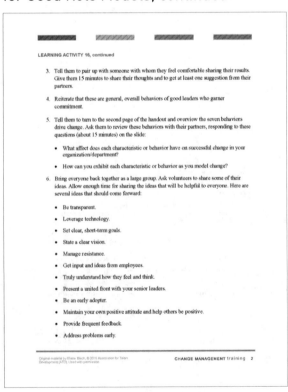

LEARNING ACTIVITY 16, continued

3. Tell them to pair up with someone with whom they feel comfortable sharing their results. Give them 15 minutes to share their thoughts and to get at least one suggestion from their partners.

4. Reiterate that these are general, overall behaviors of good leaders who garner commitment.

5. Tell them to turn to the second page of the handout and overview the seven behaviors drive change. Ask them to review these behaviors with their partners, responding to these questions (about 15 minutes) on the slide:

   - What affect does each characteristic or behavior have on successful change in your organization/department?
   - How can you exhibit each characteristic or behavior as you model change?

6. Bring everyone back together as a large group. Ask volunteers to share some of their ideas. Allow enough time for sharing the ideas that will be helpful to everyone. Here are several ideas that should come forward:

   - Be transparent.
   - Leverage technology.
   - Set clear, short-term goals.
   - State a clear vision.
   - Manage resistance.
   - Get input and ideas from employees.
   - Truly understand how they feel and think.
   - Present a united front with your senior leaders.
   - Be an early adopter.
   - Maintain your own positive attitude and help others be positive.
   - Provide frequent feedback.
   - Address problems early.

Original material by Elaine Biech, © 2016 Association for Talent Development (ATD). Used with permission.   CHANGE MANAGEMENT training   2

Learning Activity 16: Oceans of Respect for Good Role Models, *continued*

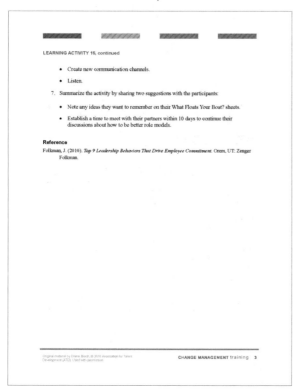

LEARNING ACTIVITY 16, continued

- Create new communication channels.
- Listen.

7. Summarize the activity by sharing two suggestions with the participants:

- Note any ideas they want to remember on their What Floats Your Boat? sheets.
- Establish a time to meet with their partners within 10 days to continue their discussions about how to be better role models.

Reference

Folkman, J. (2010). *Top 9 Leadership Behaviors That Drive Employee Commitment.* Orem, UT: Zenger Folkman.

CHANGE MANAGEMENT training   3

Learning Activity 17: Full Speed Ahead to Generate Gains

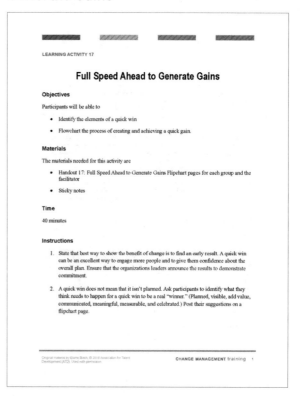

LEARNING ACTIVITY 17

Full Speed Ahead to Generate Gains

Objectives

Participants will be able to

- Identify the elements of a quick win
- Flowchart the process of creating and achieving a quick gain.

Materials

The materials needed for this activity are

- Handout 17: Full Speed Ahead to Generate Gains Flipchart pages for each group and the facilitator
- Sticky notes

Time

40 minutes

Instructions

1. State that best way to show the benefit of change is to find an early result. A quick win can be an excellent way to engage more people and to give them confidence about the overall plan. Ensure that the organizations leaders announce the results to demonstrate commitment.

2. A quick win does not mean that it isn't planned. Ask participants to identify what they think needs to happen for a quick win to be a real "winner." (Planned, visible, add value, communicated, meaningful, measurable, and celebrated.) Post their suggestions on a flipchart page.

CHANGE MANAGEMENT training   1

Learning Activity 17: Full Speed Ahead to Generate Gains, *continued*

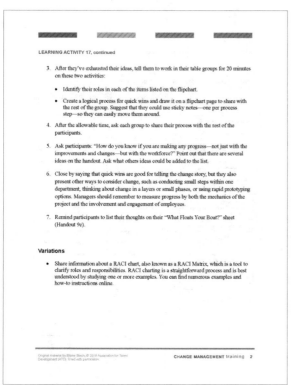

LEARNING ACTIVITY 17, continued

3. After they've exhausted their ideas, tell them to work in their table groups for 20 minutes on these two activities:

- Identify their roles in each of the items listed on the flipchart.
- Create a logical process for quick wins and draw it on a flipchart page to share with the rest of the group. Suggest that they could use sticky notes—one per process step—so they can easily move them around.

4. After the allowable time, ask each group to share their process with the rest of the participants.

5. Ask participants: "How do you know if you are making any progress—not just with the improvements and changes—but with the workforce?" Point out that there are several ideas on the handout. Ask what others ideas could be added to the list.

6. Close by saying that quick wins are good for telling the change story, but they also present other ways to consider change, such as conducting small steps within one department, thinking about change in a layers or small phases, or using rapid prototyping options. Managers should remember to measure progress by both the mechanics of the project and the involvement and engagement of employees.

7. Remind participants to list their thoughts on their "What Floats Your Boat?" sheet (Handout 9e).

Variations

- Share information about a RACI chart, also known as a RACI Matrix, which is a tool to clarify roles and responsibilities. RACI charting is a straightforward process and is best understood by studying one or more examples. You can find numerous examples and how-to instructions online.

CHANGE MANAGEMENT training   2

Learning Activity 18: Naval Slang Energizer

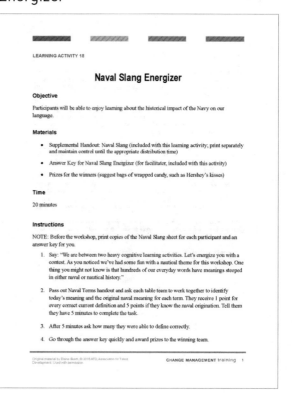

LEARNING ACTIVITY 18

Naval Slang Energizer

Objective

Participants will be able to enjoy learning about the historical impact of the Navy on our language.

Materials

- Supplemental Handout: Naval Slang (included with this learning activity; print separately and maintain control until the appropriate distribution time)
- Answer Key for Naval Slang Energizer (for facilitator, included with this activity)
- Prizes for the winners (suggest bags of wrapped candy, such as Hershey's kisses)

Time

20 minutes

Instructions

NOTE: Before the workshop, print copies of the Naval Slang sheet for each participant and an answer key for you.

1. Say: "We are between two heavy cognitive learning activities. Let's energize you with a contest. As you noticed we've had some fun with a nautical theme for this workshop. One thing you might not know is that hundreds of our everyday words have meanings steeped in either naval or nautical history."

2. Pass out Naval Terms handout and ask each table team to work together to identify today's meaning and the original naval meaning for each term. They receive 1 point for every correct current definition and 5 points if they know the naval origination. Tell them they have 5 minutes to complete the task.

3. After 5 minutes ask how many they were able to define correctly.

4. Go through the answer key quickly and award prizes to the winning team.

CHANGE MANAGEMENT training   1

Learning Activity 18, *Supplemental Resource*

Answer Key for Naval Slang Energizer

1. Mind Your Ps and Qs: If you were ever told to "mind your Ps and Qs," you knew to behave your best. In times when many sailors were illiterate, barkeepers would maintain a running chalkboard tally of the pints and quarts of ale that each sailor consumed. A "P" for pint or "Q" for quart was added next to each person's name whenever a seaman ordered another draught. On payday, a seaman had to pay up for each mark next to his name, so he was forced to "mind his Ps and Qs" or get into financial trouble.

2. Took the Wind Out of His Sails: "Taking the wind out of someone's sails" means beating them in an argument, or making them feel less confident in their actions. Originally, the term referred to a naval maneuver. One ship would pass close to its opponent and block its access to the wind. In an age of wind-powered ships, this would cause the enemy to lose maneuverability and make the opposing vessel more susceptible to attack.

3. Devil to Pay: This expression denoted the task of caulking the longest seam on a wooden ship, called the "devil." The caulking was referred to as "pay," so this unpleasant duty was called "paying the devil" and was despised by every seaman. The phrase came to denote any unpleasant job.

4. Carry On: Sailors were given a "carry on" order whenever a strong breeze came along. This order required sailors on deck to hoist every bit of canvas they could—a grueling and back-breaking task. Today, this phrase is used as a request to simply resume work.

5. Wallop: To *wallop* is to strike a major blow against an enemy or to hit incredibly hard. The term comes from the last name of English Admiral Sir John Wallop, who King Henry VIII sent to devastate the coast of France in the 1500s in retaliation for the French burning down the British city of Brighton in 1513. Wallop's complete destruction of the French coast made his name immortal.

6. Three Sheets to the Wind: The term *three sheets to the wind* is generally used to describe someone who has had too much to drink. It comes from a term that originally described a ship in a complete state of disarray, with its sails flapping in the breeze.

7. Yankee: The word *Yankee* is believed to originate with Dutch merchants. Dutchmen would refer to American sea captains as "yankers," which translates as "wranglers." This was apparently due to the Americans' ability to drive a hard bargain.

Learning Activity 18, *Supplemental Resource*

8. Knowing the Ropes: The phrase *knowing the ropes*, indicating that someone is competent at what they do, has its roots in old nautical talk. The statement, printed on a seaman's discharge, indicated that he knew the main uses of the ropes on a ship. Yet rather than indicating that the sailor was a master, the phrase meant that he was a novice who only knew the basics of sailing.

9. At Loose Ends: This is the nautical term for a rope when unattached and therefore neglected or not doing its job. Thus "tying up loose ends" indicates having done a complete job or having dealt with all the details.

10. Bamboozle: In the maneuver known as a *bamboozle*, a word first used in the early 1700s, pirates would fly the flag of a friendly nation in order to deceive passing ships into letting their guard down. The enemy ship would then attack, thereby "bamboozling" its stunned opponent.

11. Albatross Around One's Neck: An albatross is a large and long-winged seabird of the southern hemisphere capable of long flights. It was believed among seamen that albatrosses embodied the souls of dead sailors, and it was considered unlucky to kill one. The phrase alludes to Samuel Taylor Coleridge's poem, "The Rime of the Ancient Mariner," in which a sailor shoots a friendly albatross and is forced to wear its carcass around his neck as a punishment. More generally it refers to a burden someone must carry.

12. All Sewn Up: Dead sailors were "all sewn up" in a bit of canvas with a weight attached to make sure that the corpse sank deep in the water. Today this expression is used to describe something that is completed.

13. Bale Out: To *bale out* means to remove water from a vessel. Now the term is used in the sense of getting out of a bad situation such as selling the shares of a failing company.

14. Batten Down the Hatches: Now used simply to mean "get ready," the term originates from the act of securing the hatches and tarpaulins covering them on a boat with use of battens (long flat blades made of wood) in preparation for a coming storm.

15. Bite the Bullet: To bravely face up to something unpleasant, one is said to "bite the bullet." This originated from the practice of giving sailors and soldiers a bullet to bite during amputations or other surgery before the use of anesthetics.

Learning Activity 18, *Supplemental Resource*

16. Clean Slate: It was the custom in sailing ships to record courses, distances, and tacks on a log slate. The new watch would always start with a clean slate if things had been going fine, disregarding what had gone before and starting anew. In a similar way, today we refer to a new beginning as starting with a "clean slate."

17. Cup of Joe: This term comes to us from American Navy lore. Josephus Daniels (1862-1948) was appointed Secretary of the Navy by President Woodrow Wilson in 1913. During his time as Secretary of the Navy, "Joe" Daniels abolished the officers' wine, after which the strongest drink aboard Navy ships was coffee. A cup of coffee became known as "a cup of Joe."

18. Dressed to the Nines: To celebrate victories, a returning ship would approach her home waters or port "dressed" in bunting and flags. As many of the crew as possible would line up on the nine primary yards as a salute to their monarch. Today the expression is often used to describe a person who is dressed in fancy clothing.

19. Give Me Some Slack: This expression originated during the docking of a ship. One would alternately tension the line in your hands and then release. The call would be to "give me some slack" when it was your turn to "haul." Today, it still means much the same thing as when used in referenced to the boating world. The term is also now used synonymous with "give me a break."

20. Scuttlebutt: *Scuttlebutt* is synonymous with rumor or gossip. It originates from the drinking ladle with small holes or scuttles in it to reduce the small talk and wasted time at the water barrel. The holes forced the sailors to drink fast before the water ran out.

Bonus or Tie Breaker—Square Meal: This is an expression synonymous with a proper or substantial meal. It originated from the square platters that were used to serve meals aboard ships. Worth 10 points.

Learning Activity 18, *Supplemental Handout*

Naval Slang

Naval slang has left its mark on the English language. Most of us are unaware that a number of widely used words and expressions originated with sailors. Try your skill with these.

Word/Phrase	Today's Meaning	Naval Originations
Mind your Ps and Qs		
Took the wind out of his sails		
Devil to pay		
Carry on		
Wallop		
Three sheets to the wind		
Yankee		
Knowing the ropes		
At loose ends		
Bamboozle		
Albatross around one's neck		
All sewn up		
Bale out		
Batten down the hatches		
Bite the bullet		
Clean slate		
Cup of joe		
Dressed to the nines		
Give me some slack		
Scuttlebutt		

Learning Activity 19: Test the Waters With Ideas for Change-Ready Employees

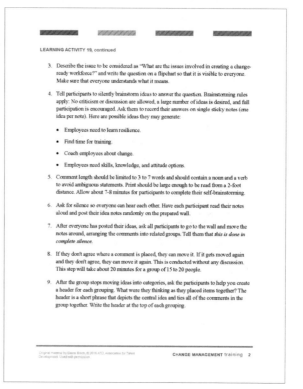

Learning Activity 19: Test the Waters With Ideas for Change-Ready Employees, *continued*

LEARNING ACTIVITY 19, continued

3. Describe the issue to be considered as "What are the issues involved in creating a change-ready workforce?" and write the question on a flipchart so that it is visible to everyone. Make sure that everyone understands what it means.

4. Tell participants to silently brainstorm ideas to answer the question. Brainstorming rules apply: No criticism or discussion are allowed, a large number of ideas is desired, and full participation is encouraged. Ask them to record their answers on single sticky notes (one idea per note). Here are possible ideas they may generate:

   - Employees need to learn resilience.
   - Find time for training.
   - Coach employees about change.
   - Employees need skills, knowledge, and attitude options.

5. Comment length should be limited to 3 to 7 words and should contain a noun and a verb to avoid ambiguous statements. Print should be large enough to be read from a 2-foot distance. Allow about 7-8 minutes for participants to complete their self-brainstorming.

6. Ask for silence so everyone can hear each other. Have each participant read their notes aloud and post their idea notes randomly on the prepared wall.

7. After everyone has posted their ideas, ask all participants to go to the wall and move the notes around, arranging the comments into related groups. Tell them that *this is done in complete silence.*

8. If they don't agree where a comment is placed, they can move it. If it gets moved again and they don't agree, they can move it again. This is conducted without any discussion. This step will take about 20 minutes for a group of 15 to 20 people.

9. After the group stops moving ideas into categories, ask the participants to help you create a header for each grouping. What were they thinking as they placed items together? The header is a short phrase that depicts the central idea and ties all of the comments in the group together. Write the header at the top of each grouping.

Learning Activity 19: Test the Waters With Ideas for Change-Ready Employees, *continued*

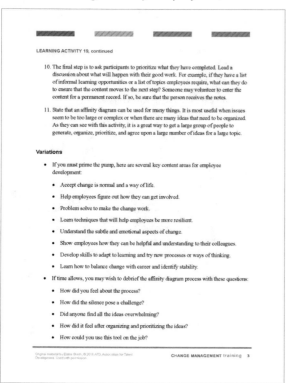

Learning Activity 20: Smooth Sailing

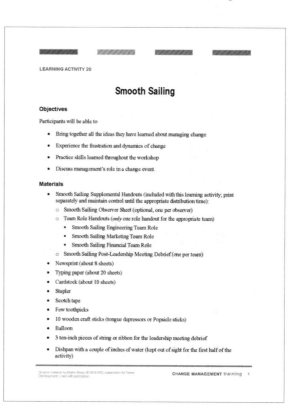

Learning Activity 20: Smooth Sailing, *continued*

Time

60 minutes

Instructions

NOTE: Before the workshop, print copies of the 5 supplemental handouts for the role play; maintain tight control until the appropriate distribution place in the activity.

1. Show Slide 43 and tell the participants that they are employees of a rapidly expanding company. The company is very agile and innovative and has been extraordinarily successful because it takes on projects at short notice that other companies cannot manage. Your company has just accepted a new project and you are in the rapid prototyping phase. Your prototype is due this week and the top brass of your company has been in numerous meetings with the customer for the past two days.

2. If you wish to have an observer or two, ask for volunteers now. Give observers the Smooth Sailing Observer Sheet.

3. Form three equal-sized teams and assign each a location. One team will serve as the engineering team for the project, one will be the marketing team, and one will be the financial team. Ask them to decide which team they would like to be. NOTE: You must have all three represented, so you may need to make an arbitrary assignment. Give each team its respective team role assignment (engineering, marketing, or financial). Also give the engineering team their construction materials (newsprint, typing paper, cardstock, stapler, scotch tape, toothpicks, balloon).

4. Tell the teams that they have 40 minutes to complete the task and be ready to meet with their leadership team.

5. After 5 minutes, stop the work and say the leadership team has said that they need representatives from each team to join them with the customers. The leaders have specifically requested these people join them immediately in the conference room. Select one person from each team—preferably one of the most engaged from each team. Tell the teams they will only be gone a short time. Have the 3 team members join you at the front of the room. And tell the teams they can get back to their tasks.

Learning Activity 20: Smooth Sailing, *continued*

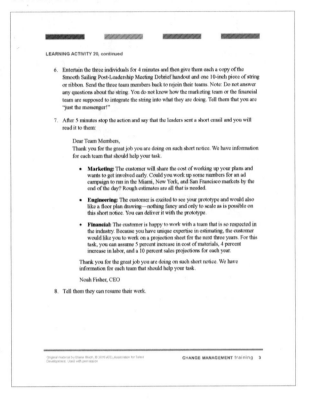

6. Entertain the three individuals for 4 minutes and then give them each a copy of the Smooth Sailing Post-Leadership Meeting Debrief handout and one 10-inch piece of string or ribbon. Send the three team members back to rejoin their teams. Note: Do not answer any questions about the string. You do not know how the marketing team or the financial team are supposed to integrate the string into what they are doing. Tell them that you are "just the messenger!"

7. After 5 minutes stop the action and say that the leaders sent a short email and you will read it to them:

> Dear Team Members,
> Thank you for the great job you are doing on such short notice. We have information for each team that should help your task.
>
> - **Marketing:** The customer will share the cost of working up your plans and wants to get involved early. Could you work up some numbers for an ad campaign to run in the Miami, New York, and San Francisco markets by the end of the day? Rough estimates are all that is needed.
>
> - **Engineering:** The customer is excited to see your prototype and would also like a floor plan drawing—nothing fancy and only to scale as is possible on this short notice. You can deliver it with the prototype.
>
> - **Financial:** The customer is happy to work with a team that is so respected in the industry. Because you have unique expertise in estimating, the customer would like you to work on a projection sheet for the next three years. For this task, you can assume 5 percent increase in cost of materials, 4 percent increase in labor, and a 10 percent sales projections for each year.
>
> Thank you for the great job you are doing on such short notice. We have information for each team that should help your task.
>
> Noah Fisher, CEO

8. Tell them they can resume their work.

Learning Activity 20: Smooth Sailing, *continued*

9. After 5 minutes, stop the action and say that the meeting between our senior leaders and the customer just ended and you have another message:

> The customer is so excited to see the prototype and hear your great information, they would like to shorten the time to complete the prototype. They know this will be a hardship and they appreciate it immensely. They have a brilliant idea to help you. They think that some inter-team collaboration will help to speed the process. Therefore we will move one team member from each team to a different team.

Proceed to assign which team member will join which team. Tell them they have 10 minutes less to complete their work.

10. Tell them to get back to work and that they have 10 minutes left, given this recent message.

11. After 2 minutes, stop the action again and say that a bit of industrial espionage has revealed an important requirement: The boat prototype must float at least 2 minutes to pass the demonstration. Say: "This is pretty important, how about if all three teams get together to ensure this will be possible." Give them the dishpan with water. Tell them they have 8 minutes to complete the testing. Expect chaos.

12. After 8 minutes ask everyone to stop their work and say, we have just received an image of what the customer hopes the boat will look like. Show the slide 44. After the groans have ended, stop the action, give everyone a round of applause and proclaim the task has been completed.

13. Have each of the teams share their roles and experiences. If you used observers, ask for their observations.

14. Lead a discussion about the activity using the discussion questions.

Discussion Questions for Debriefing

- How well do you think you managed the changes?
- Think back to how the changes affected you personally? How did you feel? What were you thinking?
- How did you respond when told a team member would leave?

Learning Activity 20: Smooth Sailing, *continued*

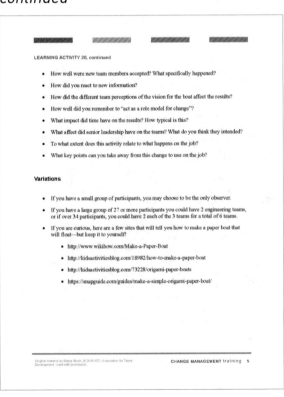

- How well were new team members accepted? What specifically happened?
- How did you react to new information?
- How did the different team perceptions of the vision for the boat affect the results?
- How well did you remember to "act as a role model for change"?
- What impact did time have on the results? How typical is this?
- What affect did senior leadership have on the teams? What do you think they intended?
- To what extent does this activity relate to what happens on the job?
- What key points can you take away from this change to use on the job?

Variations

- If you have a small group of participants, you may choose to be the only observer.
- If you have a large group of 27 or more participants you could have 2 engineering teams, or if over 34 participants, you could have 2 each of the 3 teams for a total of 6 teams.
- If you are curious, here are a few sites that will tell you how to make a paper boat that will float—but keep it to yourself!
  - http://www.wikihow.com/Make-a-Paper-Boat
  - http://kidsactivitiesblog.com/18982/how-to-make-a-paper-boat
  - http://kidsactivitiesblog.com/73228/origami-paper-boats
  - https://snapguide.com/guides/make-a-simple-origami-paper-boat/

Learning Activity 20, *Supplemental Handout*

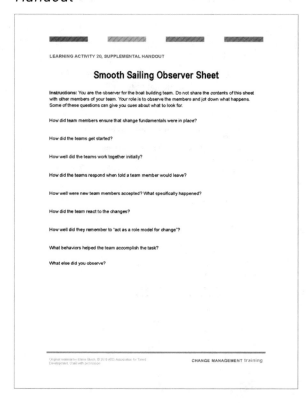

LEARNING ACTIVITY 20, SUPPLEMENTAL HANDOUT

Smooth Sailing Observer Sheet

Instructions: You are the observer for the boat building team. Do not share the contents of this sheet with other members of your team. Your role is to observe the members and jot down what happens. Some of these questions can give you cues about what to look for.

How did team members ensure that change fundamentals were in place?

How did the teams get started?

How well did the teams work together initially?

How did the teams respond when told a team member would leave?

How well were new team members accepted? What specifically happened?

How did the team react to the changes?

How well did they remember to "act as a role model for change"?

What behaviors helped the team accomplish the task?

What else did you observe?

Learning Activity 20, *Supplemental Handout*

LEARNING ACTIVITY 20, SUPPLEMENTAL HANDOUT

Smooth Sailing Engineering Team Role

You are employees of a rapidly expanding company. The company is very agile and innovative and has been extraordinarily successful because it takes on projects at short notice that other companies cannot manage. Your company has just accepted a new project, and you are in the rapid prototyping phase. Your prototype is due this week, and the top brass of your company has been in numerous meetings with the customer for the past two days.

Engineering Team

Your team is responsible for designing the prototype, something tangible that will be taken to the customer for approval. You believe the boat should be reliable, sturdy, and dependable. Here are the data points to include:

- The customer's company distributes jon boats, dinghies, and trawlers. This will be the customer's first foray into building his own boat.
- The customer owns the boat distribution company and is a friend of your company's CEO, so you really want to develop a boat that the customer wants to buy.

Your Goal for the Boat: Design a good solid, functional boat that will make the customer happy and your CEO proud.

Your Tasks:

1. Use the materials given to create a mockup of the sturdy boat you would like to present at the marketing meeting later this week.
2. The customer company seems to be very proud of its logo. It is blue and gray, and you have heard his slogan, "The big blue and gray will have you on your way!" Perhaps the new boat should reflect those colors.

You have 40 minutes.

Learning Activity 20, *Supplemental Handout*

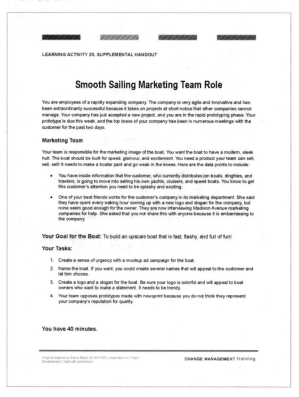

LEARNING ACTIVITY 20, SUPPLEMENTAL HANDOUT

Smooth Sailing Marketing Team Role

You are employees of a rapidly expanding company. The company is very agile and innovative and has been extraordinarily successful because it takes on projects at short notice that other companies cannot manage. Your company has just accepted a new project, and you are in the rapid prototyping phase. Your prototype is due this week, and the top brass of your company has been in numerous meetings with the customer for the past two days.

Marketing Team

Your team is responsible for the marketing image of the boat. You want the boat to have a modern, sleek hull. The boat should be built for speed, glamour, and excitement. You need a product your team can sell, sell, sell! It needs to make a boater pant and go weak in the knees. Here are the data points to include:

- You have inside information that the customer, who currently distributes jon boats, dinghies, and trawlers, is going to move into selling his own yachts, cruisers, and speed boats. You know to get this customer's attention you need to be splashy and exciting.
- One of your best friends works for the customer's company in its marketing department. She said they have spent every waking hour coming up with a new logo and slogan for the company, but none seem good enough for the owner. They are now interviewing Madison Avenue marketing companies for help. She asked that you not share this with anyone because it is embarrassing to the company.

Your Goal for the Boat: To build an upscale boat that is fast, flashy, and full of fun!

Your Tasks:

1. Create a sense of urgency with a mockup ad campaign for the boat.
2. Name the boat. If you want, you could create several names that will appeal to the customer and let him choose.
3. Create a logo and a slogan for the boat. Be sure your logo is colorful and will appeal to boat owners who want to make a statement. It needs to be trendy.
4. Your team opposes prototypes made with newsprint because you do not think they represent your company's reputation for quality.

You have 40 minutes.

Learning Activity 20, *Supplemental Handout*

LEARNING ACTIVITY 20, SUPPLEMENTAL HANDOUT

Smooth Sailing Financial Team Role

You are employees of a rapidly expanding company. The company is very agile and innovative and has been extraordinarily successful because it takes on projects at short notice that other companies cannot manage. Your company has just accepted a new project, and you are in the rapid prototyping phase. Your prototype is due this week, and the top brass of your company has been in numerous meetings with the customer for the past two days.

Financial Team

Your team is the final approver of the design. It must be built within budget. You have orders from your VP of Finance that the boat absolutely cannot go over budget like the last project. If it does, your jobs will be in jeopardy. No one else in the company knows about the budgetary issues, so it is probably best not to mention it at this time because everyone is excited about this potential contract. Here are the data points to include:

- Typing paper is half the cost of cardstock.
- Newsprint costs one-tenth the cost of typing paper.
- Wooden craft sticks are made from trees that only grow in the Amazon and are on the Convention on International Trade of Endangered Species (CITES) endangered species list.
- Tape is the most expensive material on the market and has not been proven to hold up in brackish water; it can cost roughly the same amount as all the other materials in the design.

Your Goal for the Boat: To build the cheapest boat the customer will accept.

Your Tasks:

1. Get busy immediately creating a spreadsheet that lays out the cost for building the boat comparing the three key construction materials. Consider costs for 10, 50, and 100 boats. Be sure your spreadsheet looks professional because your team will present it to the customer. Post it on a flipchart if you have time.
2. Make a list of criteria that will help keep the cost of building the boat in line with the budget; for example, the more boats you make, the cheaper they will be; the sooner you make them, the cheaper the labor costs because you already have employees on staff with the right skills. Note that you will need to share your information with the other teams later in the process.
3. Discuss the best way to share this information with the other teams when the time is announced. Create your plan and jot down a few notes about who on your team will be responsible for delivering what message.

Learning Activity 20, *Supplemental Handout*

Smooth Sailing Post-Leadership Meeting Debrief

All Teams

You just returned from the meeting that your corporate leaders are having with the potential customer. Share your perspective of what was happening with the rest of the team:

- It was a happy exciting mood.

- You just needed to answer a few basic questions.

- You did not learn anything new except that your company is not the only one building prototypes for this week's presentations.

- The one thing different is that as you walked out the door you were given a 10-inch piece of string that must be incorporated into what each team is doing.

Learning Activity 21: Build Capacity for Continuous Change and My Next Steps

Build Capacity for Continuous Change and My Next Steps

Objectives

Participants will be able to

- Explore ideas that can be implemented to prepare the organization for future continuous, complex change

- Gather ideas from colleagues for specific ideas they want to pursue

- Energize in mid-afternoon

- Capture actions for their next steps.

Materials

- Handout 21: Build Capacity for Continuous Change

- Handout 22: Action Planning: My Next Steps

- Handout 24: Additional Reading for Your Continued Development

Time

45 minutes

Instructions

1. Show Slide 46 and give an overview of Handout 21. Tell participants to review the two components of building capacity for continuous change:

   - Ensure that operational mechanisms are in place

   - Create a successful change culture.

Learning Activity 21: Build Capacity for Continuous Change and My Next Steps, *continued*

2. Ask them to review these ideas and to determine which, if any, may be lacking in their organizations. It is also appropriate if they identify another one that is more important and not on the list. If you conducted the "prouds and sorries" portion of Learning Activity 6, suggest that they review what is posted on those two flipchart pages.

3. Draw their attention to the statement on the flipchart: "I need an idea for how to . . ." Tell them to copy the statement on their index cards and then complete the prompt with one action (only one). Allow about 5 minutes.

4. Note: The activity is a version of "speed dating." Tell participants to stand and take their index card and a pen. Divide the group into two teams and line each team up so that every person on one team is facing and directly across from another person on the other team. If there are an odd number in the group, include yourself as one of the participants.

5. Label one line Team A and the other Team B. Say that Team A will state their need (I need an idea for how to...) first, and rounds will be only 90 seconds long.

6. Tell participants on Team A to state their "need for ideas" and then to listen to what their partner on Team B directly across from them has to say without interrupting them at all (no comments allowed—not even "yes, buts" or "I tried that" or "Not at our organization.") They must simply say "thank you." They may ask questions for clarity after the person has finished speaking.

7. Ask if there are any questions. Then say go and have all the Team A participants state their need to their Team B partner at the same time and have Team B participants provide input.

8. At the end of 90 seconds, call time. Have everyone in the Team B line move down one person. The individual at the end of the B line will walk to the other end of the line, so that everyone is facing a new person.

9. Repeat this process 3 more times so that everyone on Team A has stated his/her "need for an idea" to 4 different people and has received 4 different ideas. (Total time so far is less than 8 minutes.)

10. Now it is Team B's turn to state their "need for an idea" to Team A idea givers. Follow the same rules: Team B states what they need ideas about and Team A gives ideas to their partners. At the end of each round, the individual at the end of the Team B line will walk to the other end of the line and all Team B participants will move down one person. (Yes,

---

Learning Activity 21: Build Capacity for Continuous Change and My Next Steps, *continued*

Team B is the only line that moves to ensure that each participant is matched with 8 different people.)

11. Again, repeat this process a total of 4 times.

12. You may, if you wish, process this exercise ever so briefly with questions such as these:

    - How many of you obtained at least one good idea?

    - Why did this work?

    - How could you build this activity into your change management effort?

    Note, however, that there is really no need to process this activity in any way. The learning is in the process.

13. Once participants return to their seats, say that their colleagues have just thrown them a lifeline. Show Slide 47 and tell participants to turn to Handout 22: Action Planning: My Next Steps to capture the ideas they received from their colleagues. Say that they probably have a boatload of ideas at this point. Review the ideas they listed on the What Floats Your Boat? sheet as well as the other ideas they heard. Capturing their ideas in an action plan helps them turn ideas into reality. Ask: "What will help you become a change-savvy manager?" Allow about 10 minutes. If time permits, you can ask for a few ideas from participants.

14. This is a good time to point out the reading recommendations in Handout 24. Highlight a few of the books you think would be valuable to this group of managers.

Learning Activity 22: Change That Tune

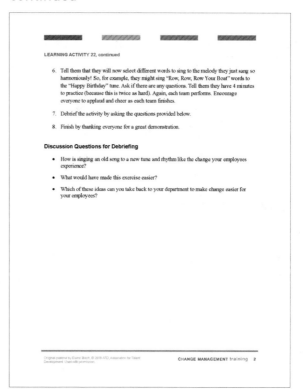

LEARNING ACTIVITY 22

Change That Tune

Objective

Participants will be able to experience one last time the feeling to do something that is uncomfortable.

Materials

- Supplemental Handout: Songs You Know (included in this learning activity; print several copies per table)

Time

10 minutes

Instructions

NOTE: Before the workshop, print several copies of the song sheet for each table group.

1. State that they have time for one more opportunity to experience what change feels like.

2. Give several copies of the Songs You Know sheet to each table.

3. Tell participants that each table team will select a song from the list. They have 2 minutes to practice singing it as a group and then they will perform for the rest of the group.

4. After the practice time, ask for volunteer groups to stand and sing their song. Ensure that everyone participates. Compliment each team on their melodious performance and lead a raucous applause for each team.

5. Ask: "Did you think that this was going to be that easy? Well, it's not. As we've discussed it is easy to do things the way we always have. Let's continue to remind ourselves that new skills, finding new ways to coordinate with others, and doing something different are difficult."

Original material by Elaine Biech, © 2016 ATD, Association for Talent Development. Used with permission.

CHANGE MANAGEMENT training 1

Learning Activity 22: Change That Tune, *continued*

LEARNING ACTIVITY 22, continued

6. Tell them that they will now select different words to sing to the melody they just sang so harmoniously! So, for example, they might sing "Row, Row, Row Your Boat" words to the "Happy Birthday" tune. Ask if there are any questions. Tell them they have 4 minutes to practice (because this is twice as hard). Again, each team performs. Encourage everyone to applaud and cheer as each team finishes.

7. Debrief the activity by asking the questions provided below.

8. Finish by thanking everyone for a great demonstration.

Discussion Questions for Debriefing

- How is singing an old song to a new tune and rhythm like the change your employees experience?

- What would have made this exercise easier?

- Which of these ideas can you take back to your department to make change easier for your employees?

Original material by Elaine Biech, © 2016 ATD, Association for Talent Development. Used with permission.

CHANGE MANAGEMENT training 2

Learning Activity 22, *Supplemental Handout*

HANDOUT 26, SUPPLEMENTAL HANDOUT

Songs You Know

Row, row, row your boat
Gently down the stream.
Merrily, merrily, merrily,
Life is but a dream.

Twinkle, twinkle, little star.
How I wonder what you are.
Up above the world so high,
Like a diamond in the sky.
Twinkle, twinkle, little star.

Mary had a little lamb.
Little lamb, little lamb.
Mary had a little lamb.
Its fleece was white as snow.

Home, home on the range,
Where the deer and the antelope play.
Where seldom is heard a discouraging word,
And the skies are not cloudy all day.

The old gray mare,
She ain't what she used to be.
Ain't what she used to be.
Ain't what she used to be.
The old gray mare,
She ain't what she used to be
Many long years ago.

The eensy weensy spider
Crawled up the water spout.
Down came the rain
And washed the spider out.
Out came the sun and dried up all the rain,
And the eensy weensy spider
Crawled up the spout again.

Happy birthday to you.
Happy birthday to you.
Happy birthday dear Changer.
Happy birthday to you.

London Bridge is falling down.
Falling down, falling down.
London Bridge is falling down,
My fair lady!

Old MacDonald had a farm,
Ee i ee i oh!
And on his farm he had some chicks.
Ee i ee i oh!
With a cluck-cluck here,
And a cluck-cluck there,
Here a cluck, there a cluck,
Everywhere a cluck-cluck,
Old MacDonald had a farm,
Ee i ee i oh!

Take me out to the ball game.
Take me out with the crowd.
Buy me some peanuts and Crackerjacks.
I don't care if I never get back.
Let me root, root, root for the home team.
If they don't win it's a shame.
For it's one, two, three strikes you're out
At the old ball game!

Yankee Doodle went to London riding on a pony.
Stuck a feather in his hat and called it macaroni.
Yankee Doodle, keep it up.
Yankee Doodle dandy.
Mind the music and the step,
And with the girls be handy.

Original material by Elaine Biech, © 2016 ATD, Association for Talent Development. Used with permission.

CHANGE MANAGEMENT training

Learning Activity 23: Nothing Will Change If You Don't

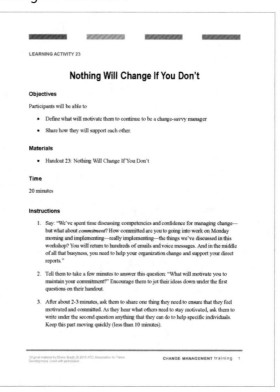

LEARNING ACTIVITY 23

Nothing Will Change If You Don't

Objectives

Participants will be able to

- Define what will motivate them to continue to be a change-savvy manager

- Share how they will support each other.

Materials

- Handout 23: Nothing Will Change If You Don't

Time

20 minutes

Instructions

1. Say: "We've spent time discussing competencies and confidence for managing change—but what about *commitment*? How committed are you to going into work on Monday morning and implementing—really implementing—the things we've discussed in this workshop? You will return to hundreds of emails and voice messages. And in the middle of all that busyness, you need to help your organization change and support your direct reports."

2. Tell them to take a few minutes to answer this question: "What will motivate you to maintain your commitment?" Encourage them to jot their ideas down under the first questions on their handout.

3. After about 2-3 minutes, ask them to share one thing they need to ensure that they feel motivated and committed. As they hear what others need to stay motivated, ask them to write under the second question anything that they can do to help specific individuals. Keep this part moving quickly (less than 10 minutes).

Original material by Elaine Biech, © 2016 ATD, Association for Talent Development. Used with permission.

CHANGE MANAGEMENT training 1

Learning Activity 23: Nothing Will Change If You Don't, *continued*

LEARNING ACTIVITY 23, continued

4. After everyone has shared what will motive them, ask them to stand and go to individuals who they can support. Encourage them to exchange email addresses and phone numbers so that they can stay in touch after the workshop.

5. Bring everyone back for final closing remarks of the workshop.

CHANGE MANAGEMENT training   2

CHANGE MANAGEMENT training

Chapter 12

Assessments

What's in This Chapter

- Three assessments to use as resources in the workshops, as pre-work prior to workshops, or as professional development

- Instructions on how and when to use the assessments

Assessments and evaluations are critical to a workshop—before it begins, as it goes on, and when it concludes. To prepare an appropriate workshop for participants, you have to assess their needs and those of their organization. Although a formal needs assessment is outside the scope of this book, the self-assessment in this chapter can help you identify what participants' current knowledge of the topic may be. This information can help you make course adjustments to fit the needs of the learners and their organization during the workshop.

Using assessments during the workshop helps participants identify areas of strength and weakness, enabling them to capitalize on their strengths and improve their weaknesses to become more effective in the workplace. You may have participants refer back to their self-assessments during the workshop to check in on participants' learning so that both of you can make needed adjustments as you go.

Finally, assessments of the workshop and the facilitator are vital both for the hiring organization and for you as the facilitator. To learn if you met the goals and expectations, you want direct responses from participants. Although negative comments can be tough to read, ultimately they allow you to continually learn and improve your skills as a learning facilitator.

The assessments in this chapter provide instructions on how to complete the assessment and when to use it in the course of the workshop, as well as an explanation of the assessment's purpose.

Assessments Included in *Change Management Training*

Assessment 1: Rate Your Managing Change Skills

Assessment 2: Change Management Training Workshop Evaluation

Assessment 3: Facilitator Competencies

Assessment 1: Rate Your Managing Change Skills

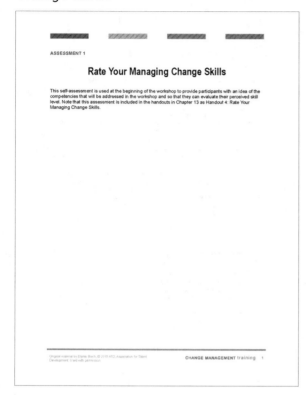

Assessment 1: Rate Your Managing Change Skills, *continued*

Assessment 1: Rate Your Managing Change Skills, *continued*

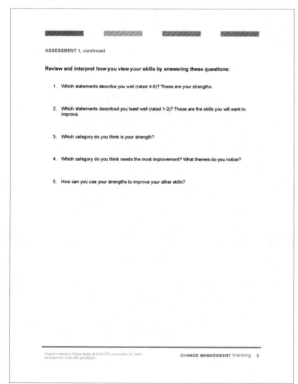

Assessment 2: Change Management Training Workshop Evaluation

Assessment 3: Facilitator Competencies

ASSESSMENT 3

Facilitator Competencies

This assessment instrument will help you as the facilitator manage your professional development and increase the effectiveness of your training sessions. You can use this instrument in the following ways:

Self-assessment. Use the assessment to rate yourself on the five-point scale, which will generate an overall profile and help determine the competency areas that are in the greatest need of improvement.

End-of-course feedback. Honest feedback from the training participants can lessen the possibility that facilitators deceive themselves about the 12 competencies. Participants may not be able to rate the facilitator on all 12, so it may be necessary to ask them to rate only those they consider themselves qualified to address.

Observer feedback. Facilitators may observe each other's training sessions and provide highly useful information on the 12 competencies that are crucial to be effective in conducting training.

Repeat ratings. This assessment can be the basis for tracking professional growth on the competencies needed to be an effective facilitator. The repeat measure may be obtained as often as needed to gauge progress on action plans for improvement.

The Competencies

Facilitators are faced with challenges anytime they lead a training session. Many skills are necessary to help participants meet their learning needs and to ensure that the organization achieves its desired results for the training. This assessment contains a set of 12 important competencies that effective training requires. Not all seasoned facilitators have expertise in all of these competencies, but they may represent learning and growth areas for almost any facilitator.

Here is a detailed explanation of the importance of each of the dozen crucial elements of facilitator competence:

CHANGE MANAGEMENT training   1

Assessment 3: Facilitator Competencies, *continued*

ASSESSMENT 3, continued

Understanding adult learners: Uses knowledge of the principles of adult learning in both designing and delivering training.

Effective facilitators are able to draw on the experiences of the learners in a training session and then give them the applicable content and tools to engage them fully and help them see the value of the learning. It is also important to address the participants' various learning styles and provide them with opportunities to solve problems and think critically so they can work through real business issues and develop additional skills.

Presentation skills: Presents content clearly to achieve the desired outcomes of the training. Encourages learners to generate their own answers through effectively leading group discussions.

Clearly, facilitators must have exceptional presentation skills. The facilitator's ability to present content effectively and in an entertaining way is one of the first things learners notice and is a large part of a successful workshop. The nature of adult learning makes it equally important that the facilitator is not just a talking head but is also adept at initiating, drawing out, guiding, and summarizing information gleaned from large-group discussions during a training session. The facilitator's role is not to feed answers to learners as if they are empty vessels waiting to be filled. Rather, it is the facilitator's primary task to generate learning on the part of the participants through their own process of discovery.

Communication skills: Expresses self well, both verbally and in writing. Understands nonverbal communication and listens effectively.

Beyond presenting information and leading discussions, it is vital for a facilitator to be highly skilled in all aspects of communication. He or she should use language that learners can understand; give clear directions for activities; involve trainees through appropriate humor, anecdotes, and examples; and build on the ideas of others. This will lead to training sessions that are engaging and highly valuable for the participants. Facilitators must also be able to listen well and attend to learners' nonverbal communication to create common meaning and mutual understanding.

CHANGE MANAGEMENT training   2

Assessment 3: Facilitator Competencies, *continued*

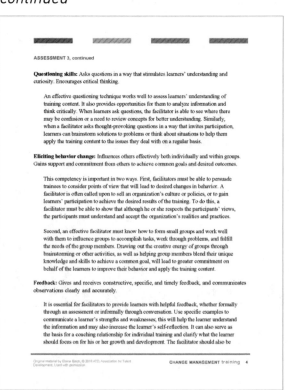

ASSESSMENT 3, continued

Emotional intelligence: Respects learners' viewpoints, knowledge, and experience. Recognizes and responds appropriately to others' feelings, attitudes, and concerns.

Because learners may have many different backgrounds, experience levels, and opinions in the same training sessions, facilitators must be able to handle a variety of situations and conversations well, and be sensitive to others' emotions. They must pay close attention to the dynamics in the room, be flexible enough to make immediate changes to activities during training to meet the needs of learners, and create an open and trusting learning environment. Participants should feel comfortable expressing their opinions, asking questions, and participating in activities without fear of repercussion or disapproval. Monitoring learners' emotions during a training session also helps the facilitator gauge when it may be time to change gears if conflict arises, if discussion needs to be refocused on desired outcomes, or if there is a need to delve deeper into a topic to encourage further learning.

Training methods: Varies instructional approaches to address different learning styles and hold learners' interest.

All learners have preferred learning styles, and one of the keys to effective training facilitation is to use a variety of methods to address them. Some people are more visual (see it) learners, and others are more auditory (hear it) or kinesthetic (do it) learners. An effective facilitator must be familiar with a variety of training methods to tap into each participant's style(s) and maintain interest during the training session. These methods may include such activities as small group activities, individual exercises, case studies, role plays, simulations, and games.

Subject matter expertise: Possesses deep knowledge of training content and applicable experience to draw upon.

Facilitators must have solid background knowledge of the training topic at hand and be able to share related experience to help learners connect theory to real-world scenarios. Anecdotes and other examples to illustrate how the training content relates to participants' circumstances and work can enhance the learning experience and encourage learners to apply the information and also to use the tools they have been given. It is also crucial that facilitators know their topics inside and out, so they can answer the participants' questions and guide them toward problem-solving and skill development.

CHANGE MANAGEMENT training   3

Assessment 3: Facilitator Competencies, *continued*

ASSESSMENT 3, continued

Questioning skills: Asks questions in a way that stimulates learners' understanding and curiosity. Encourages critical thinking.

An effective questioning technique works well to assess learners' understanding of training content. It also provides opportunities for them to analyze information and think critically. When learners ask questions, the facilitator is able to see where there may be confusion or a need to review concepts for better understanding. Similarly, when a facilitator asks thought-provoking questions in a way that invites participation, learners can brainstorm solutions to problems or think about situations to help them apply the training content to the issues they deal with on a regular basis.

Eliciting behavior change: Influences others effectively both individually and within groups. Gains support and commitment from others to achieve common goals and desired outcomes.

This competency is important in two ways. First, facilitators must be able to persuade trainees to consider points of view that will lead to desired changes in behavior. A facilitator is often called upon to sell an organization's culture or policies, or to gain learners' participation to achieve the desired results of the training. To do this, a facilitator must be able to show that although he or she respects the participants' views, the participants must understand and accept the organization's realities and practices.

Second, an effective facilitator must know how to form small groups and work well with them to influence groups to accomplish tasks, work through problems, and fulfill the needs of the group members. Drawing out the creative energy of groups through brainstorming or other activities, as well as helping group members blend their unique knowledge and skills to achieve a common goal, will lead to greater commitment on behalf of the learners to improve their behavior and apply the training content.

Feedback: Gives and receives constructive, specific, and timely feedback, and communicates observations clearly and accurately.

It is essential for facilitators to provide learners with helpful feedback, whether formally through an assessment or informally through conversation. Use specific examples to communicate a learner's strengths and weaknesses; this will help the learner understand the information and may also increase the learner's self-reflection. It can also serve as the basis for a coaching relationship for individual training and clarify what the learner should focus on for his or her growth and development. The facilitator should also be

CHANGE MANAGEMENT training   4

Assessment 3: Facilitator Competencies, *continued*

familiar with a variety of tools to gather feedback from training participants to improve the learning experience and the facilitator's own self-reflection and growth.

Motivation: Encourages learners to participate and achieve desired results. Generates enthusiasm and commitment from others.

It is the training facilitator's responsibility to inspire others to achieve the desired outcomes of a training session and to focus on their goals. Although it is generally believed that motivation comes from within, a skilled facilitator can unleash energy and enthusiasm by creating a vision that inspires the learners. Facilitators can provide meaningful learning activities and infuse fun into the training experience, and they must effectively channel participants' motivation into a commitment to achieving results.

Organizational skills: Works in an orderly and logical way to accomplish tasks. Ensures that work is correct and complete. Presents ideas logically and sequentially for learners to understand.

The importance of this competency for facilitators is twofold. First, the facilitator must have good work habits and pay attention to detail. With any training event, many factors are necessary to ensure a successful experience. Work must be done thoroughly and accurately. A well-organized training facilitator typically creates well-organized, professional training. Second, it is important for facilitators to present ideas in a logical, sequential order that allows learners to absorb new content easily and also to be able to retrieve it quickly. This also increases the probability that the learners will actually use the content. The more organized the facilitator, the better.

Time management: Plans and uses time effectively. Balances important and urgent tasks and can work on multiple tasks simultaneously.

Facilitators do many things in addition to conducting training sessions. They must also budget their time effectively to address other priorities in their work: prepare for the training, keep accurate records, analyze assessment data, design new content or activities, and report to the client organization. The most competent facilitators are able to multitask and keep the goals of the learners and client organization in view as much as possible. Good time management helps a facilitator keep track of all there is to do during any given day.

Assessment 3: Facilitator Competencies, *continued*

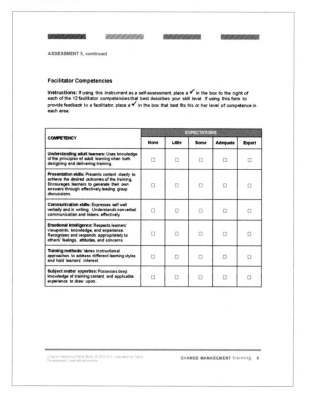

Facilitator Competencies

Instructions: If using this instrument as a self-assessment, place a ✓ in the box to the right of each of the 12 facilitator competencies that best describes your skill level. If using this form to provide feedback to a facilitator, place a ✓ in the box that best fits his or her level of competence in each area.

COMPETENCY	EXPECTATIONS				
	None	Little	Some	Adequate	Expert
Understanding adult learners: Uses knowledge of the principles of adult learning when both designing and delivering training.	☐	☐	☐	☐	☐
Presentation skills: Presents content clearly to achieve the desired outcomes of the training. Encourages learners to generate their own answers through effectively leading group discussions.	☐	☐	☐	☐	☐
Communication skills: Expresses self well verbally and in writing. Understands nonverbal communication and listens effectively.	☐	☐	☐	☐	☐
Emotional intelligence: Respects learners' viewpoints, knowledge, and experience. Recognizes and responds appropriately to others' feelings, attitudes, and concerns.	☐	☐	☐	☐	☐
Training methods: Varies instructional approaches to address different learning styles and hold learners' interest.	☐	☐	☐	☐	☐
Subject matter expertise: Possesses deep knowledge of training content and applicable experience to draw upon.	☐	☐	☐	☐	☐

Assessment 3: Facilitator Competencies, *continued*

COMPETENCY	EXPECTATIONS				
	None	Little	Some	Adequate	Expert
Questioning skills: Asks questions in a way that stimulates learners' understanding and curiosity. Encourages critical thinking.	☐	☐	☐	☐	☐
Eliciting behavior change: Influences others effectively, both individually and within groups. Gains support and commitment from others to achieve common goals and desired outcomes.	☐	☐	☐	☐	☐
Feedback: Gives and receives constructive, specific, and timely feedback and communicates observations clearly and accurately.	☐	☐	☐	☐	☐
Motivation: Encourages learners to participate and achieve desired results. Generates enthusiasm and commitment from others.	☐	☐	☐	☐	☐
Organizational skills: Works in an orderly and logical way to accomplish tasks. Ensures work is correct and complete. Presents ideas logically and sequentially for learners to understand.	☐	☐	☐	☐	☐
Time management: Plans time effectively. Balances important and urgent tasks and can work on multiple tasks simultaneously.	☐	☐	☐	☐	☐

Chapter 13
Handouts

What's in This Chapter

- 29 handouts in thumbnail format for reference
- Refer to Chapter 14 for instructions to download full-size handouts

Handouts comprise the various materials you will provide to the learners throughout the course of the workshop. In some cases, the handouts will simply provide instructions for worksheets to complete, places to take notes, and so forth. In other cases, they will provide important and practical materials for use in and out of the training room, such as reference materials, tip sheets, samples of completed forms, flowcharts, and other useful content. The handouts in this chapter could be printed together and distributed to the participants at the beginning of a workshop or, as suggested in the half-day agenda, given to participants in advance of the workshop.

Note that you will also find several *supplemental* handouts and resources in Chapter 11 with the learning activities. These supplemental handouts are unique in that the participants should *not* have access to them until specified in the activity instructions.

The workshop agendas in Chapters 1-3 and the learning activities in Chapter 11 provide instructions for how and when to use the handouts within the context of the workshop. See Chapter 14 for complete instructions on how to download the workshop support materials.

Handouts Included in *Change Management Training*

Handout 1: Managers Navigate Constant, Complex Change

Handout 2: Change Management Training Objectives

Handout 3: A Manager's Model for Change

Handout 4: Rate Your Managing Change Skills (Assessment 1)

Handout 5: Is Change a Sinking Ship?

Handout 6: It's Time to Change How We Change!

Handout 7a: Ensure the Fundamentals Are in Place

Handout 7b: Fundamental 1: Implement a Common Approach

Handout 7c: Fundamental 2: Communicate a Compelling Story

Handout 7d: Fundamental 3: Confirm Systems and Skills

Handout 7e: Fundamental 4: Involve Others

Handout 8: Determine Organizational Readiness

Handout 9a: Establish a Sense of Urgency

Handout 9b: Deep Dives

Handout 10: Your Communication Plan

Handout 11: Optimize Your Communication Plan With Social Media

Handout 12: Navigate Resistance to Change

Handout 13: Tools to Manage Relationships

Handout 14: Additional Relationship Concerns

Handout 15: Oceans of Respect for Good Role Models

Handout 16: Involve and Engage Others

Handout 17: Full Speed Ahead to Generate Gains

Handout 18: Foster Change-Ready Employees

Handout 19: Institutionalize Changes

Handout 20: Evaluate the Change Results

Handout 21: Build Capacity for Continuous Change

Handout 22: Action Planning: My Next Steps

Handout 23: Nothing Will Change If You Don't

Handout 24: Additional Reading for Your Continued Development

CHANGE MANAGEMENT training

Handout 1: Managers Navigate Constant, Complex Change

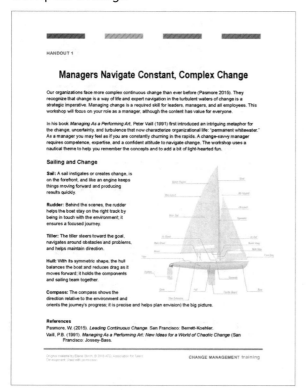

Handout 2: Change Management Training Objectives

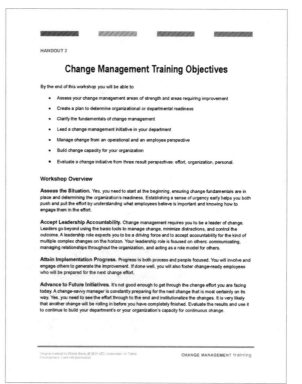

Handout 3: A Manager's Model for Change

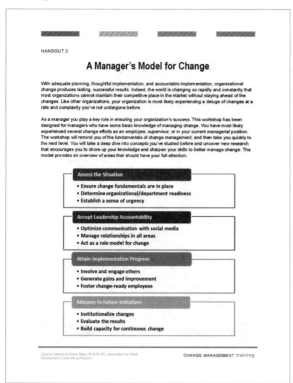

Handout 4: Rate Your Managing Change Skills (Assessment 1)

Handout 4: Rate Your Managing Change Skills (Assessment 1), *continued*

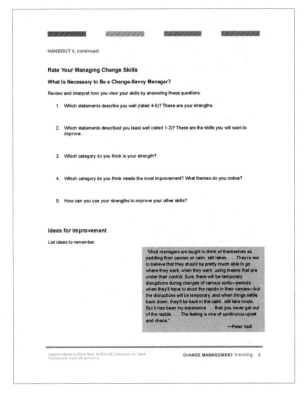

Handout 5: Is Change a Sinking Ship?

Handout 6: It's Time to Change How We Change!

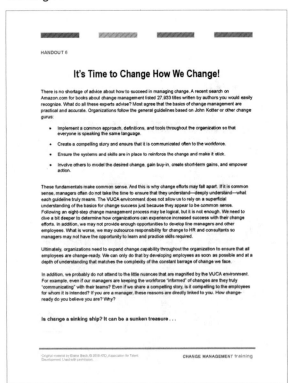

Handout 7a: Ensure the Fundamentals Are in Place

Handout 7b: Fundamental 1: Implement a Common Approach

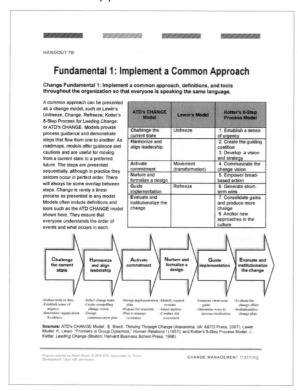

Handout 7c: Fundamental 2: Communicate a Compelling Story

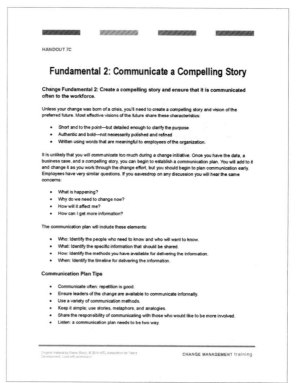

Handout 7d: Fundamental 3: Confirm Systems and Skills

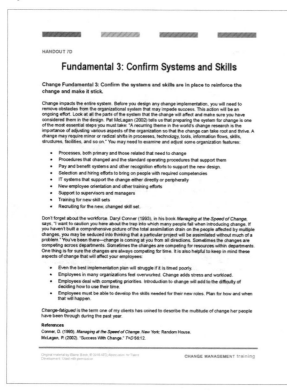

Handout 7e: Fundamental 4: Involve Others

Handout 8: Determine Organizational Readiness

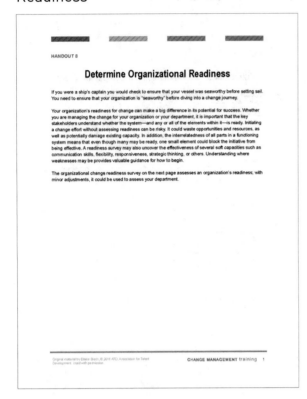

Handout 8: Determine Organizational Readiness, *continued*

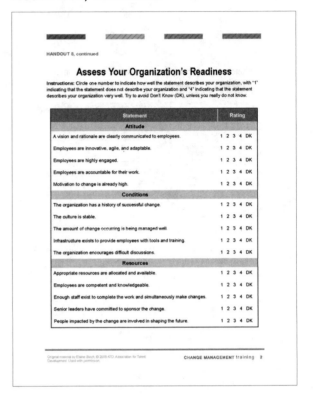

Handout 9a: Establish a Sense of Urgency

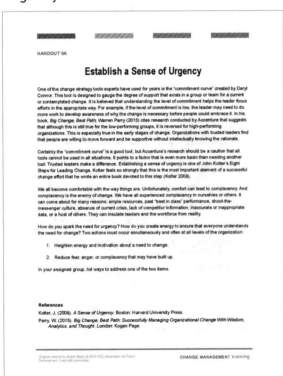

Handout 9b: Deep Dives

Handout 10: Your Communication Plan

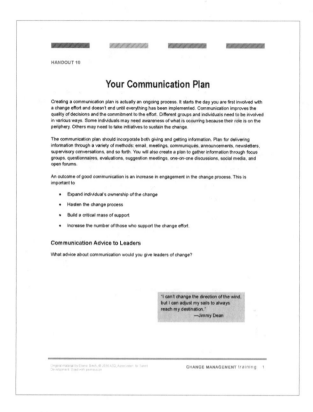

Handout 10: Your Communication Plan, *continued*

Handout 11: Optimize Your Communication Plan With Social Media

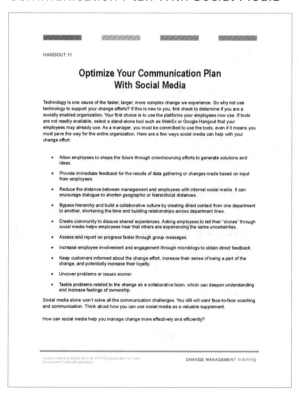

Handout 12: Navigate Resistance to Change

Handout 12: Navigate Resistance to Change, *continued*

Three Levels of Resistance

Rick Maurer (2010), the author of *Beyond the Wall of Resistance*, believes that you can identify resistance at three levels and then treat it appropriately. Level 1 is based on information such as a lack of information, disagreement with the idea, lack of exposure, or confusion. Level 2 is physiological and emotional and may come from fear of a perceived loss of power or control, loss of status or respect, feeling of too much to do, or feeling incompetent. Level 3 may come from a personal history of mistrust; cultural, ethnic, or gender differences; or a values clash.

Resistance is natural. It will occur. It is different for each individual. Think of an example of resistance. Examine it from all perceptions. Does the resistor need to know "what's in it for me"? Need clarity? Need you to acknowledge the concern was heard? Need to share important information? Need to feel a part of the change?

Is Resistance a Life Raft?

It is quite possible that the resistance is not aimed at the change effort at all. Employees feel overwhelmed on the job, frustrated that they can't keep up with their workload, stressed out, and disillusioned with the world of work. They feel as if they are drowning in work and can't handle anymore. Could their resistance simply signal a need for a life raft?

How can you help your employees stay afloat by helping them embrace change?

What reactions do you expect and what will your employee(s) need?

Will it be based more on emotions, information, or personal perspective?

What form do you think the resistance will take (stonewalling, emotional, apathy, defensiveness, minimizing, obstructing, avoiding, resisting)?

What can you do to help your employees embrace change and to realize their full potential?

Reference
Maurer, R. (2010). *Beyond the Wall of Resistance: Why 70% of All Changes Still Fail—and What You Can Do About It*. Austin, TX: Bard Press.

Handout 13: Tools to Manage Relationships

Tools to Manage Relationships

If resistance concerns you, there are two tools you can use to help or perhaps even eliminate resistance: 1) Holding On and Letting Go, and 2) Force Field Analysis.

Holding On and Letting Go is a simple 2' x 2' grid that can be used with your employees in a group or alone, with you leading it or as a personal introspection tool. It provides a method for employees to explore the advantages and disadvantages of holding on or letting go of something that seems important to them.

Kurt Lewin is credited for designing the Force Field Analysis tool. He viewed situations as being affected by "a sea of forces in motion." Some of these forces are positive and desirable, whereas others are negative and undesirable. These forces are in constant motion and produce stability, or in Lewin's words, "quasi-stationary equilibrium." Force Field Analysis is a useful tool to help identify the forces at work to produce stability or the status quo. Imagine that the center line is the status quo. Various forces impact the status quo pushing from opposite sides to hold it firmly in place. If the driving forces are favorable to the intended change and the restraining forces are those that prevent change, the key is to identify both kinds of forces, strengthen the driving forces, and weaken the restraining forces.

Holding On and Letting Go

Issue: _____

	Holding On	Letting Go
Advantages		
Disadvantages		

Handout 13: Tools to Manage Relationships, *continued*

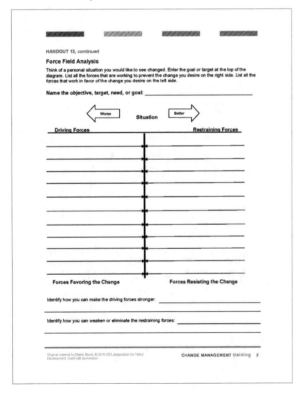

Force Field Analysis

Think of a personal situation you would like to see changed. Enter the goal or target at the top of the diagram. List all the forces that are working to prevent the change you desire on the right side. List all the forces that work in favor of the change you desire on the left side.

Name the objective, target, need, or goal: _____

⟵ Worse   **Situation**   Better ⟶

Driving Forces   **Restraining Forces**

Forces Favoring the Change   Forces Resisting the Change

Identify how you can make the driving forces stronger: _____

Identify how you can weaken or eliminate the restraining forces: _____

Handout 14: Additional Relationship Concerns

Additional Relationship Concerns

Even though we can predict human reactions with some degree of accuracy, an effort as big and complex as change cannot be addressed with a one-size-fits-all strategy. Change is personal, and resistance to change is usually an attempt to maintain the status quo. Resistance can slow or stop the organization's transition to the preferred future. As you manage change, acknowledge the inevitability of resistance and develop a plan for dealing with it. In her book *Thriving Through Change*, Biech (2007) shares the following list of practical suggestions that are appropriate for all levels in the organization:

- Identify specific reasons for resistance and act upon what you learn. It may be a misunderstanding, a fear of loss, a lack of trust, or a concern for having the skills to do what is required. Take corrective action as soon as possible.
- Ensure that everyone understands the proposed changes and that there are no misunderstandings about what or why the organization is engaged in this effort.
- Always be candid about the possible adverse effects of change.
- Create forums for open, honest, two-way communication. Listen to the feedback and act on it immediately when required.
- Provide development opportunities for your employees to learn more about planning, implementing, and monitoring change. Some may not have been through a change effort before and may not appreciate the need to communicate, address resistance, and gain commitment.
- Provide opportunities to celebrate and reward small successes and those who are responsible. This sends a powerful message that the change is important and those who have helped are valuable.
- Do not assume that everyone is on board. You may not have uncovered the strongest resistors.
- Focus on the problem, not the person.
- Consider providing stress management training to assist individuals to cope.
- Help employees say "good-byes" so they can say "good hellos." It is important to accept the discouragement or sadness that employees may be feeling. Use a ritual or ceremony even if it is as simple as telling stories about the past and acknowledging how important it was.
- Recognize that "survivors" in a downsizing may feel guilty, distrustful, or depressed.
- Offer training and education to anyone facing tasks that they have not done in the past. Training reduces stress by increasing self-confidence.
- Create many opportunities for involvement and don't turn anyone down. People advocate what they create.

Reference
Biech, E. (2007). *Thriving Through Change: A Leader's Practical Guide to Change Mastery*. Alexandria, VA: ASTD Press.

Handout 15: Oceans of Respect for Good Role Models

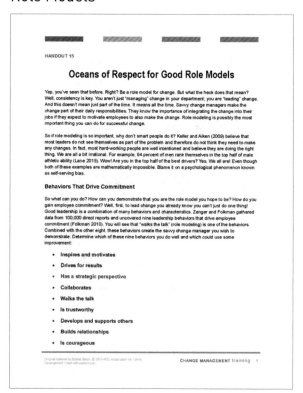

HANDOUT 15

Oceans of Respect for Good Role Models

Yep, you've seen that before. Right? Be a role model for change. But what the heck does that mean? Well, consistency is key. You aren't just "managing" change in your department; you are "leading" change. And this doesn't mean just part of the time. It means all the time. Savvy change managers make the change part of their daily responsibilities. They know the importance of integrating the change into their jobs if they expect to motivate employees to also make the change. Role modeling is possibly the most important thing you can do for successful change.

So if role modeling is so important, why don't smart people do it? Keller and Aiken (2009) believe that most leaders do not see themselves as part of the problem and therefore do not think they need to make any changes. In fact, most hard-working people are well intentioned and believe they are doing the right thing. We are all a bit irrational. For example, 94 percent of men rank themselves in the top half of male athletic ability (Lane 2015). Wow! Are you in the top half of the best drivers? Yes. We all are! Even though both of these examples are mathematically impossible. Blame it on a psychological phenomenon known as self-serving bias.

Behaviors That Drive Commitment

So what can you do? How can you demonstrate that you are the role model you hope to be? How do you gain employee commitment? Well, first, to lead change you already know you can't just do one thing! Good leadership is a combination of many behaviors and characteristics. Zenger and Folkman gathered data from 100,000 direct reports and uncovered nine leadership behaviors that drive employee commitment (Folkman 2010). You will see that "walks the talk" (role modeling) is one of the behaviors. Combined with the other eight, these behaviors create the savvy change manager you wish to demonstrate. Determine which of these nine behaviors you do well and which could use some improvement:

- Inspires and motivates
- Drives for results
- Has a strategic perspective
- Collaborates
- Walks the talk
- Is trustworthy
- Develops and supports others
- Builds relationships
- Is courageous

CHANGE MANAGEMENT training 1

Handout 15: Oceans of Respect for Good Role Models, *continued*

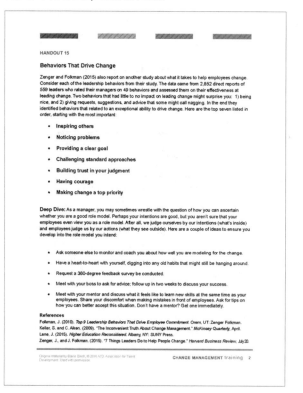

HANDOUT 15

Behaviors That Drive Change

Zenger and Folkman (2015) also report on another study about what it takes to help employees change. Consider each of the leadership behaviors from their study. The data came from 2,852 direct reports of 559 leaders who rated their managers on 49 behaviors and assessed them on their effectiveness at leading change. Two behaviors that had little to no impact on leading change might surprise you: 1) being nice, and 2) giving requests, suggestions, and advice that some might call nagging. In the end they identified behaviors that related to an exceptional ability to drive change. Here are the top seven listed in order, starting with the most important:

- Inspiring others
- Noticing problems
- Providing a clear goal
- Challenging standard approaches
- Building trust in your judgment
- Having courage
- Making change a top priority

Deep Dive: As a manager, you may sometimes wrestle with the question of how you can ascertain whether you are a good role model. Perhaps your intentions are good, but you aren't sure that your employees even view you as a role model. After all, we judge ourselves by our intentions (what's inside) and employees judge us by our actions (what they see outside). Here are a couple of ideas to ensure you develop into the role model you intend:

- Ask someone else to monitor and coach you about how well you are modeling for the change.
- Have a heart-to-heart with yourself, digging into any old habits that might still be hanging around.
- Request a 360-degree feedback survey be conducted.
- Meet with your boss to ask for advice; follow up in two weeks to discuss your success.
- Meet with your mentor and discuss what it feels like to learn new skills at the same time as your employees. Share your discomfort when making mistakes in front of employees. Ask for tips on how you can better accept this situation. Don't have a mentor? Get one immediately.

References
Folkman, J. (2010). *Top 9 Leadership Behaviors That Drive Employee Commitment.* Orem, UT: Zenger Folkman.
Keller, S. and C. Aiken. (2009). "The Inconvenient Truth About Change Management." *McKinsey Quarterly,* April.
Lane, J. (2015). *Higher Education Reconsidered.* Albany, NY: SUNY Press.
Zenger, J., and J. Folkman. (2015). "7 Things Leaders Do to Help People Change." *Harvard Business Review,* July 20.

CHANGE MANAGEMENT training 2

Handout 16: Involve and Engage Others

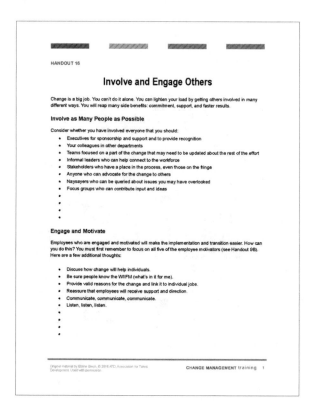

HANDOUT 16

Involve and Engage Others

Change is a big job. You can't do it alone. You can lighten your load by getting others involved in many different ways. You will reap many side benefits: commitment, support, and faster results.

Involve as Many People as Possible

Consider whether you have involved everyone that you should:
- Executives for sponsorship and support and to provide recognition
- Your colleagues in other departments
- Teams focused on a part of the change that may need to be updated about the rest of the effort
- Informal leaders who can help connect to the workforce
- Stakeholders who have a place in the process, even those on the fringe
- Anyone who can advocate for the change to others
- Naysayers who can be queried about issues you may have overlooked
- Focus groups who can contribute input and ideas
-
-
-

Engage and Motivate

Employees who are engaged and motivated will make the implementation and transition easier. How can you do this? You must first remember to focus on all five of the employee motivators (see Handout 9B). Here are a few additional thoughts:

- Discuss how change will help individuals.
- Be sure people know the WIIFM (what's in it for me).
- Provide valid reasons for the change and link it to individual jobs.
- Reassure that employees will receive support and direction.
- Communicate, communicate, communicate.
- Listen, listen, listen.
-
-
-
-

CHANGE MANAGEMENT training 1

Handout 16: Involve and Engage Others, *continued*

HANDOUT 16, continued

Develop Teams

Whether you call them guiding teams, improvement teams, transition teams, change teams, or implementation teams, teams are good! They provide great ideas to the process and give employees a way to be involved. Even more important, teams are a way to help develop your employees. Consider these tips for team success:

- Select the right people with the right skills and the right attitude.
- Use a facilitator to ensure efficiency and increases effectiveness.
- Create a charter for guidance that defines the purpose, boundaries, timeline, and role of the team.
- Encourage frank discussion at all meetings.
- Invite the change leader (CEO, president) to attend the first meeting to define the vision and answer any questions.
- Build strong relationships among the members; use a team-building expert if necessary.
- Make decisions by consensus as much as possible.
-
-
-

> "Change is disturbing when it is done to us, exhilarating when it is done by us."
> —Rosabeth Moss Kanter

CHANGE MANAGEMENT training 2

Handout 17: Full Speed Ahead to Generate Gains

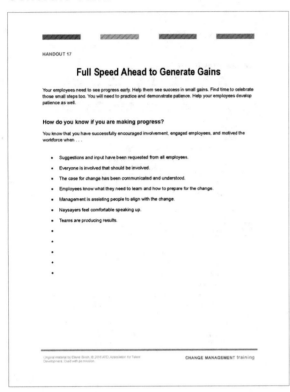

Full Speed Ahead to Generate Gains

Your employees need to see progress early. Help them see success in small gains. Find time to celebrate those small steps too. You will need to practice and demonstrate patience. Help your employees develop patience as well.

How do you know if you are making progress?

You know that you have successfully encouraged involvement, engaged employees, and motived the workforce when . . .

- Suggestions and input have been requested from all employees.
- Everyone is involved that should be involved.
- The case for change has been communicated and understood.
- Employees know what they need to learn and how to prepare for the change.
- Management is assisting people to align with the change.
- Naysayers feel comfortable speaking up.
- Teams are producing results.
-
-
-
-

Original material by Elaine Biech, © 2016 ATD, Association for Talent Development. Used with permission.

CHANGE MANAGEMENT training

Handout 18: Foster Change-Ready Employees

Foster Change-Ready Employees

Give your employees a gift; help them learn to adapt, appreciate, and embrace the new reality of constant, complex change in today's VUCA world. Today's organizations need to change often in order to survive. The workforce needs to have the skills to deal with the changes that will transform their organizations. Organizational survival is at stake, and the workforce needs to be ready for the change.

What Skills and Messages Do Employees Require?

Employees are more likely to support changes when they are involved. In addition, employees must believe that their organization and managers will provide support for change in the form of resources and information. They require information about the cost benefit of any change. And finally the employee must understand the reason for changes and the vision for the future.

Open communication, corporate transparency, and trust have a tremendous impact on people's acceptance of and willingness to support corporate change and change themselves. If you can start building a positive and supportive environment prior to the change, you will have a head start on the change implementation.

Also help your employees cope with their feelings and attitude toward change. Having change-ready employees is not just about them having certain skills, knowledge, and behaviors. You also want to win their thoughts, feelings, and beliefs. Ignoring the underlying mindsets of employees leads you to address the symptoms rather than the root cause. If you are skeptical about the value of employees' mindsets, might I remind you of the Roger Bannister story. Prior to 1954 the four-minute mile was considered impossible. Once the mindset, along with the four-minute mile, was broken it left no barriers for others. We are talking about the same mindset in your employees. Employees with a can-do attitude are essential to organizational change success.

It's also important to help your employees understand how they can personally cope with the changing business world. Changes create a need for them to be adaptive. An organization can help employees understand that changes are not just about operational procedures but also about personal adaptation. Providing them with the skills to be resilient will be welcomed when the time comes that it is needed. Don't wait to get your employees involved in learning more about organizational change. Your employees must be prepared and ready to keep up with the speed of change in your organization. The sooner they become a part of your change-ready department the better!

Original material by Elaine Biech, © 2016 ATD, Association for Talent Development. Used with permission.

CHANGE MANAGEMENT training 1

Handout 18: Foster Change-Ready Employees, *continued*

Develop Employees

Developing employees to be change ready should start before (if possible) a major change initiative. It might begin with a formal training event where employees learn about the organization's change process, tools, and how to be involved. Follow this with fieldwork that links the content directly to the employees' jobs and requires them to put into practice new mindsets and skills back on the job. Employees' supervisors might be involved to coach, correct, and reinforce. Employees might have one-on-one sessions with their supervisors to learn how they can use what they learned on the job. Supervisors can recommend resources that employees could read or suggest they visit their internal customers to discuss a recent success.

Developing employees includes a coaching plan that is active during and after any change effort. The coaching plan teaches employees skills and provides instruction for using change management tools. During the change, employees should have opportunities to participate in a change team to practice their skills.

The condition of a sailboat and its gear is important—especially in a race. If the hull is not smooth, it creates drag in the water, slowing the boat speed. If the sails are old and stretched out, they do not generate as much lift, and you don't go as fast. If the rigging is in the wrong place, the crew loses efficiency while maneuvering, and the boat loses the race. Our businesses are also in a race—a race to beat the competition. Develop your employees so that they can keep up with changes and make efficient and effective contributions. They need to have the most current skills—knowing what to do, when to do it, and where to do it. Ensuring you have change-ready employees will help your organization stay in the race.

> "You can't stop the waves, but you can learn to surf."
> —Jon Kabat-Zinn

Original material by Elaine Biech, © 2016 ATD, Association for Talent Development. Used with permission.

CHANGE MANAGEMENT training 2

Handout 19: Institutionalize Changes

Institutionalize Changes

John Kotter calls this step "anchoring new approaches in the culture." Many experts in the field of change assert that new approaches are fragile and subject to regression until the changes have a stronghold on the organization's culture. Leaders must make a conscious effort to demonstrate how the changes have improved corporate performance. Behaviors may revert back, former processes may creep back in, and old familiar relationships may take over. Geoff Bellman (2000), in *The Beauty of the Beast*, states that we have "spent years preparing not to change." He suggests that creating dialogue around some of these issues is a good way to create awareness and head off regression.

After going through all that you have to do to manage change, you will want to ensure the change sticks and becomes a part of the way you do business. What can you do to ensure that the changes will last and become a part of the culture? John Kotter suggests that it isn't over until the change has roots. And it actually goes beyond roots. Who hasn't planted trees that had perfectly good roots. Without constant care for quite some time the tree will wither and die. Like a tree, you will want to keep the roots growing and healthy. That means constant attention over time—in some instances years. Remember, people are very good about creating workarounds to stall change!

Find Roots for Your Change Implementation

These ideas will help ensure that your change effort continues to grow and become a part of the culture:

- Keep everyone involved in the process.
- Continue to discuss the effort.
- Report on successes—large and small.
- Share and save success stories.
- Reward those who achieved success.
- Remove old ways so that employees have no choice.
- Continue to discuss the benefits of the change.
- Continue to use a communication plan.
- Find new ways to celebrate successes.
- Establish red flags for regressive behavior.
- Articulate the connections between new behaviors and organizational success.
- Ask people for their ideas for refining what has been done, or for ideas about new interventions.
- Use the credibility and success of this effort to address other processes, procedures, roles, and other parts of the organization that do not align with the vision.
- Adjust procedures, pay/benefit systems, or other recognition efforts to support the new design.
- Implement a monitoring plan and assign someone the responsibility to report on it regularly.
- Establish a follow-up plan that focuses on key transition areas.
- Let people go who do not comply.

Reference: Bellman, G. (2000). *The Beauty of the Beast: Breathing New Life Into Organizations.* San Francisco: Berrett-Koehler.

Original material by Elaine Biech, © 2016 ATD, Association for Talent Development. Used with permission.

CHANGE MANAGEMENT training

CHANGE MANAGEMENT training

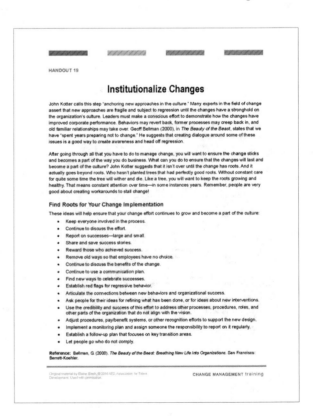

Handout 20: Evaluate the Change Results

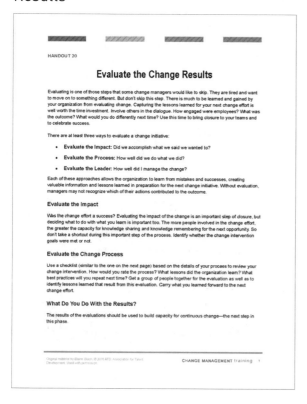

Handout 20: Evaluate the Change Results, *continued*

HANDOUT 20, continued

Evaluate the Change Process

Event or Action	Partially Successful	Successful	Completely Successful
A solid rationale for change was provided.			
Costs were predicted and an adequate ROI was determined.			
The leaders of the change were willing volunteers.			
A shared vision was created.			
Commitment to change was created.			
Everyone who wanted to be involved had an opportunity.			
The right people were selected for the teams.			
A comprehensive implementation plan for the change was prepared.			
The change focused on results not activities.			
Changes were completed with a minimum of interruption to the workforce.			
Customers experienced no interruption of services.			
Employees received training, development, and coaching as needed.			
The change can be linked directly to the organizational strategic plan.			
Monitoring and adjusting occurred in response to problems in the process.			
Progress was tracked and published.			
Clear success metrics were identified.			
Change has been institutionalized with formal policies, systems, and structures.			
Top management is committed to continued success of the change.			
Employees are pleased with the results.			

Source: ebb associates Inc.

Handout 20: Evaluate the Change Results, *continued*

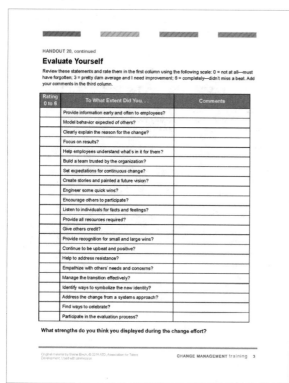

Handout 21: Build Capacity for Continuous Change

HANDOUT 21

Build Capacity for Continuous Change

Your ultimate goal should be to ensure that your organization has the capacity for making changes in the future. Change will occur. Ensuring that the organization has the strategies, systems, and processes in place to address them efficiently and effectively will be critical. The days of one big change at a time will never return. Ensure that your organization has plans in place so the workforce can manage numerous change initiatives simultaneously.

Ensure Operational Mechanisms Are in Place

In his book, *Big Change, Best Path*, Warren Parry (2015) identifies 10 business drivers that make an organization "change smart." The top four are business leadership, systems and processes, vision and direction, and passion and drive. Create a capacity for change that has these operational mechanisms in place:

- A budget for change
- A budget to develop change-ready employees
- Investment for continuous learning about competitors and changes in the industry
- A plan for developing all employees
- A solid communication plan that is fast and factual
- Change processes that everyone understands and uses
- A clearly defined vision
- Defined skills your organization requires 10 years from now.

Create a Successful Culture of Change

You must also drive a sense of urgency into the culture. A successful change culture accomplishes the following:

- Rewards innovation and risk taking
- Expects managers to be mentors and coaches
- Builds leader commitment and alignment
- Allows people to learn from their mistakes
- Removes barriers to change and fighting for resources
- Ensures people know that leaders/managers trust them
- Focuses on the credibility and visibility of leaders
- Is agile, flexible, and quick to decide
- Engages employees at all levels to participate and make decisions
- Develops employees at all levels to ensure they are ready for their next jobs
- Builds leaders' capacity to lead change
- Encourages peer sharing and peer support
- Builds trust and support across department lines and hierarchies
- Makes change everyone's responsibility
- Addresses leaders mindsets, styles, and behavior.

Reference

Parry, W. (2015). *Big Change, Best Path: Successfully Managing Organizational Change with Wisdom, Analytics, and Insight.* London: Kogan Page.

CHANGE MANAGEMENT training

Handout 22: Action Planning: My Next Steps

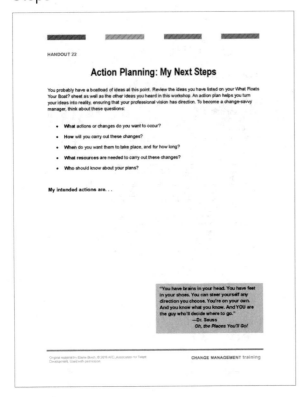

Action Planning: My Next Steps

You probably have a boatload of ideas at this point. Review the ideas you have listed on your What Floats Your Boat? sheet as well as the other ideas you heard in this workshop. An action plan helps you turn your ideas into reality, ensuring that your professional vision has direction. To become a change-savvy manager, think about these questions:

- What actions or changes do you want to occur?
- How will you carry out these changes?
- When do you want them to take place, and for how long?
- What resources are needed to carry out these changes?
- Who should know about your plans?

My intended actions are. . .

> "You have brains in your head. You have feet in your shoes. You can steer yourself any direction you choose. You're on your own. And you know what you know. And YOU are the guy who'll decide where to go."
> —Dr. Seuss
> *Oh, the Places You'll Go!*

Original material by Elaine Biech, © 2016 ATD, Association for Talent Development. Used with permission.   **CHANGE MANAGEMENT** training

Handout 23: Nothing Will Change If You Don't

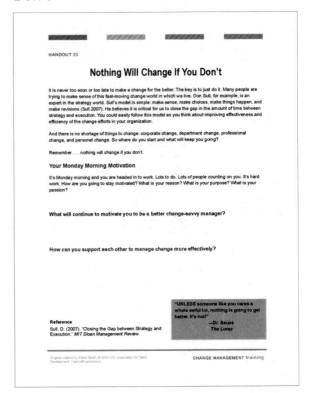

Nothing Will Change If You Don't

It is never too soon or too late to make a change for the better. The key is to just do it. Many people are trying to make sense of this fast-moving change world in which we live. Don Sull, for example, is an expert in the strategy world. Sull's model is simple: make sense, make choices, make things happen, and make revisions (Sull 2007). He believes it is critical for us to close the gap in the amount of time between strategy and execution. You could easily follow this model as you think about improving effectiveness and efficiency of the change efforts in your organization.

And there is no shortage of things to change: corporate change, department change, professional change, and personal change. So where do you start and what will keep you going?

Remember . . . nothing will change if you don't.

Your Monday Morning Motivation

It's Monday morning and you are headed in to work. Lots to do. Lots of people counting on you. It's hard work. How are you going to stay motivated? What is your reason? What is your purpose? What is your passion?

What will continue to motivate you to be a better change-savvy manager?

How can you support each other to manage change more effectively?

> "UNLESS someone like you cares a whole awful lot, nothing is going to get better. It's not!"
> —Dr. Seuss
> *The Lorax*

Reference
Sull, D. (2007). "Closing the Gap between Strategy and Execution." *MIT Sloan Management Review*.

Original material by Elaine Biech, © 2016 ATD, Association for Talent Development. Used with permission.   **CHANGE MANAGEMENT** training

Handout 24: Additional Reading for Your Continued Development

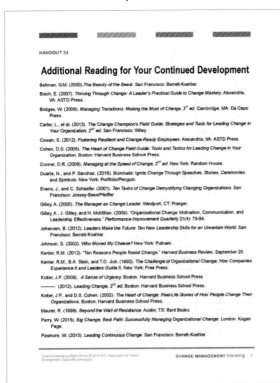

Additional Reading for Your Continued Development

Bellman, G.M. (2000). *The Beauty of the Beast*. San Francisco: Berrett-Koehler.

Biech, E. (2007). *Thriving Through Change: A Leader's Practical Guide to Change Mastery*. Alexandria, VA: ASTD Press.

Bridges, W. (2009). *Managing Transitions: Making the Most of Change*, 3rd ed. Cambridge, MA: Da Capo Press.

Carter, L., et al. (2013). *The Change Champion's Field Guide: Strategies and Tools for Leading Change in Your Organization*, 2nd ed. San Francisco: Wiley.

Cowan, S. (2012). *Fostering Resilient and Change-Ready Employees*. Alexandria, VA: ASTD Press.

Cohen, D.S. (2005). *The Heart of Change Field Guide: Tools and Tactics for Leading Change in Your Organization*. Boston: Harvard Business School Press.

Conner, D.R. (2006). *Managing at the Speed of Change*, 2nd ed. New York: Random House.

Duarte, N., and P. Sanchez. (2016). *Illuminate: Ignite Change Through Speeches, Stories, Ceremonies, and Symbols*. New York: Portfolio/Penguin.

Evans, J., and C. Schaefer. (2001). *Ten Tasks of Change Demystifying Changing Organizations*. San Francisco: Jossey-Bass/Pfeiffer.

Gilley, A. (2005). *The Manager as Change Leader*. Westport, CT: Praeger.

Gilley, A., J. Gilley, and H. McMillan. (2009). "Organizational Change: Motivation, Communication, and Leadership Effectiveness." *Performance Improvement Quarterly* 21(4): 75-94.

Johansen, B. (2012). *Leaders Make the Future: Ten New Leadership Skills for an Uncertain World*. San Francisco: Berrett-Koehler.

Johnson, S. (2002). *Who Moved My Cheese?* New York: Putnam.

Kanter, R.M. (2012). "Ten Reasons People Resist Change." *Harvard Business Review*, September 25.

Kanter, R.M., B.A. Stein, and T.D. Jick. (1992). *The Challenge of Organizational Change: How Companies Experience It and Leaders Guide It*. New York: Free Press.

Kotter, J.P. (2008). *A Sense of Urgency*. Boston: Harvard Business School Press.

——— . (2012). *Leading Change*, 2nd ed. Boston: Harvard Business School Press.

Kotter, J.P., and D.S. Cohen. (2002). *The Heart of Change: Real-Life Stories of How People Change Their Organizations*. Boston: Harvard Business School Press.

Maurer, R. (1996). *Beyond the Wall of Resistance*. Austin, TX: Bard Books.

Parry, W. (2015). *Big Change, Best Path: Successfully Managing Organizational Change*. London: Kogan Page.

Pasmore, W. (2015). *Leading Continuous Change*. San Francisco: Berrett-Koehler.

Original material by Elaine Biech, © 2016 ATD, Association for Talent Development. Used with permission.   **CHANGE MANAGEMENT** training   1

Handout 24: Additional Reading for Your Continued Development, *continued*

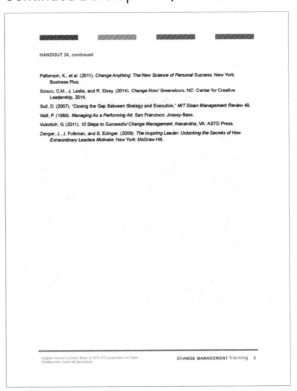

Patterson, K., et al. (2011). *Change Anything: The New Science of Personal Success*. New York: Business Plus.

Scisco, C.M., J. Leslie, and R. Elsey. (2014). *Change Now!* Greensboro, NC: Center for Creative Leadership, 2014.

Sull, D. (2007). "Closing the Gap Between Strategy and Execution." *MIT Sloan Management Review* 48.

Vaill, P. (1989). *Managing As a Performing Art*. San Francisco: Jossey-Bass.

Vukotich, G. (2011). *10 Steps to Successful Change Management*. Alexandria, VA: ASTD Press.

Zenger, J., J. Folkman, and S. Edinger. (2009). *The Inspiring Leader: Unlocking the Secrets of How Extraordinary Leaders Motivate*. New York: McGraw Hill.

Original material by Elaine Biech, © 2016 ATD, Association for Talent Development. Used with permission.   **CHANGE MANAGEMENT** training   2

Chapter 14

Online Supporting Documents and Downloads

What's in This Chapter

- Instructions to access supporting materials

- Options for using tools and downloads

- Licensing and copyright information for workshop programs

- Tips for working with the downloaded files

The ATD Workshop Series is designed to give you flexible options for many levels of training facilitation and topic expertise. As you prepare your program, you will want to incorporate many of the handouts, assessments, presentation slides, and other training tools provided as supplementary materials with this volume. We wish you the best of luck in delivering your training workshops. It is exciting work that ultimately can change lives.

Access to Free Supporting Materials

To get started, visit the ATD Workshop Series page: www.td.org/workshopbooks. This page includes links to download all the free supporting materials that accompany this book, as well as up-to-date information about additions to the series and new program offerings.

These downloads, which are included in the price of the book, feature ready-to-use learning activities, handouts, assessments, and presentation slide files in PDF format. Use these files to deliver your workshop program and as a resource to help you prepare your own materials. You may download and use any of these files as part of your training delivery for the workshops, provided no changes are made to the original materials. To access this material, you will be asked to log into the ATD website. If you are not an ATD member, you will have to create an ATD account.

If you choose to re-create these documents, they can only be used within your organization; they cannot be presented or sold as your original work. Please note that all materials included in the book are copyrighted and you are using them with permission of ATD and/or the author. If you choose to re-create the materials, per copyright usage requirements, you must provide attribution to the original source of the content and display a copyright notice as follows:

© 2016 Elaine Biech. Adapted and used with permission.

Customizable Materials

You can also choose to customize this supporting content for an additional licensing fee. This option gives you access to a downloadable zip file with the entire collection of supporting materials in Microsoft Word and PowerPoint file formats. Once purchased, you will have indefinite and unlimited access to these materials through the My Downloads section of your ATD account. Then, you will be able to customize and personalize all the documents and presentations using Microsoft Word and PowerPoint. You can add your own content, change the order or format, include your company logo, or make any other customization.

Please note that all the original documents contain attribution to ATD and/or and this book as the original source for the material. As you customize the documents, remember to keep these attributions intact (see the copyright notice above). By doing so, you are practicing professional courtesy by respecting the intellectual property rights of another trainer (the author) and modeling respect for copyright and intellectual property laws for your program participants.

ATD offers two custom material license options: *Internal Use* and *Client Use*. To determine which license option you need to purchase, ask yourself the following question:

Will I or my employer be charging a person or outside organization a fee for providing services or for delivering training that includes any ATD Workshop content that I wish to customize?

If the answer is yes, then you need to purchase a *Client Use* license.

If the answer is no, and you plan to customize ATD Workshop content to deliver training at no cost to employees within your own department or company only, you need to purchase the *Internal Use* license.

Working With the Files

PDF Documents

To read or print the PDF files you download, you must have PDF reader software such as Adobe Acrobat Reader installed on your system. The program can be downloaded free of cost from the Adobe website: www.adobe.com. To print documents, simply use the PDF reader to open the downloaded files and print as many copies as you need.

PowerPoint Slides

To use or adapt the contents of the PowerPoint presentation files (available with the Internal Use and Client Use licenses), you must have Microsoft PowerPoint software installed on your system. If you simply want to view the PowerPoint documents, you only need an appropriate viewer on your system. Microsoft provides various viewers at www.microsoft.com for free download.

Once you have downloaded the files to your computer system, use Microsoft PowerPoint (or free viewer) to print as many copies of the presentation slides as you need. You can also make handouts of the presentations by choosing the "print three slides per page" option on the print menu.

You can modify or otherwise customize the slides by opening and editing them in Microsoft PowerPoint. However, you must retain the credit line denoting the original source of the material, as noted earlier in this chapter. It is illegal to present this content as your own work. The files will open as read-only files, so before you adapt them you will need to save them onto your hard drive. Further use of the images in the slides for any purpose other than presentation for these workshops is strictly prohibited by law.

The PowerPoint slides included in this volume support the three workshop agendas:

- Two-Day Workshop
- One-Day Workshop
- Half-Day Workshop.

For PowerPoint slides to successfully support and augment your learning program, it is essential that you practice giving presentations with the slides *before* using them in live training situations. You should be confident that you can logically expand on the points featured in the presentations and discuss the methods for working through them. If you want to fully engage your participants, become familiar with this technology before you use it. See the sidebar that follows for a cheat sheet to help you navigate through the presentation. A good practice is to insert comments into PowerPoint's notes feature, which you can print out and use when you present the slides. The workshop agendas in this book show thumbnails of each slide to help you keep your place as you deliver the workshop.

NAVIGATING THROUGH A POWERPOINT PRESENTATION	
Key	**PowerPoint "Show" Action**
Space bar or Enter or Mouse click	Advance through custom animations embedded in the presentation
Backspace	Back up to the last projected element of the presentation
Escape	Abort the presentation
B or b	Blank the screen to black
B or b (repeat)	Resume the presentation
W or w	Blank the screen to white
W or w (repeat)	Resume the presentation

Acknowledgments

This book allowed me to continue to develop my own talents. It draws upon what I've learned from my clients, my ATD colleagues, and other authors who continue to research and write so the rest of us can continue to learn. I read several books every week, so keep 'em coming! You all inspire me.

Thank you to everyone at ATD and TPH who always make me look better than I thought possible: Cat Russo, fabulous friend and passionate publisher, for inviting me to share another book in this series; Jacki Edlund-Braun, editor extraordinaire who reviews my work with the most critical as well as creative eye of anyone I've worked with; Tora Estep, whose keen attention to detail helped put the quality in QC; Courtney Vital Kriebs who shared time from her busy schedule for a knotty philosophical discussion; Tony Bingham, who allows me to continue to play in the fabulous ATD world; and the rest of the team at ATD Press.

About the Author

Elaine Biech, president of ebb associates inc, a strategic implementation, leadership development, and experiential learning consulting firm, has been in the field more than 30 years helping organizations work through large-scale change. She has presented at more than 100 national and international conferences and has been featured in publications such as *The Wall Street Journal, Harvard Management Update, Investor's Business Daily,* and *Fortune.* She is the author and editor of more than 70 books, receiving national awards for two of them.

Among her extensive body of published work are many ATD titles, including its flagship publication *The ASTD Handbook: The Definitive Reference for Training and Development* (editor, 2014). Other ATD/ASTD titles include *New Supervisor Training* (2015); *The Book of Road-Tested Activities* (copublished with Pfeiffer, 2011); *ASTD Leadership Handbook* (2010); *ASTD's Ultimate Train the Trainer* (2009); *10 Steps to Successful Training* (2009); *ASTD Handbook for Workplace Learning Professionals* (2008); and *Thriving Through Change: A Leader's Practical Guide to Change Mastery* (2007), to name just a few.

Elaine specializes in helping leaders maximize their effectiveness. Customizing all of her work for individual clients, she conducts strategic planning sessions and implements corporate-wide systems such as quality improvement, change management, reengineering of business processes, and mentoring programs. Elaine is a consummate training professional, facilitating training on a wide range of workplace and business topics. She is particularly adept at turning dysfunctional teams into productive teams.

As a management consultant, trainer, and designer, she has provided services globally to organizations as diverse as Joint Strike Fighter, Outback Steakhouse, China Telecom, Johnson Wax, FAA, Land O' Lakes, McDonald's, Lands' End, China Sinopec, Chrysler, Federal Reserve Bank, Lockheed Martin, PricewaterhouseCoopers, Banco de Credito Peru, Minera Yanacocha, Newmont Mining, American Family Insurance, Hershey Chocolate, U.S. Navy, NASA, Newport News Shipbuilding, Kohler Company, ATD, American Red Cross, Association of Independent

Certified Public Accountants, the University of Wisconsin, the College of William & Mary, and hundreds of other public and private sector organizations to prepare them for current challenges.

A long-time volunteer for ATD, she has served on ASTD's National Board of Directors, was the recipient of the 1992 ASTD Torch Award, the 2004 ASTD Volunteer Staff Partnership Award, the 2006 Gordon Bliss Memorial Award, and in 2012, the inaugural CPLP Fellow Program Honoree from the ASTD Certification Institute. Elaine was instrumental in compiling and revising the CPLP study guides and has designed five ASTD Certificate Programs. She was the 1995 Wisconsin Women Entrepreneur's Mentor Award recipient and has served on the Independent Consultants Association's (ICA) Advisory Committee and the Instructional Systems Association (ISA) Board of Directors. Elaine is currently a member of the Center for Creative Leadership's Board of Governors and Berrett-Koehler's worldwide curator for Advances in Leadership and Management.

About ATD

The Association for Talent Development (ATD), formerly ASTD, is the world's largest association dedicated to those who develop talent in organizations. These professionals help others achieve their full potential by improving their knowledge, skills, and abilities.

ATD's members come from more than 120 countries and work in public and private organizations in every industry sector.

ATD supports the work of professionals locally in more than 125 chapters, international strategic partners, and global member networks.

1640 King Street
Alexandria, VA 22314
www.td.org
800.628.2783
703.683.8100

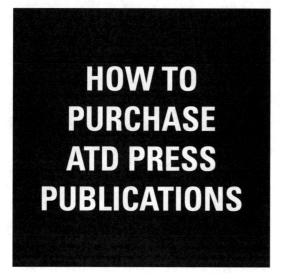

HOW TO PURCHASE ATD PRESS PUBLICATIONS

ATD Press publications are available worldwide in print and electronic format.

To place an order, please visit our online store: www.td.org/books.

Our publications are also available at select online and brick-and-mortar retailers.

Outside the United States, English-language ATD Press titles may be purchased through the following distributors:

United Kingdom, Continental Europe, the Middle East, North Africa, Central Asia, Australia, New Zealand, and Latin America
Eurospan Group
Phone: 44.1767.604.972
Fax: 44.1767.601.640
Email: eurospan@turpin-distribution.com
Website: www.eurospanbookstore.com

Asia
Cengage Learning Asia Pte. Ltd.
Phone: (65)6410-1200
Email: asia.info@cengage.com
Website: www.cengageasia.com

Nigeria
Paradise Bookshops
Phone: 08033075133
Email: paradisebookshops@gmail.com
Website: www.paradisebookshops.com

South Africa
Knowledge Resources
Phone: +27 (11) 706.6009
Fax: +27 (11) 706.1127
Email: sharon@knowres.co.za
Web: www.kr.co.za

For all other territories, customers may place their orders at the ATD online store: **www.td.org/books**.

0215145.62220